THE COAST OF SUMMER

Books by Anthony Bailey

FICTION

Making Progress (1959)
The Mother Tongue (1961)
Major André (1987)

NONFICTION

The Inside Passage (1965)
Through the Great City (1967)
The Thousand Dollar Yacht (1968)
The Light in Holland (1970)
In the Village (1971)
A Concise History of the Low Countries (1972)
Rembrandt's House (1978)
Acts of Union (1980)
Along the Edge of the Forest (1983)
Spring Jaunts (1986)
The Outer Banks (1989)
A Walk Through Wales (1992)
The Coast of Summer (1994)

AUTOBIOGRAPHY

America, Lost & Found (1981)
England, First & Last (1985)

THE

COAST

OF

SUMMER

SAILING NEW ENGLAND WATERS

FROM SHELTER ISLAND

TO CAPE COD

ANTHONY BAILEY

Michael di Capua Books
HarperCollins Publishers

HarperCollins books may be purchased for educational, business, or sales promotional use. For information, please write: Special Markets Department, HarperCollins Publishers, Inc., 10 East 53rd Street, New York, NY 10022.

FIRST EDITION

Designed by C. Linda Dingler

Library of Congress Cataloging-in-Publication Data

Bailey, Anthony.
    The coast of summer : sailing New England waters from Shelter Island to Cape Cod / Anthony Bailey. — 1st ed.
        p.   cm.
    "Michael di Capua books."
    ISBN 0-06-118004-1
    1. Sailing—Atlantic Coast (New England). 2. Atlantic Coast (New England)—Description and travel. I. Title.
    GV776.A84B35   1994
    797.1'24'0974—dc20   93-36722

94 95 96 97 98 ❖/HC 10 9 8 7 6 5 4 3 2 1

Health, south wind, books, old trees, a boat, a friend.
Ralph Waldo Emerson,
Journals, February 1847

For 'tis a chronicle of day by day, / Not a relation for breakfast.
Prospero, in Shakespeare's
The Tempest, Act V, Scene 1

AUTHOR'S NOTE

WRITING—as I hope I am—for English-speaking readers anywhere, who may not use precisely the same words or spellings of words for nautical maneuvers or material, I've had to take decisions that may offend some here and some there. I have stayed faithful to the English spelling of "gybe," the maneuver by which a yacht with the wind astern changes direction and the main boom is brought over from one side of the boat to the other. The American "jibe" leads to problems, particularly with the present participle "jibing," which looks to me as if it has something to do with only a jib, a foresail, or else with the act of refusing to do something, as a horse might when refusing a jump. "Gybing" doesn't present this difficulty. To redress the balance, I've gone along with American usage for the fuels gasoline (a.k.a. petrol) and kerosene (paraffin to the British). I have also stuck with the time-honored feet and fathoms for measuring depth of water instead of the metres (meters!) that are now found on British and of course European

AUTHOR'S NOTE

charts. I've decided that elaborate explanations of many nautical terms may put off those who know about the sea without enlightening those who are new to it. (For the latter, however, two items: a halyard—halliard in Britain—is used to haul up a sail and let it down; a sheet is not a sail, but rather the rope or line for pulling it in and letting it out.) The flag flown by British-owned ships, merchant and private, large and small, is referred to as both the Red Ensign and, more familiarly, the Red Duster.

Since the time of the cruise with which this book is mostly concerned, several years ago, some details may have altered: the identities of harbormasters, the times of bridge openings, the characteristics of lights and beacons, the price of rental moorings. As this book goes to press, Monomoy is no longer an island, but is connected to Cape Cod. The land changes, and so does the sea bottom. There's now less left of the *Longstreet,* the target shipwreck which made such a good seamark on the approach to Wellfleet Harbor. I'm told that Ultra Heat Treated Milk, whose lack I bemoan, is making a tardy but welcome appearance in the United States.

During thirty years, our summer sailing has been supported by friends who have looked after children, driven us to and from boats, and provided shelter, meals, hot water, and good company. Some are mentioned in the following pages. A few are no longer living. But my gratitude, now and always, goes to Paul Brodeur; Betty Richards; Jon and Marianne Swan; Bill and Shelly White; Rod and Lucia Johnstone; Maria and John McVitty; Rosemary Gutwillig; Robyn Dodson; Yaacov Adam; Rust Hills and Joy Williams; Jim and Betsy Wade Boylan; Cynthia Lichtenstein and Charles Miller; Penney, Henry, and Paula Chapin; Belinda Coote; Peter and Shirley

Wood; Buell and Margaret Hollister; Eloise, Tony, and Ann Spaeth; Stephen Jones; Rob and Didi Cowley; Ed and Ann Moore; Charles and Alisa Storrow; Janet Groth and Al Lazar; Elizabeth Dixon; Jack and Sarah Totten; Doralyn Bibby; Emily and Sybby Lynch; George Shafnacker; and Ray and Isabel Avellar. This book is for them all.

JULY

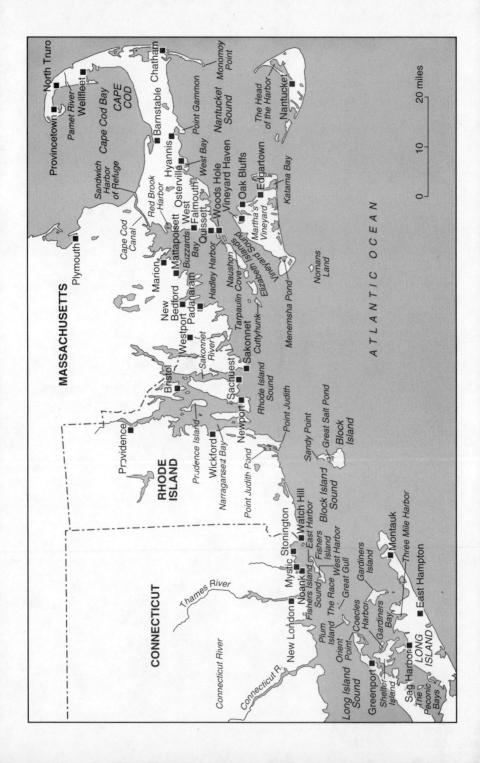

1

SAILING PEOPLE who live in houses often envy those who live on boats. But those who dwell afloat all year round miss one great thing: the annual pleasure of throwing off a land-based existence in exchange (however briefly) for a seagoing life that will rock them with different demands and buoy them up with different delights. Yet that happy transition may not be easy. In my case, I have two hurdles to clear as I set out in July to spend the rest of the summer on the water. First, I live in London near the Thames, not far from where Queen Bess dubbed Francis Drake a knight, but my boat is three thousand miles away on the New England coast, within cruising range of the *Mayflower*'s landfall. I have been leading a transatlantic life since childhood, sometimes perforce, more often by choice. For ten years from 1961, my wife, Margot, and I, and eventually four children, lived in the seaside village of Stonington in southeastern Connecticut and went sailing when we could.

Almost every summer since we moved back to old England in 1971, I have sailed New England's cruising grounds aboard three successive boats, each kept in as frugal a fashion as such far-flung ownership permits.

A long day flying westwards brings me to Logan Airport. In the slow line at Immigration or amid the exhaust fumes at the Bonanza bus stop, I tell myself I'm fortunate: I was not on the *Mayflower,* or indeed on almost any other vessel in previous centuries that took uncomfortable weeks, sometimes distressing months, to carry immigrants and visitors to these shores. Occasionally Margot has flown over with me, but most times, cleverly, she arrives a few weeks later, after I've got the boat sorted out and had a single-handed shakedown cruise. Often a Stonington friend—for example, our former neighbor Betty Richards—will meet me at the bus depot outside Providence. In the early dusk of this latitude, with the muggy heat of the day still lying heavily on the land, I come at last to Stonington, up over the road bridge spanning the shoreline railroad track, and proceed along Water Street. From Betty's car I catch enticing glimpses of the harbor down the side streets. But I turn down her offer to take me to the club, from whose dock I'd be able to see if *Lochinvar* is on her mooring. Jet lag is beginning to have its sandbag effect; tomorrow will be time enough.

The second hurdle, impeding me from actually sailing away once I've got here, is the friendly grip the land maintains on my boat. *Lochinvar,* as it happens, has not yet been launched—though the hard-pressed crew at Dodson's Boat Yard has moved her from the club parking lot, where she sat all winter, and has promised to have her anti-fouled and rigged and in the water the day after tomorrow. (The reader will have to get used to my staunch traditionalism on one point: boats and ships are feminine, as they were for the ancients, and are therefore alluded to in these pages as "she," even when they have masculine names.) Moreover, Betty, who is putting me up for the next few days, says that I have invitations waiting. Old friends in the village, not seen for nine months, proffer drinks and meals and catching-up conversation. And there are errands to be run for provisions and equipment: grapefruit juice, cannelloni, and tomato paste; a new fire extinguisher and batteries for radio and flashlight; a chart of Nantucket Sound to replace the salt-soaked old one, which has lost crucial depth indications. Lucky the man who can set sail without first going shopping.

On *Lochinvar*, bobbing on her mooring at the head of the yacht-filled harbor, the cabin overhead is speckled with mildew; a fine layer of dust and sand has penetrated the interior; lockers must be cleaned before pots and pans and cans are stowed in them. The VHF radio and elderly loran, which was a gift, have to be connected to the boat's wiring and their antenna. On deck, I oil blocks and winches. I check turnbuckles, shackles, cotter pins. I feel I am making progress when, on the calm evening of a day when I at last seem to be on American time, I hump the sailbags on board and—happily in contact with sailcloth and rope—bend on the mainsail and working foresail (the number-two genoa jib). "Bending on," in the latter's case, means sliding the luff of the sail into a groove on the roller-furling gear while hauling away on the halyard, attaching each of the jib sheets with a bowline knot, and then rolling in the gently flapping sail. The main is a bit more of a handful for one person. When finally the foot and luff slides are all in place and the foot of the main is stretched out along the boom, I plan to insert the four fiberglass battens which stiffen the leech, the curved trailing edge of the sail, before furling the mainsail and putting on its cover. But during a winter checkup a local sailmaker has made neat new batten pockets, and as they are slightly longer than the old ones, he has provided new battens; I can see that the top batten will be too stiff for a position where a supple curve is called for. This means a dinghy trip ashore and a walk into the village to the basement workshop of a friend. A few minutes' use of his bandsaw reduces the width of the batten's midsection and renders it more flexible. Back on *Lochinvar,* the next task is choosing books for the shelf over the port berth in the main cabin. Some books kept in friends' attics go aboard every summer and never get opened, but maybe this is their year. Guides to birds and seashells are much consulted. Some books, like Robert Fitzgerald's translation of the *Odyssey,* are old companions and can't be left behind.

Lochinvar may already be taking shape in the reader's imagination. In which case, a few quick words. Despite the romantic name (from the ballad by Sir Walter Scott which begins, "Oh, young Lochinvar is come out of the West, / Through all the wide Border his steed was the best . . ."), *Lochinvar* is a doughty, even homely-looking craft. Twenty-seven feet long, she was built in 1967 of fiberglass (with teak trim) by the Painesville, Ohio, firm of Douglass and McLeod, whose ancestors clearly came from north of the borders. Douglass and McLeod built well. Moreover, boats of that early fiberglass period tended to be constructed more heavily than they are today—when boatbuilders seeking economy and speed know how little they can get away with (at least for the first few years). Therefore her decks are not like trampolines and her hull doesn't flex when going over well-spaced combers. She has, to date, never suffered the outer-skin blistering from osmosis which affects many fiberglass craft. *Lochinvar* is of a class called Tartan 27, designed by the celebrated New York naval architects Sparkman & Stephens; she shares some of the family characteristics of S&S boats of her time, being short-ended but with fairly heavy displacement, which gives her good carrying capacity. Yet she draws only 3 feet 6 inches with her centerboard raised into her long keel, and this enables her to reach the shallower bays and ponds. She is also, board down, extremely weatherly—in other words, she sails fast and close to the wind, which makes not only for speedy passages but for an ability to sail out of trouble.

Down below, our floating summer home has bunks for five and consequently decent room for two people who know each other well. Starting in the bow, there's a compartment for the anchor rode; two fo'c'sle berths with water tank and lockers below and an opening hatch above; a hanging locker for clothes to starboard and an enclosed marine toilet—the head or heads—to port; then the saloon, or main cabin, with a galley of sink, stove, and cupboards on the starboard side followed by a spacious quarter berth. On the port side is a sitting area which can be converted into a small double-bunk by dropping the folding table into place and adding cushions. The decor is white-painted cabin sides and overheads with mahogany joiner work and bulkheads. A kerosene lamp with a glass chimney provides both light and warmth, while several 12-volt electric lights, powered by the boat's batteries, provide just light—though I'm a bit miserly about their use, fearing the batteries will lack the punch to start the engine when needed. The saloon has "standing headroom"; I am just under six feet tall and my hair brushes the underside of the cabin top. Some masochists—that is, most people who own small boats, and I have been numbered among them—say that the important thing in a boat is sitting headroom and for the rest you can kneel or crawl; but being able to stand erect in a boat is—I now admit—a blessing, particularly when cooking or dressing or pulling on foul-weather gear or simply being cooped up below on a miserable day. As in most boats of this size, steps over the engine box lead up to the cockpit via a companionway and sliding hatch.

These commissioning chores and shore entanglements are useful in braking the pace at which I have been scurrying to this point in the year, getting writing projects finished and domestic matters—house, dog, cat, and bank account—organized so that they can manage without my direct attendance for several months, and then flying here at 600 miles per hour. Pottering around on the boat, I am adjusting to boat speed. For although one of the thrills of sailing lies in getting your boat to go as rapidly as it can from place to place by manipulation of the natural elements (the moving air, the favoring current), this pleasure arises from a movement which, compared to most other forms of modern transport, is not very fast at all. In a sailing boat you can spend all day—or indeed all day and all night—covering a distance which might take only an hour or so by car. You may not even reach your intended landfall; the wind and tide may prompt you to go somewhere else. So, in these first few days in Stonington, I am gradually divesting myself of our contemporary need to travel as fast as possible to a definite spot and preparing to reaffirm the importance of the voyage over the place voyaged to. The means used to reach any destination will enhance it, and wherever a passage brings me, I will be able to curl up for the night in my own snail shell of a cabin.

After several days, people in the village are asking predictable questions. They have only just finished exclaiming, "When did you get back here?" and "How was your winter?" Now it is (from the same people): "When are you setting off on your cruise?" and "Where are you sailing to this year?" To the first, I answer cautiously, "Oh, in a day or so," because you never know what last-minute hitches there will be. To the second, I reply, with an airy gesture, "Oh, somewhere east," or "Maybe west to start with." I have a superstitious disinclination to be specific. I fear that if I name a place I will not get there. But in my own mind I have already determined the direction of my shakedown cruise: west it will be.

Tasks continue to present themselves, like a leaky icebox that needs repair with duct tape, insulation board, and epoxy glop. But one morning the water tank is filled, the fuel tank is topped up, and a block of ice is packed around with milk and other perishables in the still imperfect icebox. I have consulted the *Eldridge Tide and Pilot Book*, the indispensable annual nautical almanac that tells the sailor when tides and currents change along this coast, and whose yellow paperback format is comfortingly constant. In the community center's thrift shop I've bought a replacement boat kettle for fifty cents. I have turned down an invitation to a party in two days' time I would really like to attend. The forecast from my weather radio is for continued heat and humidity but no alarming winds. It is time to sail.

2

EVEN SO, the morning has gone before the last fiddling job has been done and everything—I hope—is in place. There are only a few hours of westbound current still to run up Fishers Island Sound; for wind, light airs from the south. I tie the oars in the dinghy, now on its painter astern, hoist the mainsail, and lower the centerboard. *Lochinvar* pivots like a weathervane into the fragile breeze. Then I unfurl about a third of the jib, uncleat the mooring pennant, and, backing the exposed section of jib, make the bow swing to starboard so that I can—by dashing aft and taking the tiller and pulling in the starboard jib sheet—sail away on the port tack, just clearing the stern of *Whimbrel,* a gray J–24. (*Whimbrel's* mooring seems a bit closer each season; as the harbor gets more crowded, my territory feels threatened, or—possibly— my eyesight weakens.) I unroll the rest of the jib. As *Lochinvar* tacks slowly out through the moored fleet of yachts lying this way and that, I keep a keen watch around the jib, which obscures the helmsman's view of upcoming obstacles. We miss by a foot a transom here, a bowsprit there, and cause people varnishing hatches or reading *The New York Times* to lift their heads as *Lochinvar*'s sails briefly enshadow them and her bow wave rustles by.

Beyond the fish dock, where draggers and lobster boats tie up, a wide channel is free of moorings, and I have boatroom for a leisurely prospect of the village waterfront. Stonington stands on its promontory in the bright afternoon light, a motley, tight-packed collection of buildings. It is a mini-Manhattan, except that here most of the structures are wooden and the few visible towers are those of churches. The only really large building is the old factory, which in recent years made molds for plastic squeegee bottles and in the past turned out cannons, rifles, potbelly stoves, and much of the world's silk-making machinery. It is now owned by a Japanese real-estate entrepreneur who paid an over-the-odds price in the hope of getting a zone change that would allow him to build condos and private yacht slips. Opposed by those who still believe real work has a meaningful place in the village, which like many pretty places is in danger of becoming a geriatric retirement haven, this hope is so far unfulfilled. I feel grateful for having no similar real-estate problems; a boat is all the waterfront property I need. On the factory breakwater two youths are fishing. Children play on the little public beach, their mothers sun themselves and gossip, and the lifeguard sits proudly in his high white wooden chair. Off Stonington Point I tack *Lochinvar* once more and take my departure. It is 2:32 p.m. The Stars and Stripes on the point flagpole flaps idly, in need of real wind.

Lochinvar still has to pass through the broad west-facing gap between the two main breakwaters, whose immense granite blocks protect the harbor from the south. The breakwaters date from Stonington's nineteenth-century heyday as a commercial port. Whaling and sealing ships sailed from here. Cargo schooners busily plied this coast. In Stonington passengers arrived by train from Boston and Providence to be carried overnight in large paddle-wheel steamers to New York. (The engineer in charge of building the Providence-Stonington railroad was Major George Washington Whistler, and sometimes, as I look at the misty nocturnal paintings of the Thames, painted by his son James, who spent part of his childhood in the village, I see Stonington water, Stonington light.) *Lochinvar* skirts the east end of the inner breakwater and threads her way among the lobster-pot buoys. The gulls perched on the breakwater stones, waiting for incoming draggers to disgorge fish scraps, are unalarmed. Calm though it is, a slight surge lifts *Lochinvar* as I free the sheets a little for a close reach down Fishers Island Sound. A glance south to check the tilt of a navigation buoy—yes, leaning westward still.

This seven-mile-long body of water, partly enclosed on the south by a line of reefs and Fishers Island, has a well-founded reputation for making things difficult for the unwary. *Atlantic Coast Pilot,* sixth edition, says: "The entire area is exceedingly treacherous, characterized by boulder patches which rise abruptly from deep water." In 1814, Captain Thomas Hardy, commanding a small flotilla of British ships-of-war in an attack on Stonington, had trouble with what he described as "the shallowness of the water." After several days of desultory bombardment of the village, the British ships departed, their boats going ahead to sound the way for the larger vessels. Nevertheless, the *Ramillies,* Hardy's flagship, ran aground, and it took her crew ten hours of putting out anchors, dumping drinking water, and moving heavy cannon and shot from bows to stern, before the *Ramillies* could be kedged off into deeper water. (Hardy later lived in Greenwich, England, a street away from where we presently live; I think of him as a neighbor.) Even now, when the perils of the Sound are marked by lighthouses and buoys, a walk around the local boatyards during the summer presents the sight of craft hauled out with mangled propellers, damaged rudders, or dented keels, the results of contact with the treacherous boulder patches.

I sail through Fishers Island Sound—my local waters for thirty-two years—with a chart always open on the cockpit seat beside me. Familiarity breeds insouciance; the chart reminds me of perils a lack of care entails. Often when sailing, one's concentration becomes very parochial: the immediate vicinity of air and water engrosses the senses; one buoy may look much like another; a larger disorientation bemuses the navigator. During a race in Fishers Island Sound last year I suddenly dragged my attention from the quivering luff of the jib just in time to see a horseshoe of rocks a boat's length ahead. Quick! Down with the helm! Hard a-lee! The jib, taken aback, pulled the bows round, out of danger. A near thing. The chart told me that in my racing concentration *Lochinvar* had nearly run onto the rocks of West Clump. "We were going faster than I thought," I said in limp explanation to my crew.

This afternoon, telling myself it's too early in my cruising season to do anything so stupid, I note the seamarks on the route *Lochinvar* is taking down the sound. Latimer's, the lighthouse marking the reef of that name and the chain of clumps stretching down the middle of the sound, is broad on the port bow. The lighthouse is unmanned, like all such aids nowadays; but the sight of its tall brown-and-white conical iron tower makes me think of Frank Jo Raymond, an all-purpose photographer, artist, and fisherman who used to row to and from Stonington on his tours of duty as helper to his uncle, the keeper of the light. Frank used to say that he got $93.50 a month, plus 45 cents a day for food, when he started the job in 1923, at the age of sixteen. He learned to play the clarinet and saxophone while out at Latimer's. He also taught himself to paint as he looked out on Fishers Island Sound, and though he turned out many pictures, which he exhibited locally, he couldn't bear to part with any of them. Close to starboard is a shoal called Eel Grass Ground, but it creates no danger for shallow-draft craft like *Lochinvar.* Farther north, sunlight catches the windows of a train approaching the bridge over the entrance to Quiambaug Cove. The cove runs a mile inland, a haven for ducks and egrets and my friends Rust and Joy, who have a house on its east shore. The coastline here is low, green with outcrops of gray stone—"the soft green breast of the New World" were Scott Fitzgerald's words for this seaboard. It seems as always an unassertive beginning for a great continent. The most conspicuous landmarks are ecclesiastical: a monastery on Enders Island, the spires and towers of churches in Mystic and Noank. The natives here are not quite post-Christian yet. Somewhat closer to hand, lying athwart the entrance to the Mystic River, is Ram Island, where a big private house has recently been built on the site of a nineteenth-century hotel—old-timers in Noank remember boxing matches being held out here, for large purses. After the hotel was abandoned, it was dismantled and carted off to Noank by the Noankers, and bits of it are to be seen in various houses there, pointed out now and then by the owners.

As *Lochinvar* slips westward, ghosting a little faster than the still-helpful current, the afternoon doesn't seem suitable for going far. Yet I don't want to spoil this inaugural sail by using the engine. The logical spot for the night is West Harbor, Fishers Island. So at Ram Island Reef I harden in the sails to make for the gap of navigable water between West Clump and Flat Hammock. The Hammock is a crescent moon of sand in whose lee boats anchor for weekend picnics; but no one is here today. Just west of Flat Hammock are the two islets known as the Dumplings. Steep-to and uninhabited South Dumpling is thick with scrub and small trees; North Dumpling is bare except for a small lighthouse, the light now automatic, the house converted and extended for private use. I recognize the impulse of wanting to live in a lighthouse, but as always when sailing past, I wonder how the new occupants manage to co-exist with the automatic foghorn.

The current is slackening as *Lochinvar* fetches into West Harbor. I tack over to the shore of the island south of Clay Point and then back to Hawks Nest Point, where the narrow entrance channel curves in with a parcel of rocks to starboard. Before reaching this I put the boat into the wind for a few moments, furl the jib, and go forward to ready the anchor. I haul out fifty feet of anchor line and coil it on the foredeck so that it will snake free when the anchor goes over the side. A choice of two anchors gives me a Danforth, a modern design which stows flat and is effective in stiff mud and sand, or an old-fashioned Fisherman, which, though more of a nuisance on deck, is also more reliable on seabeds foul with rocks or rich with eelgrass—an increasingly common condition on this coast. I plump for the Fisherman and its fathom of very heavy chain, which I shackle to the nylon anchor rode. Then I direct *Lochinvar* under main alone to what seems to be a good spot for the night, clear of other moored and anchored yachts, and drop the hook in what will be about nine feet of water at low tide.

Arriving in port, a sailor has duties before going ashore that can be either skimped or done properly. Even though nobody but me will appreciate the results, I furl the mainsail as tightly as I can, coil the mainsheet and hang it tidily from the boom end, and tie the halyards out to the shrouds so that they won't rattle against the mast during the night. (I'm the sort of person who expands into all available space in a house, but a boat brings out qualities of neatness and organization in me. Margot, whom I'm missing, is affected otherwise, treating a boat as a way of escape from her usual household responsibilities and thus, now and then, exasperating her tidy-ship husband.)

When all's snug, I row ashore to the yacht club dock. On the way, I appraise some of the other boats in harbor: the small fleets of lean Inter-Club racers and buxom Bullseyes; the giant ketch *Barlovento*, belonging to Henry duPont. I look for, but don't see, *Maid of Honor*, the elegant brass-funneled pinnance which was a tender to *Endeavour*, one of the British prewar America's Cup challengers, and is sometimes here. After I've found somewhere to tie up the dinghy, I take a stroll around the west end of the island. Fishers—called so by the locals, who spurn the apostrophe—has an air of difference for anyone arriving from the Connecticut mainland. In part this is the effect of money. The local phonebook lists—without addresses—duPonts, Kinsolvings, Roosevelts, Lorillards, Houghtons, and Rockefellers, among others. People who summer on Fishers (and winter in such places as Jupiter Island in Hobe Sound, Florida) may have tried Newport and the Long Island Hamptons and found them wanting. However, if Fishers is more private, some of the houses on it aren't exactly inconspicuous little hide-aways. Whitecaps, once owned by the Simmons mattress family, at the east end of the island, is a full-scale Newport-sized imitation-French château. Until it burned down a few years back, Windshield, belonging to John Nicholas Brown, flaunted an all-glass modernity. John Hay Whitney has his own seaplane ramp, and many of the island's several thousand wealthy summer residents fly to Fishers' little airport in their own planes. But the island's 300-strong year-round population and the servants of the summer folk make do with the ferryboat which runs between New London and Silver Eel Pond, near the western tip of Fishers.

Most of the big houses and the golf course lie on the eastern two-thirds of the island; a road gate makes a point of distinction. But even at the west end, you feel as if you're on a private estate. The roads are quiet, and few have names. Wild roses grow along the verges and veteran trees shade spacious lawns. In terms of government Fishers is an outpost of the Long Island town of Southold, twenty miles to the west, and the fact that I'm now in New York State and no longer in Connecticut is brought home by the golf course–like terrain. Fishers is a long link in the chain of islands that reaches out from the North Fork of Long Island to Napatree Point, the western tip of the state of Rhode Island. The ghastly possibilities of this stepping-stone arrangement were noticed in the 1960s by highway enthusiasts, who proposed a system of roads and bridges connecting New York City and Rhode Island via Long Island and the rocky outcrops and islands to the east. This notion was acclaimed by Long Island potato farmers, construction engineers, highway interchange developers, and two powerful men: Henry Barnes, the New York City traffic chief, and Robert Moses, chairman of the Triborough Bridge and Tunnel Authority. It was opposed by the operators of the New London–Orient Point ferry, which the scheme would have put out of business, and by yachtsmen who envisioned restrictive mast clearances under low bridges spanning some of the gaps, for example in Plum Gut and Watch Hill Passage. Many vehement objectors lived in the path of the proposed route, particularly on Fishers, where a great swath of the island paradise would have been given over to the superhighway. Whether this opposition caused the scheme to fade is unclear. Moses's interest shifted westward to other possible Long Island Sound bridges; they didn't get built either. Connecticut state legislators shelved their proposals for taking over Fishers Island (where secessionary feelings had been strong) from New York State and got on with their own fantasies— which at that point included a plan for an international "jetport" in the state's eastern boondocks.

This evening, instead of motels and fast-food outlets, a single, elderly inn and a family-run vegetable stand grace the roadside. On the weathered wooden stand, tomatoes, lettuce, and zucchini are for sale. In the Pequot Inn I have a glass of beer, but apart from a young couple tête-à-tête at the far end of the bar I'm the only customer, the bartender is wrapped up in his accounts, and after listening to the sound system's melancholy rendition of "Autumn Leaves," I feel more cheerful back out-of-doors. Through the window of a delicatessen I see a plump, Mediterranean-looking girl patting ice cream into a sugar cone for a bony, blond young woman; the local class structure is evident in physiognomy, I decide (perhaps quite unjustly). Farther on, I saunter by the old brick barracks and defensive structures of Fort Wright, named after Horatio G. Wright, a Civil War general of little note; it was built to defend this part of the coast against the Spanish, in case they got this far from Cuba during their war with America in 1898. The fort served a purpose during the First World War, when it was used for training soldiers before they were shipped to France. Then I swing back past the low contemporary brick building of Union Chapel, where the notice board advertises the times of the Sunday service and the name of the minister. I'm disappointed that it is not the Reverend W. Lloyd Williams.

Last July, my good friends Joy Williams and her husband, Rust Hills, brought me out here one Sunday to attend a service conducted by Joy's father, who was then minister at the chapel. Our craft was Rust's Boston Whaler, which took us from Quiambaug Cove, west of Stonington, across Fishers Island Sound—a fast, jarring, and noisy ride. However, Rust throttled back to a more sabbatical pace for the passage up West Harbor, through the moorings, and then through Goose Inlet into the inner cove, where we tied up to a simple stone dock. This belonged to the Dawson family, friends of the Reverend Williams and his wife. On the lawn outside a modest shingle house, Al Dawson was taking his ease in an Adirondack chair. He greeted us with a wave and apologized for not getting up; he was eighty-two and recovering from pneumonia. He pointed out his son and daughter-in-law, who were clamming a little way along the cove shore; he thought they wouldn't be going to church today. (By the time we returned they had collected 110 clams.)

It was a warm morning. On our short walk to the chapel half a dozen cars cautiously passed us—we were exercising the privilege of pedestrians on small islands by walking in the road. Joy told me that the present Union Chapel had replaced a wooden church which had burned down not long before. I admired the simple square shape of the new chapel with its stumpy shingled spire and, within, a varnished wooden ceiling. Wooden pews in a church can be mortifying, but these cosseted the flesh with cushions. Some windows were open, allowing a pleasant cross breeze. One of my few dark memories from childhood is of fainting during Mass in a stuffy church in Chatham, on Cape Cod, where I was spending the summer with the Spaeths, my guardians during the Second World War. Union Chapel was full. There were about forty people in the congregation, of all ages, two-thirds female, and (according to Joy) mostly year-round residents; several middle-aged black women had jobs as housekeepers for summer people. The service was straightforward. After an initial silence for reflection came an organ prelude. Then there was a friendly greeting from the tall and dignified Reverend Williams, followed by hymns and prayers. Hymns, in my fitful experience, are not always to one's taste: sometimes boring, sometimes syrupy or tuneless, but once in a while tremendously stirring. And so it was here, as after several forgettable or regrettable numbers we gave full vent to "Guide me, O thou great Jehovah!," the splendid work of an eighteenth-century Welshman, the Reverend William Williams of Pantycelyn.

Our Reverend Williams's sermon, however, was rooted in Scotland, a country which he and his wife had recently visited. I knew that Joy was nervous about her father's ability to preach. He had had a great reputation as a preacher but had suffered a mild stroke and developed cataracts, which made it difficult for him to read his notes. In our pew there was an almost tangible willing, hoping, and praying that he would not make mistakes. But the sermon was faultless. Reverend Williams leaned confidingly over the lectern and told us of an experience he and his wife had had on a Scottish country road with a flock of Scottish sheep, and he moved from this to the need for shepherds and particularly the Good Shepherd. At the end there was the sort of hush that in a church replaces applause. Joy smiled proudly.

I think if I ever take up regular churchgoing, it will be with the Congregationalists, who seem to have a much more direct line to the Almighty than most sects. I'll miss the sonorous mysteries of the Latin Mass, which has been almost completely phased out, anyway. I'll miss the impressive language of the Anglican Book of Common Prayer; I find its updated version painfully flatfooted. But I shan't miss the incense and the kneeling and the embarrassing faux-camaraderie of shaking hands with or hugging nearby strangers, not to mention having to endure the guitar-accompanied sing-alongs that some churches go in for these days. At Union Chapel none of these forms of religious observance was practiced. The handshakes and how-do-you-do's were saved for afterward, over coffee and cupcakes in the vestibule, accompanied by spontaneous and friendly conversation.

Back on *Lochinvar* after my walk, I enjoy my first run-through this summer of my evening on-board routine.

Furling and stowing my (British) Red Ensign, though the sun has already set and my ensign etiquette is tardy. Lighting the cabin lamp and readying the anchor light, to be lit later. Checking anchor line, halyard lashings, the proximity of other boats. Changes are better made now than of necessity in the small hours. Then firing up the galley alcohol stove and having a rum-and-tonic in the cockpit as the corned-beef hash bubbles in the frying pan. Stars are hazily appearing over the masthead. Onshore, in houses big and small, at the duPonts' and the Dawsons', windows are lighting up. From the entrance buoy off Hawks Nest Point a red light flashes every four seconds to guide boats coming and going in the dark.

3

WEST HARBOR is snug unless the wind happens to shift into the north and turn fresh. I've spent a bumpy night here when it has done just that. But last night was uneventful. I'm up early. Once again, there's a difference to my slothful habits on land. Dew lies wet on deck when I stick my head out of the forehatch before six. The anchorage is mirror calm and the summer houses crowding Groton Long Point, more than two miles away across the Sound, are melded in a gray blur. While making coffee and toasting English muffins (a lengthy job on my stand-up toasting rack over an alcohol stove burner), I listen to the weather radio. My confidence in the U.S. National Weather Service is not absolute—its forecasts seem to be comprehensively right about two out of three times, its predictions of wind strengths and directions often appear premature or out-of-date—but I'd rather know what its gruff announcers have to say than be ignorant of it. This morning the forecast is for a light northerly wind becoming variable in the afternoon. With this in mind, over muffins and marmalade I consult the tides and currents in *Eldridge*.

My plan for today depends in part on what the yellow pilot book tells me about the Race, the boisterous stretch of water that lies between Race Point at the western tip of Fishers and Little Gull, smallest and farthest east of the islands that extend from the North Fork of Long Island. What makes the Race exciting is the immense amount of Long Island Sound's water that is sluiced out on the ebb tide and brought back on the flood. This body of water moves through a space constricted not only laterally but vertically. At this threshold, the Sound's floor climbs abruptly from depths of as much as three hundred feet to a ledge a mere fifty feet or so below the surface (though there are some even higher underwater summits on which the projected bridge might have planted its clumsy feet). Over this ridge the outgoing tidal current surges and then tumbles down into considerable depths. One effect of this submarine ascent and fall is a vehemently disturbed surface. In a contrary wind, the waves can be steep enough to make you wish you were somewhere else. In a calm, it is easier to see the whirlpools, which can waltz a boat around giddily, or—if you are trying to get across the Race from east to west, or west to east, as I generally am—watch helplessly as the water carries you sideways. My hope today is to cross the Race at slack water, when the ebb has ceased to run and the flood has not yet begun to pour in.

Lochinvar tacks out of West Harbor, one of the first boats underway. I round North Hill and, easing sheets in the unstrenuous breeze (indeed from the north), lay a solitary course just south of west; the few other yachts to be seen are heading eastward down Fishers Island Sound. It's going to be a sultry day. On a boat, direct exposure to the sun has to be taken in especially small doses, and I've smeared sunblock cream on nose and cheeks and the backs of my hands; I wear a faded striped cotton shirt with long sleeves; an old beach towel lies on the cockpit seat ready to cover my bare knees and shins. My broad-brimmed white cotton hat, bought in the cricket department of Lillywhites clothing store in Piccadilly Circus, is somewhat Aussie in appearance though made in China. Any day now, I expect doctors (who keep changing their minds about the effects of butter, margarine, red meat, and wine) to tell us that sunlight is good for us. Meanwhile, in order to come here, I ride annually in jumbo jets, which deplete the ozone layer and increase harmful radiation. And I know that whatever precautions I take, in a week or so the light of our fiery star beating down from above and reflected up off the sea will have turned my face, arms, and legs the color of an old suede shoe.

On a broad reach *Lochinvar* slides across the Race. After the confines of harbor and Sound, there's a sudden roominess: the Connecticut coast low to the north, various lumps of Long Island distant to the west and south, and to the southeast the open sea. A mile ahead, crossing my bow, a submarine moves toward New London, a long, black, mostly immersed cylinder with its conning tower standing up like a shark's fin. Menace and obsolescence seem to ride together there. What ploughshares, I wonder, does General Dynamics have in its seemingly one-track mind for beating out of this particular sword? Other, smaller craft are on the move—powerboats, approaching from the coast. The Race is a prime fishing spot, and soon, when the current has started to run, fifty or sixty sportfishing boats will be jock-eying for position, gunning forward into the current, then dropping back, their skippers watching the gulls and the competing boats.

Often the morning breeze poops out at midday; today it does so in mid-morning. The sails barely hold their shape. I can sense the watery mass about to turn and sweep *Lochinvar* northwest. I point her bow farther south to allow for the expected set from the flood current. I shift to the slightly shadowed lee side of the cockpit and peer forward and up at the luff of the jib, striving to get the last thrust from the fading wind. I don't want to turn the motor on, but I may end up in Bridgeport if I don't. (*Lochinvar*'s auxiliary engine, a gasoline-powered Universal Atomic Four, is power-ful and not too noisy or vibration-making, as boat engines go. However, when requested to start, it occasionally has quirks for which mechanics make various explanations, such as "The problem's in the ignition switch"; "It may be the solenoid"; or "It's only a bit of damp.") Unlike some yachts-men, who turn on the engine the moment their boat speed drops below 5 knots, I continue to have a sailor's conviction that I am out here to use the wind, and that the best voyages are those completed under sail alone.

More than halfway across the Race, with the green bell buoy marking Valiant Rock already astern and clanging lethargically, it seems to me that the light tower on the rocky outcrop which is Little Gull Island is no longer on my starboard bow, where it should be. Willy-nilly I am now steering straight for it. The current has turned, the flood is pouring in, and *Lochinvar* is being carried into Long Island Sound. I look for signs of hope, but the surface of the water is still glassy and the sails have given up trying to determine which way the wind is blowing. The only movement is that of the boat going sideways. There is nothing for it. I go through the engine-starting routine: click on the master switch; run the blower for several minutes to ventilate the bilges; twist the lever that turns on the fuel supply; pull out the choke halfway and the throttle a smidgeon; make sure the gear level is in neutral; and then turn the ignition key. Nothing but silence. I turn it back and—hoping hard—turn it on again. The whir of the starter. The engine fires. "Just a little damp," I say to myself. Choke in a little. I step aft and look over the transom to make sure that cooling water is gushing from the exhaust pipe. Then I push the throttle in until the engine is just ticking over and put the gear lever forward.

By this time *Lochinvar* has been swept downtide, north of Little Gull. So I take the route of least resistance and steer along the north side of the island, bare stone with an empty brick house and granite light tower, and then past the rocks which lie between Little Gull and Great Gull, its big brother to the west. The current is surging around these rocks, making me grateful for the engine. Without it, I would have had to try to anchor—not easy where the bottom falls steeply away to considerable depths. On Great Gull, the remains of another Spanish-American War fort are surrounded by bayberry bushes and numerous white boxes on legs, resembling dwarf fire-watching platforms, for terns, not gulls, to nest and breed in. The 17-acre islet is owned by the American Museum of Natural History, though it looks as if it belongs to the terns. They have been given subsidized housing here so that ornithologists can study their habits. As *Lochinvar* passes, many of the terns are busy fishing, restless white-and-gray birds which, like swallows, are difficult to track in flight, so rapid are their gliding, diving, and climbing movements. There are no ornithologists to be seen.

There is a longish, shallower gap before the next, much larger island, Plum Island. And since the current is less fierce here than in the Race, now astern, or Plum Gut, some way ahead, and the water is deep enough for *Lochinvar,* I steer through this opening toward my preferred course south of these islands into Gardiners Bay. The one obstacle to look out for is Old Silas Rock, a substantial boulder poking well above the surface at this early stage of the flood tide, the sort of rock a mermaid would sit on to comb her damp tresses. (I assume an early, elderly settler named Silas came to grief here.) The current pushes *Lochinvar* toward Old Silas, so near that I can see mussels and kelp growing on it; but then we're by, and heading across 14 feet of water over Bedford Reef. Along the south shore of Plum Island the effect of the current, thrusting toward Plum Gut, is favorable. I switch off the engine, the fuel, the electricity. I fancy I detect the first signs of the afternoon onshore breeze, a few cat's-paws from the southwest streaking the glazed surface. I trim the sheets in anticipation. For a while, *Lochinvar* maintains steerageway from the momentum the engine has given her. This is, in fact, one of the frequent occasions at sea when hope overwhelms experience: I know from previous passages that this is a notorious flat spot, a bit of the earth's waters that Aeolus sometimes forgets about altogether.

Plum Island is a little over two miles long. In the 1930s, there was talk of making it the site of an East Coast Alcatraz. The island has a high ridge for a backbone, two tall water tanks, an official sort of flagpole, and several

large industrial-looking buildings and many partly under-
ground sheds with tall ventilators. These structures are part
of the Animal Disease Laboratory of the Department of
Agriculture; visitors are not encouraged to land. I find
myself holding my breath as I sail by, fearing some violent
strain of anthrax, scrapie, or cowpox will waft out and
infect me. Today I am grateful to be upwind, in such wind
as there is. One recent summer, disarmament experts from
the United Nations came out to Plum Island to see if its
facilities could be used for making offensive biological
weapons and to discuss with island scientists methods of
monitoring the similar researches of other nations.
(Scientists who work here say that the worst threat is the
Plum Island mosquito, presumably an indigenous nuisance
and not the result of a mad experiment gone wrong.)

For the yachtsman, Plum Gut—the westernmost portal to
Long Island Sound in these parts—is the prime anxiety.
Seven currents thrash together here. Tides occasionally rip at
an alleged 10 knots. (*Lochinvar*, flat out under power, can
do between 5 and 6.) *Lochinvar* is moving at barely 2 knots
in what I hope is a consistent zephyr as she passes Pine
Point, the southern tip of Plum Island. Two miles off our
port beam I sight what looks like Stonehenge surrounded by
water, another former Spanish-American War battery named
Fort Tyler, built in the shallows north of Gardiners Island,
storm-damaged during construction, and used, in the more
recent past, for bombing practice; known as "the Ruins," it
is marked on the chart as a "danger area" and always presents an eerily ambiguous shape, though today no bombing
aircraft can be seen or heard. In any event, Plum Gut is hint-
ing at giving me a near-enough experience of Scylla and
Charybdis. The current is by now running through it at

about the same speed *Lochinvar* is making through the water. A big red-and-black buoy on Midway Shoal, in the southern entrance to the Gut, provides a marker by which I can judge how *Lochinvar* is being swept into the Gut and by its northwestward tilt and bouncing motion indicates the force of the current. The next aid to pilotage is the old iron light tower on the reef that extends from Orient Point, the very tip of the North Fork; white water breaks on the rocks around the rusty tower.

As I notice this, *Lochinvar* coasts into another hole in the little breeze. Sideways motion is suddenly much greater than forward motion. My basic geometry tells me I should compensate by heading at an even broader angle off my intended course—say, directly toward the Ruins—though this will point *Lochinvar* straight to where the wind has been coming from. I watch the white swirl of water around the rocks become more and more distinct. And just to rub in the Bard's wisdom that when troubles come, they do so not as single spies but in battalions, a large vessel appears, steaming straight for me. This is the ferry from New London, big enough to carry a half century of cars, a score of trucks, and a battalion if not regiment of tourists. Dark gray diesel exhaust blurts upward from its funnel. Its steep bow wave appears even more intimidating than the waves around the rocks.

I rapidly consider my options. One: Turn the engine on again. Two: Toss out the anchor—it's only twenty-two feet or so of water here. I know that power (the ferry) should give way to sail (me), but this rule is generally set aside in narrow channels, where maneuvering room for big vessels may be constrained (like here). And can I really be said to be sailing, not just lying dead in the moving water? At this moment, as I reach toward the ignition key, I feel a puff of air on my cheek. The boom lifts, the mainsheet goes taut. *Lochinvar* pulls forward. The salutary little breeze lasts five minutes and Orient Point glides past. The ferry, perhaps avoiding a craft whose intentions are uncertain, takes a wide swing around us before heading into its jetty not far from the Point.

For the next few hours I slowly negotiate these waters of the north part of Gardiners Bay. The bay is bounded top and bottom by the twin forks of Long Island; by Shelter Island to the west, hanging like a walnut in the jaws of a nutcracker; and, to the east, by Gardiners Island, hovering less substantially in the wider space between Plum Island and Montauk. All around the land is unemphatic: sandy beaches, low sandy cliffs. The waters of the bay are generally only 4 to 6 fathoms deep. (In England, we have been deprived of the fathom, a measure of a man's height, in favor of the Napoleonic meter, which one can only describe as a bit more than a yard; obstinately, I go on using the term "fathom" when I can.) On a fickle day like this, when I am reduced to whistling traditional marching tunes like "Men of Harlech" and "Lilliburlero" to raise the wind, it is hard to imagine the bay in quite different mood. Often a hot wind blows out of the west as the heat of the day builds up on the concrete and asphalt of western Long Island. When the ensuing sirocco hits the bay, the lee rail is soon under, spray flies, and things are to be heard falling off the windward cabin shelves as you tie in a reef and bilge water quietly soaks into the leeward bunk cushion. I've been here then. But I've also been out here during the Off Soundings race series, on a seemingly flat afternoon when nothing looked like changing, and my old friend Yaacov (born in prewar Palestine) performed an Arab wind dance on the foredeck of the Alden schooner *White Wing* and within minutes a goodly breeze was whisking us along, almost privately, through the fleet.

Today, whistling, singing, and swearing produce only erratic puffs. The afternoon is hot and sticky. These are the trying times in which persistence and patience are the higher virtues. All the same, after 2:00 p.m. it is never absolutely calm. Light and variable airs take *Lochinvar* westward along the bay beach of the North Fork toward Greenport. I have plenty of time to regard the creosoted timber bulkhead of a small marina, just west of the ferry landing, and to make out the barely perceptible marina entrance. But the tall jib of a mobile crane rises over the marina, an ever useful landmark. I had bought my previous boat, *Clio,* on the North Fork and during the 1980s shared the use of her with various people, including my friend Rusty, who lives in Greenport. For several years *Clio* wintered in Greenport, and when summer came, I would fly from London to JFK, get out to Greenport by train, bus, or car, and then next day sail *Clio* eastward to Stonington, my suitcase on a bunk forward. I had convinced myself it was more enterprising to arrive in Stonington by sea.

I began by keeping *Clio* where I had first found her, in Henry Pierce's boatyard in Stirling Basin. Henry, a crusty Yankee, ran a low-key, low-overhead operation; he would send out bills to his customers roughly once a year, and sometimes these bills were for work done more than a year before. Unfortunately, he then decided to sell out to a New England boatyard chain. My impression was that Henry's successors sent out bills within days of the work being done, if not actually in advance; that services Henry had never charged for suddenly had commercial value; and that the rates for everything were doubled. More cynical or realistic fellow customers said that the new bunch had to do this, having paid such a whopping purchase price to Henry, who in one swoop got a splendid return for his years of low charges.

Looking for a new winter home for *Clio*, through Rusty's local knowledge I found Robert Douglass. He and his family lived on a sort of farm in Orient village, between Greenport and Orient Point. From this base, Douglass and his father ran a marine salvage and heavy lifting business with a mobile crane and large flatbed trailers. He also repaired boats and engines and stored boats out of season in part of his farmyard. There were, however, difficulties to get by before becoming a customer. Several KEEP OUT signs greeted Rusty and me as we drove into the Douglass spread in the quaint village and saw two weather-beaten houses, several huge truck-trailer rigs, boat cradles, children, a barking dog, many chickens, and an inquisitive pony. Douglass himself was a burly, affable, but taciturn man covered in fiberglass dust. He didn't seem eager for new business, and I had to put myself forward strongly. Douglass made clear that his services were modestly priced but not very flexible. If *Clio* came early into the farmyard in the autumn, she would be boxed in by other boats and would have to be launched after them. But my mention of Henry Pierce, from whom Douglass said he had learned a lot, and of living in London, too far away for me to constitute a nuisance, were points in my favor. I was admitted to the privileged circle. At the end of that season, all I had to do was sail into Orient Point marina and unload *Clio*'s gear, and the next day Douglass would unstep the mast and lift her out of the water with his crane and carry her off to his farmyard to spend the winter among his ponies and chickens. As waterfront land in many places becomes too overtaxed and built up with condominiums for moderately priced boatyards, boat owners are having to consider storing their boats inland. Robert Douglass was in the vanguard of this development.

It was exciting, arriving at Orient Point marina for the first time on an afternoon when Gardiners Bay was being buffeted by a strong southwesterly. I ran over from Coecles Harbor on Shelter Island, where I'd spent the last sad, happy night of the summer at anchor. It was a gray day, and like today, I found it hard to see the marina entrance. Moreover, I had no idea what I would find inside the entrance. Would there be room to round up and drop sail? Boats have no brakes. If you don't want to slam into other craft, tied up cozily at floats and docks, you should make careful preparations before blasting into an unknown harbor, especially one as small as this promised to be. Half a mile offshore, I brought *Clio* into the gusty wind and hove-to, jib hauled to weather, main slackened, tiller tethered to leeward. The short Gardiners Bay chop jolted *Clio* about, and I had to use one hand for the job, one for the ship. I got out docklines and made them fast to cleats fore and aft. I tied a couple of fenders to the cabin-top handrails so that I could get at them quickly. I started up the engine, which was a balky old Evinrude outboard situated in a well just abaft the helmsman, with a line holding the gear lever from misbehaving by jumping out of gear, as was its wont. When the Evinrude was coughing out its customary haze of exhaust on starting, I set up the topping lift and dropped the main and furled it informally on the boom. I made the anchor and some line ready for quick use if necessary (the idea of the engine failing was large in my mind). I left the jib up, but made sure the sheets were able to run free whenever I let them go. By this time *Clio* had drifted into shoal water; the little combers were a lighter, crueler blue. I put up the helm and ran toward the marina under the pulling jib. As *Clio* closed rapidly on the entrance, which looked about as wide as a garage door, another question loomed: What do I do if a sportfishing boat comes charging out as I go in?

But none did. In the entrance, I let the jib sheet fly and went in on momentum and the effect of the wind from astern on boat, spars, and shaking sail. I had a few seconds then to take in the possibilities, which were indeed circumscribed. It was a very small marina: several floats crammed with powerboats, a quayside restaurant, and a narrow channel running past the restaurant with a space—the only empty boat space visible—alongside the bulkheading. But there was no room to turn *Clio* into the wind and stop her. I waggled the helm first this way, then that, in an attempt to slow her down, to put off for an extra instant or two the inevitable impact. There was no way to anchor. The whirring engine, thrust into reverse, provided no help at all. It would have been helpful if several experienced people had appeared on the rudimentary dockside and held out eager hands for my lines. As it was, I steered *Clio* toward the space, conscious of the broad stern of the powerboat moored just over a boat length ahead, aware of the dent even so small a boat as *Clio* could make, and managed to loop a bight of my stern line over the head of a piling as it came by. There was a thump, a bit of varnish gone at the toe rail, the sting of a splinter in my right thumb, and a sharp snatch as the line took the strain. Then *Clio* was surging back a little. I dashed forward and got a bowline onto another post. I was there.

Along the North Fork shore, past Orient Beach and Long Beach, *Lochinvar* ghosts. I feel relieved that I'm not attempting Orient Point marina in a breeze today. The main hazard this afternoon is the fish weirs which are strung out from this shore but have wooden posts visible above the surface. I steer a course outside these traps and south of the "shoaling" the chart reports off Long Beach Point. The breeze slowly improves. The thin overcast clears into late-afternoon sun and the wooded slopes of Shelter Island form a Hunter's Green setting, left of stage, to the right of which I head. *Lochinvar* is then hard on the wind that comes around Hay Beach Point, and is actually heeling slightly, and doing all of 3 knots with a chuckling bow wave, as I clear (by half a boat length) the end of the Greenport breakwater. It's a well-known phenomenon, the breeze that picks up as you are about to moor or anchor. Off the entrance to Stirling Basin, I furl the jib and then, ignoring *Clio*'s old haunts inside that haven, direct *Lochinvar* toward the area between a fish dock and a substantial 1920s waterfront house with wide porches. Off this I anchor and exchange waves with Rusty when she appears on her lawn. Once all is furled and properly disposed, I row ashore.

4

FOR A LONG TIME Greenport was one of those places that couldn't seem to make up its mind whether it was going backward or forward. I liked this state of civic dither about "improvement." A few houses were renovated while others fell apart. Venerable wharves and rotting jetties, remnants of Greenport's heyday in the first half of the nineteenth century as one of the principal Atlantic whaling ports, conspicuously balanced a few modern marine facilities. (Whales, as it happens, have actually been caught in the entrance channel to Greenport, though you'd think they'd instinctively keep clear of those who slaughtered their kin in distant oceans.) But in the last few years, Greenport, like other waterside towns in the eastern megalopolis, has been getting fixed up. At the water end of Bay Avenue, Rusty's tree-lined street, a clutch of dove-gray, balconied condominiums has been built. In Stirling Basin, several marinas with swimming pools, restaurants, and—in one case—even a hotel attached look after boat owners who may not want to go too far from plug-in shore connections and the reassuring proximity of their own kind. Yet the town itself remains a dandy place to stroll around, as Rusty and I do the morning after my arrival.

I've known Rusty since 1955. She was one of the first people I met on arriving in New York from England that year. She worked in the business department of a magazine where I started as a cub reporter and she made an immediate impression on me. Wiry, with straight dark-red hair, she'd come from Utah via Cornell. Her laconic humor was new to me; she was pretty in a way that seemed equally original. Unfortunately for any romantic aspirations of mine, she married Bob, also ex-Cornell. But Rusty and I have remained good friends ever since. She became godmother to my first child. With two children of her own, retired from a publishing job and no longer married, she still does occasional book-production projects when not out-of-doors, skiing, boating, and trekking in the Himalayas. When we meet, even after a year or so, we take up exactly where we've left off.

It is a few minutes' walk along Bay Avenue into the heart of Greenport. Most buildings are low and some have façades that, like those in a Western movie town, look more substantial than the premises behind. The assorted shops and eating places have a variety that you don't find in malls or shopping precincts, designed for convenience, productive of banality. The mixture here includes sailmaker and bookshop, Greek restaurants and hardware stores, station and ferry dock. My wristwatch, which is *Lochinvar*'s chronometer, a seven-year-old Timex "Camper," has ceased to function, but Greenport's large drugstore provides a replacement. In Preston's, the waterfront ships' chandlery, where I used to get something for *Clio* every year, as if to propitiate the local gods, I purchase a rigging knife. In the nearest hardware store I buy a rugged one-gallon water container to replace a former spring-water jug which has sprung a leak. (*Lochinvar*'s drinking water is kept in such bottles and canisters; the water in the 30-gallon tank is for washing and washing up.)

Rusty and I lunch in the Coronet Café, where the food and drink are classic American: no granola, but pancakes and waffles, burgers and meat loaf, sundaes and shakes, all yummy and cheap. There's a view of the street corner: pickup trucks going by with dogs in back; rotund North Fork oldsters walking by in terry-towel shirts and visored terry-towel sun hats; a shop window across the street with a sign advertising shotgun shells. We talk about publishing, about magazines now and then, with rueful fondness for the past and as much charity for the present as veterans can muster. We gossip about old friends. And we reminisce about boats. First, a 16-foot Comet-class day boat which we shared one summer in the late fifties, when Rusty, Bob, and I rented a cottage in Centerport on the north shore land as a refuge from Manhattan heat. The Comet, named *Boat* by us as a blunt acknowledgment of its impermanence in our lives, was decked with hardboard, which in the course of the summer began to roll up at the edges. The seams of the bottom planking never became tight; bailing was part of sailing. Then *Caliban:* after five years of own-ing this jaunty 24-foot sloop, I sold her to Rusty and our friend, Penney, with wishes for many happy voyages and a warning that the keel bolts should be checked. Rusty and Penney kept *Caliban* for a few more years and then sold her, with my help, to the British naval liaison officer at the New London submarine base. Once again, since R. and P. had done nothing about them, the advice was given to have the keel bolts checked. The British commander had a good time with *Caliban* for the two summers he was in New England and then, not being allowed to ship her home free as part of his goods and chattels, sold her to a retired U.S. naval captain. Was anything said about the keel bolts? The U.S. captain launched *Caliban* the following spring, and as she went into the water her keel fell off; salvage operations were costly. Anglo-American relations took a tumble. I was ashamed yet thankful: there but for the grace of God went—as boat-owner—I.

Despite the partial protection of Greenport breakwater, this Bay Avenue anchorage isn't a perfect spot to lie overnight. Although it's at a safe distance from the raucous music coming from the outdoor bars of the town waterfront, I'm nearly rolled from my bunk by wake from passing craft. This morning, taking rough bearings on Rusty's house and the end of the breakwater, I wonder if *Lochinvar* has moved since I anchored her. She seems to be lying closer to the fish dock. For security, I'd used the heavy Fisherman, but I know that it can fall in such a way that one end of the stock digs in rather than one of the flukes. Sometimes, if the boat sails herself around during the night, the chain can get wrapped around an upright fluke or stock and exert pull in the wrong direction. Sure enough, as I get under way in the early afternoon, the anchor comes up tangled in its own chain. I make a resolution to do a more thorough job of setting anchor this summer so that *Lochinvar* doesn't end up against fish docks or on the beach during the night.

Today's voyage is short. I motor half a mile to Dering Harbor, on the northwest side of Shelter Island, facing Greenport. Here there's excellent protection except from a severe northwester. There are also plenty of moored craft, and it takes me a while to find a spot to anchor, close to the eastern shore. Then I drop the Fisherman with care as *Lochinvar* drifts astern, letting out about forty feet of line before giving the engine a quick nudge in reverse to dig in the hook, and finally paying out a further few fathoms of line. I let out a length of line roughly five times the depth of water; ten times is my ideal, say a hundred feet in ten feet of water; but scope here as in many harbors is restricted by the proximity of other boats on short but sturdy mooring chains. However, the afternoon is quiet and the harbor—on an island well named Shelter—prompts a secure feeling. Dering Harbor is, in fact, one of five harbors on the island: others are Coecles on the east side, Smith Cove on the south, West Neck Harbor on the southwest corner, and, near the southern tip of the island at Mashomack Point, Majors Harbor, despite its name more of a cove open to winds and wake.

In late afternoon, I've no quarrel with where I am. A few boats are motoring in and out. Sailing dinghies are lying becalmed off the yacht club dock, on the northwest side of the harbor. Outside in the channel, ferries bustle to and from Greenport. The warmth of the day is steaming off the wooded slopes. I row ashore and, with the permission of the youth manning the gas dock, tie up the dinghy at its head. I walk around the village by the harbor and up into the twisting roads of Shelter Island Heights, which are lined with big Victorian houses, summer residences for the most part, many with gingerbread trim on gables, eaves, and porches. I glimpse people closing screen doors, passing windows, or going upstairs on private errands.

Apart from their pleasing scale, the islands of this coast share a number of features. If you read the histories loyal residents have assembled, you find many themes—and chapter headings—in common. The original inhabitants. The first settlers (European, that is). Early religious controversies. Notable families. Times of war. Shipwrecks, pirates, and smugglers. Island industries and trade. Wildlife. Nature. Summer visitors. In these histories we usually learn that the native "Indians" gave up their rights to the islands for what now seem ridiculous payments: for "a coat, a barrel of biscuits, and a hundred fishhooks," in the case of Plum Island; "ten coats of trading cloth," for Gardiners Island; and evidently not much at all to the Manhansets when they gave up Shelter Island. At any rate, one of the first white settlers, Stephen Goodyear, sold it in 1651 for about $80 worth of sugar. Nathaniel Sylvester, one of the new purchasers, was shipwrecked with his bride on the Rhode Island coast as they arrived from England. They were no doubt relieved to reach Shelter Island, where they built a house with chimneys of Dutch brick and planted English flowers in the garden.

Goodyear proceeded to offer sanctuary to persecuted Quakers, though like other landowners at the time it didn't bother him that he was the owner of slaves. His slaves rowed the Sylvester daughters to church every Sunday in Southold, a couple of miles west of Greenport. Over a hundred years later, in the year of the Declaration of Independence, a census listed 33 slaves among the 171 inhabitants of the island, most of whom probably received their freedom by the New York State manumission act of 1788.

The island was once covered with a forest of white oak, but much of this soon went. Shipbuilding consumed many trees, and during the Revolutionary War others were used for firewood. Frederick Mackenzie, a British officer in Rhode Island, wrote in his diary on December 8, 1777: "Thick weather . . . Wind S. . . . About 4 this Evening came in the Wood fleet from Shelter Island, under convoy of the *Unicorn*. The vessels have brought about 300 cords of wood for the use of the troops, and about 400 for the inhabitants. A considerable quantity of Poultry, Pigs, Corn, Potatoes, Butters, and other articles, has also been brought for sale." Hay Beach Point is so called, it is believed, because there the British loaded their ships with fodder. In the early nineteenth century many Shelter Island men went whaling, at least until tempted west by the California gold rush of 1849. ("None made a fortune," writes our Shelter Island historian Ralph G. Duvall.) Part of the urge to go West or to sea may have come from the presence on the island of determined religious proselytizers. Among the eighteenth-century visitors was the eager English evangelist George Whitfield, who often preached sixty hours a week to large congregations. He wrote one night from Stirling, as Greenport was then called, to Thomas Dering, with whom he used to stay on Shelter Island, complaining that he had missed the last ferry to the island. By the mid-nineteenth century there were not only evangelists on the island but revivalists, Methodist summer camps, and the Columbian Temperance Society, whose ladies' choir, according to Duvall, helped "to stay the hand that grasps the poisonous cup as with a magic charm by the sweet power of song." Despite these drawbacks, many Shelter Islanders eventually returned to the island as to a bourne they never again wished to leave. The last words of island Captain Ben Cartwright, who had spent his life chasing whales and menhaden, were "Safe in port."

A "pot works" for extracting oil from menhaden once stood near the west side of the entrance to Dering Harbor, but was a smelly nuisance and was moved to the South Fork. Phosphate, guano, and fish scrap were all island products valued as fertilizers, particularly on tobacco and cotton fields. But despite its pungent odors, the island became popular as a resort; ferries ran to and from East River piers in Manhattan, and a big hotel, the Manhanset House, was built in 1874. It proclaimed in its brochure that "precautions against fire are extraordinarily complete and extensive," but despite these precautions it burnt down in 1896. Soon rebuilt, it burnt down again in 1910. The New York Yacht Club set up an outpost on the east side of Dering Harbor. Among summer residents of the island was Mary Mapes Dodge, editor of the *St. Nicholas Magazine* and author of *Hans Brinker, or the Silver Skates.* Another was Eben Horsford, professor of chemistry at Harvard, who invented a popular baking powder and experimented with the efficacy of pouring oil—no doubt from menhaden—on troubled waters. He founded the Shelter Island Library and proclaimed his belief that the Norse, in the Viking Age, had settled in New England.

I row back to *Lochinvar* in fading light. A few mosquitoes are out and about—I hear them before I see them. From time to time the surface of Dering Harbor is violently ruffled and a thousand gleaming darts, almost electric, appear just under the troubled surface. Occasionally one of the tiny fish, in a desperate bid to escape the large jaws behind it, leaps, plunges, and then—gulp!—is gone. As I open a bottle of

Bulgarian red and cut up onions, mushrooms, and ham for a carbonara sauce, the lights are coming on in the big houses around the harbor and on a few other boats. My radio brings in the World Service of the BBC. The news has the usual quota of ecological disasters, terrorist incidents, famines, and civil wars. *Lochinvar* swings to her anchor line in Shelter Island. Safe in port.

5

NOT EVERYONE wants to be stuck in the Garden of Eden. I know of one man who happily moved into an inherited Shelter Island house and began to fix it up, until his wife left him. She couldn't stand life on the island. The fact that ferries run eighteen hours a day didn't help. A friend of mine who spent wondrous childhood summers on the island says the place is now too stuffy. There's no longer a phosphate works near Hay Beach Point or a shipbuilding yard in West Neck Creek. The atmosphere of well-to-do, well-behaved ease is near total. In the 1890s two young men started a paper, the *Shelter Island Tribune*, and had a story for their first issue when lightning struck St. Mary's Episcopal Church and it was consumed by fire. But the paper had failed by the following summer. "Unfortunately important happenings on the island were rare," remarks Mr. Duvall. (Even so, in that decade fires also destroyed an island store, the post office, the telegraph office, the library, and twice, as noted, the

Manhanset House Hotel.) I'm aware that my impressions are those of a bird of passage and that there must be another point of view. If it's quiet, and not suffering the attentions of arsonists, most locals like it that way. And maybe on Shelter Island, as in most places, there are private dramas, sometimes inflammatory enough for those concerned. One recent summer resident, a Borax magnate, lost several spectacular fortunes in distant states.

I get up once during the night to see how *Lochinvar* is lying. Overhead, stars; all around, stars reflected on calm water. And morning comes with sparkling sun and a northwest breeze. The halyards, despite their restraints, are trying to ping against the mast. It will be a good day to circumnavigate Shelter Island. The breeze is so inviting that I set off counterclockwise, tacking out of Dering Harbor toward Fanning Point at the west end of Greenport, and not bothering to consult *Eldridge*. I do have to worry, though, about a ferry, chuntering across from Greenport with four cars and a small truck and clearly expecting *Lochinvar* to keep out of its way. (Ferries like these seem to be exceptions to the "all boats are feminine" rule, perhaps because they seem like bits of floating bridge. Anyway, for this ferry I use the unisex "it.") There's a two-foot spot marked on the chart off Fanning Point, so I come about again and, close-hauled on the starboard tack, set *Lochinvar* forging across the wide mouth of Pipe's Cove, freeing off a little to get round Conkling Point on the North Fork and then hardening up to shave past Jennings Point on Shelter Island's northwest tip. I reflect on the scanty immortality of having one's name attached to a geographical feature. Who were Fanning, Pipe, Conkling, and Jennings?

It's not a day when I feel any desire to make the fastest

passage to my ultimate destination. Once I get around Jennings, rather than bearing off in order to follow the Shelter Island shore south, I stand across Southold Bay. On the chart Town Creek and Jockey Creek on the west side of the bay have their allure, but single-handed, with the tide ebbing, I don't fancy exploring these dead-end shallows. I bear away to clear Paradise Point on Great Hog Neck. For a little while *Lochinvar* is running by the lee; that is, with the wind coming over the port quarter and the mainsail out on the port side. I can feel the breeze on the wrong side of my neck. To avoid an uncontrolled gybe—mainsail and boom crashing over as the wind gets in front of the sail, with a good chance of the boom end lifting and hitting the backstay—I choose the right moment to conduct the gybe. I watch the wind-ruffled water astern for the smooth patch that indicates a slight lull. Then I tug in the sixty feet or so of mainsheet as quickly as I can through the triple purchase blocks and move the tiller over to the port side. "Gybe oh!" *Lochinvar* dips her bow and tries to round up a little as the mainsail flicks over my head. But the whole maneuver is quite well mannered. My scalp is intact. The backstay isn't carried away.

These little exercises are among sailing's pleasures, like negotiating a mountain overhang or riding a horse over a big ditch. But they aren't always a success. Among the boats out this morning is a small catamaran. It shoots out of Noyac Bay to the south, rounds up near *Lochinvar,* and then goes foaming past. The young man at the helm gives me, in exchange for my wave, a curt nod; he has the mainsheet in his teeth and an air of preoccupation mixed with pride. In a few minutes the catamaran is halfway to Shelter Island, whisking along with one hull lifted clear of the water, our young hero stretching out his weight to hold the boat down. Suddenly a gust hits. The effect is of slow motion, the windward hull lifting, lifting. Why doesn't he let the mainsheet go? The cat flips. The young man falls onto the now horizontal mainsail, but slides off into the water before the sail can submerge completely and the boat turn upside down, mast pointing bottomward. I change course, wondering how to help. But a small motorboat is heading toward the catamaran and stands by as the young man swims around to windward and rights his craft.

For the next few hours I'm in waters that are new to me, the two Peconic Bays, Little and Great. A strong ebb current is running eastward in the narrow passage between Cedar Beach Point on the north side and the thin carrot-shaped sandspit which pokes out from the South Fork. But there's a flicker of a back eddy close to Cedar Beach Point, and some five feet of water, and *Lochinvar* makes use of this to gain entrance to Little Peconic. Then I head north of Robins Island. This is a large teardrop-shaped piece of seemingly unspoiled landscape, with vivid green scrub-oak woods and tan cliffs. On the west side of the island the cliffs are decorated with sinuous natural markings that look like Celtic scrollwork or African tribal incisions. Rusty had told me that Robins was currently the subject of a fight. Despite the declared intentions of Suffolk County to preserve the island in its "natural state," the present owner, a German businessman named Claus Mittermayer (who has a home on Shelter Island), wanted to sell Robins for the construction of houses on thirty of its acres, the remaining 400 acres to be kept as a "nature haven." Mr. Mittermayer's company bought the island for $1.35 million in 1979 and was hoping California developers would now purchase it for $15.2 million. Mr. M.'s view was that the island's timber had been cleared several times in the past for cattle and sheep grazing, and that brickmaking, iron smelting, and game hunting had gone on there. Local environmentalists, however, held that the proposed "nature haven" would benefit only the rich buyers of the proposed mini-estates on Robins; that a brown tide caused by run-off pollution, probably resulting from overdevelopment, was back in the Peconic Bays for the seventh year running; and that there was no such thing as partial development or a partial wildlife refuge. Right now, according to one conservationist, the deer on Robins were so tame they'd eat out of your hand.

The narrows of North Race, with shallows on each side, involve some quick tacking around the top of Robins—today, no sign of deer or developers. Then *Lochinvar* is in Great Peconic Bay, which seems like a spacious inland lake. This morning she shares this splendid sailing territory with only two other boats. If I have a complaint about the scenery, it's to do with a certain sameness—the shores are continuous, thickly wooded, low sandy hills. There are few landmarks other than an occasional spire, water tank, or radio tower lifting above the trees. Looking west, the similar cliffs and woods of each segment of bay make you feel as if you're staring into a mirror facing another mirror, in which what you see is repeated over and over into limitless distances. Yet if you press closer to these apparently uniform shores, you find many diverse creeks and ponds. The ditchlike entries to them are hard to pick out, until you get near them. Most of these snug little refuges have marshy borders, a few private landings, and some moorings for unpretentious craft. "Gunkhole" is the North American term for these intimate recesses, a term that suggests garbage and glop rather than birds and crabs, reeds and marshgrass and rich mud. On the south shore of Great Peconic, what you might think is the entrance to such a creek reveals itself as more important: it has a flashing green light on its entrance buoy, a pair of small breakwaters formalizing the entry, and inside, it is spanned by a number of road and rail bridges. This is the Shinnecock Canal, which makes a connection with the bays and inlets on the Atlantic shore of Long Island; it also makes the eastern part of the South Fork in effect an island, though not many of the residents may be aware of this. The canal current can run at 5 knots. If any craft with a mast, such as *Lochinvar*, wants to pass through the canal, it must use the wharfside crane to remove the spar before shooting under the bridges.

This isn't in my plans today. I run back into Little Peconic via South Race, south of Robins Island, the last of the ebb proving useful as, once again, midday brings a diminishing breeze. *Lochinvar* slides northeastward past North Sea Harbor—a long way in distance and atmosphere from the North Sea—and past Wooley Pond and Fresh Pond. The tide is slack by the time I reach the passage into Noyac Bay, whose sand cliffs shimmer and stand high as in a mirage. It's slow going across to Shelter Island, working the final puffs of the morning breeze to the point of Shell Beach at the left-hand side of the entrance to West Neck Harbor. The tip of the point has to be rounded close at hand; you can see the shoal reaching out from the other shore. I point *Lochinvar* up into the harbor, and when she has ghosted some way in—propelled, it seems, less by breeze than by my desire for lunch—I fling the hook overboard.

But in deference to a sign at the harbor entrance, I do so not too close to the beach. Clam diggers are working the inside of the point, their buckets floating inside inner-tubes; evidently the rights of shellfishermen supercede those of yachtsmen (and shellfish). But my stance on this is wobbly: my lunch includes crab salad, bought in Greenport, together with pita bread, an apple, and a can of Ballantine ale. Like most Europeans, I complain about New World beer, bread, and apples, in my case missing the Young's bitter, granary rolls, and Cox's orange pippins I can buy in Greenwich. Not that I'm grumbling today. West Neck Harbor is lovely. There's only one other visitor at anchor. I came here in *Clio* eight years ago and glimpsed one of the last of the big men-haden boats pulled into the shore, all rust and peeling paint, with ivy and honeysuckle growing around its stanchions. But there's no sign of it today when I get some post-lunch exercise in the dinghy. From the harbor, two creeks—one long, one short—separate two snug coves. The cove at the end of Menantic Creek has a neat little marina packed with prosperous powerboats. *Lochinvar*'s dinghy is neat, little, but less redolent of money. It looks like a shorter version of the flat-bottomed punt Pogo and his fellow cartoon characters used to paddle around their Southern bayou, with names like *Rosey M. Banks* and *Good Ol' Rosey* painted on its sides. My dinghy was built by my Stonington friend Charles Storrow from a design by L. Francis Herreshoff. I sometimes think it should have painted on it *L. Francis H.* and *Good Ol' Charlie.* It has a shippy-looking rope fender around its gunwales and is painted a creamy beige, which contrasts nicely with *Lochinvar*'s royal-blue topsides. It also rows well with seven-foot oars, which are long enough to put power in one's strokes.

Back on board, an early-afternoon stretch-out on a cockpit seat becomes a siesta. I'm wakened by the breeze disturbing the tilt of my hat, which has been forming a shady lean-to over my brow and nose. Time to move on. Going out of the harbor, I admire a fine Victorian white clapboard house on the edge of the island, with green roof, dormer windows, tower, and adjacent stone barn, but then must concentrate. There's the beginnings of a flood current, foul against me, in the narrows by South Ferry. On several occasions with *Clio* the wind faltered as I was attempting this passage under sail. Ferries running between Shelter Island and the North Haven peninsula of the South Fork muscled in from both sides. On the last such occasion, as *Clio* dallied and the ferries pounced, I looked back at the outboard, wondering whether it was time to start it, and happened to notice the bronze plaque which the importers of the boat had fixed to the aft cockpit coaming. It said, *Sailmasters Inc., South Ferry Road, Shelter Island, NY. Clio* had been built in Holland, but this was her American home.

Despite nerves set on edge by the ferries, as I sail through I continue to hope that no bridges get built here and at North Ferry, as Suffolk County bureaucrats now and then propose. There's something in the shift from road to ferry to road again that emphasizes the fact that you are going to an island. The sense of going somewhere different is even stronger if you haven't got a car. Nine Septembers ago, I left *Clio* on a mooring in Sag Harbor, just east of here, for Rusty to use for a few weeks before laying her up at Pierce's. Yaacov had just bought a house in Sag Harbor and kindly offered to drive me to Orient Point, to catch the ferry to New London on my way back to Stonington. But I said that dropping me here at South Ferry would be fine; I

could then make my way across Shelter Island to North
Ferry, and ride the jitney bus from Greenport to Orient
Point. Taking the ferry here gave me a chance to look at the
crossing from the ferry captain's point of view, as the current set his craft sideways and yachts dawdled or rushed to
the east and west. I was the only foot passenger among the
half-dozen cars and single truck on board. The voyage was
over before it occurred to me that, while on board, I should
have tried to hitch a lift across Shelter Island. But how was I
to know who was driving to the middle of the island and
who was going to North Ferry? I was embarrassingly lum-
bered with two heavy canvas bags full of personal gear. I
walked off the ferry and stood at the roadside. The last few
vehicles from the ferry rumbled past and ignored me. The
ferry sat there with its bulwark gates open to receive its new
load of southbound customers. I pondered the enigmatic
sign: ROAD ENDS AT FERRY. At the ferry office in a little hut I
asked about taxis, without success. It was a question of
walk or wait for the next ferry. When it came, I cast away
pride and stuck out my thumb, trying not to look like a villain. Cars went by; their numbers dwindled fast. The last
was an immense immaculate white convertible, a 1950s
Chevrolet with its top down. It rolled off the ferry ramp
and stopped.

"Going far?" asked the blond young man at the wheel.

"Just to North Ferry," I said.

"Hop in."

His companion, also young, also blond, also male, got
out and pulled forward the back of the front seat so that I
could get into the rear with my bags. The seats were glossy
red leather. All the chrome shone.

It was a ten-minute drive along the quiet island roads,

under the tall trees, in the big boatlike Chevy, the golden locks of the lads in front touseled by the slipstream. Not much talking goes on in an open convertible. My samaritans exchanged a few words now and then. They seemed in accord with one another, contained in their partnership. They didn't ask me any questions. When we arrived at North Ferry, I said, "That was really good of you. I hadn't fancied a hike with these bags . . ." But they didn't wait to hear more. Quick smiles, quick waves, and then the car was turning back into the island. Do our guardian angels appear like this, in open Chevrolets, on summer islands? Were they just keeping their hands in for more urgent situations? Or were they the spirits of the place, the *genii loci,* who had decided that in these days of declining public transport the island's reputation for looking after strangers in need must be upheld?

The afternoon breeze doesn't falter today. *Lochinvar* romps past South Ferry and turns south, as I harden the sheets. Sag Harbor lies at the foot of the next stretch, where the channel begins to bend to the east—but it's too soon to drop in there. I'd phoned Yaacov from Greenport, and he's expecting me tomorrow. So, ignoring the too-open Majors Harbor, I gybe around Mashomack Point and run up the eastern shore of Shelter Island. I make sure I avoid two submerged rocks off Cedar Point and Nichols Point. Then I follow the channel into Coecles Harbor. This harbor—which the old books call Coeckles—has a narrow entrance; much intricately shaped space within, with various inner bays, coves, deeps, and shallows; and a secretive atmosphere. It is landlocked and tree-locked. Mashomack Forest grows down to its shores, and ospreys, ibises, egrets, herons, bald eagles, ducks, and oystercatchers call it home.

I choose to anchor a good way from the entrance, close to the southern shore of the harbor, sheltered from the northwest by a curving spit on which stands a house topped with a cupola. From here, as evening comes on, I watch a few other boats sniffing their way in, after a day afloat, pondering where to settle for the night. I hear the crickets in the old woods tune up and frogs start to bellow. And then—the one drawback of Coecles—squadrons of pesky midges and hungry mosquitoes fly onto the scene. (They would attack Margot first if she were here.) Still, after dinner, protected by long sleeves, long trousers, and Deep Woods Off, I sit in the cockpit and appreciate the nearby dark enclosing woods and above me the dizzy shimmer of the Milky Way. A shooting star flares across the sky and I make a wish. If I reveal it, it won't come true. Do people in other galaxies have boats and, anchored, look up at the stars in their night? If not, what is their reason for existence?

6

A MOIST MORNING at Coecles. Warm drizzle is pock-marking the water surface. The wet-leaved trees look tropi-cal. There are places where this coast seems northern, almost like Nova Scotia, say, and certainly more northern than you would expect for the same latitude as Lisbon. Yet in other places it seems like the Deep South, perhaps a backwater behind the Georgia Sea Islands. I draw my head back in and close the hatch, in no hurry to get under way. Sag Harbor, my day's destination, is all of three miles from here. I consult the port-side bookshelf and pull forth a late Conrad, *The Rover,* whose hero is a loner. This novel has cruised with *Lochinvar* for two summers now. I always hope for time for reading; but in these parts, summer day-light disappears fast, the flickering oil lamp glows warm rather than bright, and the effect of fresh air, sun, and early rising is to make one's eyelids droop heavily by 9:00 p.m. For this reason, some books are never opened. Others are easy to dip into; the *Odyssey* is of this kind and I know it well enough to pick up the thread quickly. Now I have at least an hour before the day sorts itself out. There's time to become absorbed in the fate of the old French seaman, Peyrol, dragged out of seclusion on the coast near Toulon by momentous events.

In fact, it is 11:00 when the rain clears, the sun shines, and I break out the anchor—it has been the Danforth's turn to prove its worth. No breeze at all, but the Atomic Four comes to life without hesitation. The engine, by behaving so well, has surely used up one of its trouble-free starts, like one of a cat's nine lives. With the ebb current under her, *Lochinvar* pops out of Coecles and then turns south and into the tide being disgorged around the south side of Shelter Island. I steer close to Cedar Point, which has a small abandoned lighthouse but no cedar trees. The Danforth is waiting unlashed on deck with fifty feet of line. This is not sound practice when sailing, but I want to make anchoring easy again close to the beach behind Cedar Point. There I take a solitary walk along the sand and find pink slipper shells. My guidebook, *Seashells of the World,* says that the male slippers are much smaller than the female, "but may change their sex and grow to a larger size." It's a disturbing evolutionary prospect: small men, dissatisfied with their biological lot, maybe will not just change gender but become big, strapping women. With the beach to myself, I slip into the water for a leisurely swim. This as always is to go back rather than forward in the current of creation—to rejoin my aquatic ancestors, male and female and both, who millions of years ago first slithered out of the water onto a beach like this.

Peanut butter and raspberry jam on pita bread for lunch.

A pulpy peach gets thrown overboard half-eaten. The afternoon is as windless as the morning and hotter. I power slowly south, watching out for the spits, shoals, and rocks in the approaches to Sag Harbor. On reaching the harbor breakwater, I flick on the VHF radio and rehearse a request for a mooring. I'm no good at public speaking. I dislike breaking into the babble of fishermen talking to one another, yachtsmen talking to marinas, to try to catch the ear of the local harbormaster—who has no inkling of my existence until my nervous voice bursts on him from the ether. *Clio* and *Caliban* had no such gadgetry. In my inexperience, I forget the protocol: do I first say the name of the speaker or the intended recipient of the message? One begins on Channel 16 and then switches to another channel. The basic rule is brevity. I press the transmission button and say, "This is *Lochinvar,* calling Sag Harbor harbormaster. Over." And lo, through the static the harbormaster tells me to switch to a channel which I just happen to have. (Adding to the complications of this procedure, there are more channels in use than *Lochinvar* has on its elderly set, making each contact a gamble.) The harbormaster doesn't call *Lochinvar* by name, but I assume he's replying to me. In a few minutes an emissary of the mooring service appears in an outboard-powered inflatable dinghy and leads me to a mooring.

I've arrived here before and had room to serve myself without benefit of radio. Today the town's marinas and docks are jammed with yachts, and the moorings that crowd the area between docks and breakwater at first sight look generally in use. Once I hailed a boatyard launch, paid for a mooring, but then after tying up at the yard in the quiet southeastern corner of the harbor, to load water and

ice, was told I could stay at their float for that night. On
another occasion, a slow survey of the moorings revealed
several empty ones; a further investigation of the pennant of
one such mooring showed a season's growth of green slime
and weed. Deduction: no boat was using this mooring.
Corollary: it was unlikely that, in the small hours, I'd be
woken with the fearsome shout "You're on my mooring!"
The disadvantages were a foredeck covered with slippery
gunge and tiny creatures slithering as fast as they could for
the scuppers and a quick plunge into their element, and
maybe a lingering doubt about the reliability of the mooring
tackle; how long was it since the links of chain and connecting shackles had been overhauled? Still, I decided that on a
calm evening, for just one night, it was worth the risk.
Today, however, unsure when I'll get back to *Lochinvar*
from a liberty trip, and perhaps also in a do-it-properly
mood, I hand over my twenty dollars in return for a clean
mooring pennant. Then I row ashore and call Yaacov.

Yaacov is an old friend whom I seem to see nowadays only
when sailing. In the late 1950s, when Margot and I had a
small apartment on West Seventy-fifth Street in Manhattan,
Yaacov lived two blocks away. I met him at an art gallery; he
and I were the only people to turn up at the opening of an
exhibition, so we started talking. It became clear that we
were both interested in boats and Yaacov had access to one, a
40-foot cutter kept at City Island. I went sailing with him.
Yaacov was born in Poland, grew up in Palestine (under the
prewar British mandate government), served during the
Second World War in several Allied navies, did a stretch in a
Russian prison, and went to university in California. Since
then he had lived mostly in New York, between trips home to
Israel. He usually seems to have several jobs going at once:

teaching navigation, providing marine expertise for filmmakers, writing a readers-aid column for a yachting magazine, doing underwater surveys of African harbors, and delivering yachts across the Atlantic. Part of his apartment was a marine workshop, and where most people would have museum posters or mobiles, bits of rigging hung from the walls. For a few years he was married to a beautiful woman named Nina, a jewelry designer, but she didn't like the sea and enjoyed taking taxis everywhere, horrifying the thrifty Yaacov. Nonetheless, though divorced, they've remained good friends. Yaacov helps Nina with her tax returns and sometimes mends her shoes. He has often helped Margot and me in other ways. When our first child was about to be born, it was Yaacov who drove us across town to the hospital in his little Renault Dauphine, crashing red lights. Yaacov—as described in another place—also gave me a hand in fitting out my thousand-dollar dory-yacht, *Billy Ruffian*.

From time to time you get the impression that Yaacov's marine doings are only some of his activities. For instance, the last time I saw him, he said, "Oh, I was in Tunis in March, but I had to leave a bit quickly. I passed this woman in the street. I hadn't seen her for twenty years. PLO. I could tell she recognized me. I got the next plane out—the one after that would have been too late." It sounded like a yarn based on a movie he'd seen. But not long afterward a Stonington acquaintance said to me, "I ran into your friend Yaacov last spring—in Tunis, of all places. I couldn't work out what he was doing there."

Yaacov meets me at the town dinghy dock by the sewage pumping station. Shorts—leather sandals—a sandy mustache—an ingenuous smile. "You'd better bring your oars from the dinghy," he says, implying that otherwise they won't be here when I return. I show him my canvas bag containing *Lochinvar*'s anchor light, which has sprung a leak and needs his attention. His car is an elderly but stylish Alfa Romeo, which I remark on as we drive through town. "I bought it from a friend," says Yaacov, as he banks around a corner. "It was her son's. He went off to get detoxed. I helped her by buying it. It was rusting in her drive."

Yaacov, a twentieth-century man, is gifted with the waste-not want-not instincts of an early Yankee. As we walk around his house, and its garden running down to Sag Harbor Cove, various objects found, given, or bought for a song come into view: a stack of slightly clouded Thermopane windows; central-heating radiators; dinghies; a new bathtub; a large ship's compass. A story goes with each item. For a start, though, there's the story of Yaacov's house. Ten years ago, Yaacov was driving through this part of town in his car—then a clapped-out Karmann-Ghia, stuffed with boat gear and paint cans—when it broke down. It was a problem he couldn't fix. The man who answered the door of the nearest house let him phone a garage. While Yaacov waited for a tow, the man asked him what he was doing in these parts.

Yaacov said, "Looking for a house to buy."

"My mother's just died," said the man. "She left me this house. I'm thinking of selling it."

He named a sum. Yaacov said that he had only half that to spend. Within ten minutes they had agreed on a price.

The old lady's house had been a rather run-down summer place. Now it looks like what Robinson Crusoe might have had if the departed inhabitants of the island on which he came ashore left the makings of a hundred yard sales. It is a work in progress. There's a spacious workshop in the cellar.

Over the garage there's a semiprivate suite, about to be inhabited for the rest of the summer by a woman from an Upper East Side art gallery whom Yaacov—still attending vernissages—met last week. There's a deck from which you can see through thin trees to the cove.

"No boat right now?" I ask. Yaacov used to have a 28-foot Yugoslav double-ender, *Haviva,* planked with Mediterranean pine; it resembled the caiques of the eastern Mediterranean on which Yaacov sailed as a boy.

"No time," he says. He is adjusting compasses for Montauk fishing boats; he is a consultant for an international youth sail-adventure project called Operation Drake; he teaches a yacht skippers' proficiency class at a Manhattan college twice a week; he has the house to work on. Telephone calls punctuate our talk. A nearby friend wants Yaacov to help him assemble a table-tennis table which has just arrived, unassembled, with inscrutable instructions. An elderly multimillionairess in East Hampton wants Yaacov to accompany her to a benefit ball next week. A younger woman (so I assume from Yaacov's more enthusiastic expression) invites him to dinner tonight here in Sag Harbor, and Yaacov (adopting a rather highfalutin accent) explains my presence: "An Englishman . . . here on his yacht . . ." I get invited, too. At some point we retire to the cellar, and Yaacov hammers, solders, and files the bottom of my beloved old riding light, which has been leaking kerosene. Meantime, I tell him about Wales, where I have been walking. Yaacov tells me that at the end of the war his ship docked in Swansea and he met a Welsh girl he really should have married. But he was only twenty then. It seemed too soon to marry. His voice betrays the feeling that it is too late to marry now. To cheer him up, I recall visits he made to

Stonington when we were living there in the sixties. He had cut a bit of a dash with local society (or at least its female half). "That old Jaguar you had," I say. "One of your semi-mobile paint lockers. You parked it in somebody's driveway on Wamphassuc Point all one summer."

"She finally made me take it away," says Yaacov. Then he reflects. "Maybe I should go to Stonington again."

Later that night—we are staying out of cars after drinking a good deal of wine—Yaacov rows me and my oars and lamp back to the dinghy dock. I balance his small dinghy by sitting in the bow while he sits on the stern thwart, facing forward to row. There is something unpretentiously salty about this. We pass along the cove, under the road bridge, and into the main harbor. Dim shapes of silent yachts loom up and vanish. It's a misty night, the stars obscured. When I've boarded my dinghy, Yaacov rows beside me in his until he's sure I've found the unlit *Lochinvar*. Then, with a "Cheerio" and "Good sailing!" he rows back to the cove. I decide not to read a little Conrad before sleeping. I hardly need to, it occurs to me. Yaacov *is* the Rover.

7

SAG HARBOR is in many ways a sister to Stonington. A small port town with many colonial, Federal, and Greek Revival houses, it was attacked, as Stonington was, by the British during the War of 1812, though here the British actually sent in a landing party and burned some of the wharves. In the first half of the nineteenth century, Sag Harbor's ships sailed the world, whaling and trading; sixty-three whalers left from here in the year 1845 alone. In the same year, the Sag Harbor ship *Manhattan,* under the command of Captain Mercator Cooper, rescued some Japanese fishermen and put them ashore in the port of Yedo (now Tokyo), Japan, thus becoming the first United States vessel to gain entry to that hermetic country. Another Cooper, the author James Fenimore, lived in Sag Harbor from 1819 to 1823, and based the adventures of his character Natty Bumppo on those of local skipper David Hand. The town's last whaler, the *Myra,* sailed in 1871. Whaling days are memorialized now in cemetery gravestones and exhibits in the Whaling Museum on Main Street, with its four-columned portico and whale-jawbone entrance; there's an awful lot of scrimshaw, the making of which kept the hands busy while waiting for the shout "Thar she blows!" Now the town, like many places whose fortune resides in its proximity to water and a quaint architectural inheritance, seems to make its living from leisure and nostalgia, from yachting people and buyers of antiques. It also has the common small-town worries: the high-school dropout rate, the cost of cable TV, the leaking roof at the new firehouse, and how to turn the town dump into a recycling center.

In the morning I shop for milk, salami, bread, plums, and ice. Back on board there are a few niggling jobs to be caught up with. Every boat has an item of equipment which serves as a focus for frequent effort and exasperation. On *Clio* it was the switch of the electric pump on the fresh-water pressure system. On *Lochinvar,* whose fresh-water pump is manual, the troublemaker is the speed log. This has a gauge in the cockpit that registers the boat's speed in knots. The needle on the dial is moved by current from a tiny generator worked by an equally miniature paddle wheel sticking out from the hull underwater. This paddle wheel gets clogged with weed, but can be cleaned in two ways. You either rig a line under the boat from side to side, put on a face mask, hold your breath, and swim down; then clutch the line with one hand while brushing the paddle wheel with an old toothbrush until it spins freely. Or you can move the companionway steps and box at the forward end of the engine, and lift aside two heavy batteries. This makes it possible to get at the speed log fitting, a solid plastic cylinder in which the paddle wheel is fixed. A screw ring holds the cylinder tight where it passes through the hull. Before removing the paddle-wheel cylinder, you have to have at hand a similar-sized temporary plug. Then—skip these details if they're too much for you, but this is what sailing's all about—then I unscrew the hold-down ring, push a small screwdriver through a hole drilled horizontally through the cylinder, and heave, just so much, so that the cylinder starts to come up out of its tube, hold the plug ready, and then pull the cylinder all the way out. A stout green column of water jets upward inside the boat. For an instant I can see the water under *Lochinvar*'s hull and have a vision of sinking. Then I push in the plug; it wobbles for a moment against the jetting water. Then I've got it in and push it down. The inflow stops. Everything in the boat around me is wet.

There are a few strands of eelgrass and what look like some flakes of anti-fouling paint which I remove from the paddle wheel. I spin it to ensure it's free. Then the removal procedure in reverse: plug out; jet of water; shove in paddle-wheel cylinder; tighten down screw ring. Back go the batteries, engine box, steps. Sponge the cabin sole and starboard bunk, which was in direct line of the geyser. Pump the bilges dry. Hope that does the trick. If it doesn't, as is sometimes the case, it leads to another problem: the wiring from the paddle-wheel generator to the gauge is loose; the cables have to be disconnected and their ends cleaned of corrosion and grime before being refastened to the terminals (which should also be wire-brushed) and sealed with Vaseline. And all this for one instrument! On previous boats I estimated how fast I was going. *Lochinvar* came with a speed log and I'm a captive of its needs. When I have dried myself off after one or other of these performances, I have to admit that the log is a help, not just when trying to get extra speed from the boat by experimenting with sail trim, but when navigating in poor visibility. If you know exactly what speed you've been doing, you have a better idea of how far you've gone and therefore where you are.

Where I am now, as I look around at noon conditions, is where I think of staying. It's overcast, with a squally south-easterly. But I'm expected in East Hampton tonight. Three Mile Harbor, which I intend to sail to, is a little closer to that town, and anyway, a touch of nasty weather provides a work-up for really nasty weather. I stow everything as firmly as possible. I tie the oars in the dinghy, put the plug in the sink, and turn off the sea cock on the drainpipe. I tie a single reef in the main and leave the jib rolled up for the time being. There's just room enough astern to get away without the engine. I make sure the mainsheet is uncleated, so that the mainsail isn't penned in. I drop the mooring, hasten aft, and put the tiller hard over to port so that *Lochinvar* as she drifts back tucks her stern over to star-board. The wind coming over the starboard bow fills the main. *Lochinvar* gathers way. I slowly ease the sheet for a moment, heading toward the breakwater, then quickly haul in the sheet, gybe, and run out of Sag Harbor.

Once outside, going east and to windward, I need center-board and jib. Now and then the lee rail dips under. Now and then the not unfamiliar thought occurs: Perhaps I should have put in the second reef. In the gusts I have to let out the main, so that the forward third of it luffs, back-winded, and the boat drives along on the jib and the aft part of the main. The sail shakes noisily, setting up a sympa-thetic vibration in my sailor's conscience: I know that this luffing and shaking isn't good for anything except the repair business of sailmakers. Once around Mashomack Point I can bear off with full sails. But this is only five minutes of relief, for *Lochinvar* is soon abreast of Cedar Point and I need to come hard on the wind again. Meanwhile I have to stay off the shallows north of the Point and away from the rocks the chart calls dangerous—indeed, that is their name, Dangerous Rocks.

I don't want to get too far out into Gardiners Bay, which today I'd call rough. The waves get more wicked out of the lee of the land, where low cliffs back the beach that curves in a shallow bay between Cedar Point and Hog Creek Point. The entrance to Three Mile Harbor is mid-curve, at the east end of Sammy's Beach, but *Lochinvar* can't lay it with the wind where it is. A tack in, another tack out, therefore, and when the occasional sea breaks over the bow and cascades aft, wet-faced I come about again and head inshore. Jetties at either side protect the entrance, and in here *Lochinvar* consents to point high enough to scramble over the outgoing current. Once well inside, I roll up the jib and saunter along the channel under the main.

Three Mile Harbor may have seemed that long to those who named, it but in fact it's just over two miles from the entrance to the foot of the innermost cove. Several marinas and boatyards are on the port hand not far from the entrance; at one of them, the Maidstone Boatyard, I was a reluctant customer some years ago when *Caliban*'s center-board pennant parted en route to Montauk after a visit to Three Mile and we had to return for repairs. To starboard, the channel is banked by a bulging spit that continues far-ther south into the harbor in the form of a shoal. (Worth remembering, in case you're tempted to make a right turn too soon.) In the past, I've anchored *Caliban* and *Clio* up in the northwestern corner of Three Mile, where it's a short row in and a quick walk from the marsh covered with sea lavender to the delights of Sammy's Beach: nice sand and good swimming, though I recall some nettlesome jellyfish there on one visit. Today I keep going down toward the southern end of the harbor, where there's still room to anchor among the moorings. At the very end, there is a cove where I've left *Clio* at anchor, though I now see in Duncan and Ware's *Cruising Guide* that anchoring there isn't permitted. I've also berthed *Clio* in one of the small marinas on the creek that winds to this cove, on an occasion when I hadn't brought a dinghy. But I'm not fond of marinas. I've never become handy at the backing in you have to do to enter a slip (if you want your stern to the dock). I'm not good at rigging the cat's cradle of lines that are needed to hold the boat in place between pilings as the tide rises and falls. Moreover, marinas are claustrophobic: they pen you in, with their showers and washing machines and shore current. I don't enjoy having to listen to the clang and clatter of halyards on alloy masts. And there can be other problems from being so closely attached to the land. A New York surgeon I know kept his handsome 35 foot Nielsen yawl in one of these marinas, where a trim lawn divides the slips from the road to East Hampton. It seemed a convenient and attractive spot to him, until one night a car came off the road at high speed and crashed on his deck, demolishing both masts, the cockpit, and the cabin top.

After the hook has dug in well, I row up the creek to the town dock and leave the dinghy among a pack of its colleagues. Finding the right spot to leave one's tender sometimes needs prospecting for; the float or section of wharf designated for itinerants' dinghies isn't always evident. "You can't leave that dinghy there!" is the welcome I've had in several harbors. But there is no such problem here. A phone call to Eloise Spaeth's house in East Hampton is answered by Eloise's granddaughter Megan Doherty, an artist; she'll drive over to collect me. While I wait, I fill up my empty water bottles and leave them in the dinghy ready to take back to *Lochinvar.*

I enjoy the contrast between my boating life, whose independent character is exemplified by those water bottles, and the fancy shore life I now and then dip into. The apparently simpler boating life is just as privileged as the other, maybe more so. In East Hampton, summer generates an expensive social ferment. For three months, there are parties, exhibition openings, charity dances, and private dinners. Artistic people mingle with industrialists and financiers in a potent, glamorous mix of creativity and money. This is all staged in an attractive if rather elongated small town. What was a farming village became a summer resort in the nineteenth century, and early in the twentieth many artists followed the painter Thomas Moran in coming to live here; as in other places, the rich and influential followed the artists, if only seasonally. Now, old coffee-colored shingle houses are squeezed among chic shops and restaurants, and in the surrounding former potato fields more recent mansions and great estates vie for place. East Hampton claims as one of its sons the versifier John Howard Payne, who grew up in a house overlooking the tree-surrounded village green, and who wrote the song "Home, Sweet Home"—"Be it ever so humble, there's no place like home." But I wouldn't say that East Hampton's big feature is humility.

However, its respect for originality in the arts and the presence of so many artists makes the place attractive for many art lovers. Eloise Spaeth and her late husband, Otto, first came out here in the late 1940s. Otto had owned a machine-tool factory in Dayton, Ohio, and during the war they had taken me, a child evacuated from Britain, into their family. Both Otto and Eloise cared greatly for art; their house was full of wonderful pictures and pieces of sculpture. When they moved from Dayton to a Manhattan apartment, they also built a summer house here, a striking contemporary version of the shingle style. (It stands, in a little road called Spaeth Lane, behind the dunes near the Maidstone Club, where Otto used to play golf.) After Otto's death, Eloise built a smaller house backing on the golf course and within sound of the sea. Here, where Megan drops me, one is likely to bump into museum curators, art critics, and various Spaeth children and grandchildren. Although she is ninety, Eloise looks and acts at least twenty years younger; she continues to buy work by little-known artists; she's in touch with many well-known artists whose early careers she and Otto helped foster.

After Eloise and I have a cup of tea on her upstairs, outside deck and exchange family news, I take a walk on the beach. Beyond the surf, beyond the swell rolling in diagonally from the southeast, a fishing vessel slowly drags its nets. The gray afternoon, humid wind, and lively sea appear to have kept most beachgoers away. I stride happily along, for a while walking on damp sand and then, for a change of pace, on dry. The ocean stretches away southward. Back at Eloise's I swim in her small, warm pool, listening to chirruping birds and a pair of golfers discussing the approach to the next hole. In my best shore-going rig of navy blazer and tan trousers, white shirt and tie, I accompany Eloise to the East Hampton Guild Hall, whose art gallery has an opening tonight. "Local Artists" are being shown, though these aren't exactly the usual Sunday painters. The works are by Pollock, Krasner, Solomon, Ernst, Steinberg, Gottlieb, de Kooning, et al. As at such occasions elsewhere, few people in the talkative throng are looking at the pictures. But here, the gallerygoers have an air of being at the center of the universe. Nowhere else is so *in* or *with it*.

Eloise and I have a quiet supper together. At one point she suddenly asks, as if it is something that she—as my wartime foster mother—really ought to know, "How did you ever get started with boats and sailing, anyway?"

"You've forgotten. It was that camp in Michigan you sent me and Tony Spaeth to. Camp Fairwood, on Torch Lake. Our first summer there, in carpentry lessons, we each had to build a little wooden punt. They were basic boats, low and almost square, and we paddled them around in the swimming area. The next summer we were actually taken out in proper sailboats. We were shown how to tack and gybe, how to take the helm and trim the sheets, when to duck our heads and how to hike out. I was impressed by being able to use the wind, and then by the sound, the feel of water. I thought it was wonderful."

8

IN HIS MAGISTERIAL STUDY *Influence of Seapower Upon History*, Admiral Alfred Thayer Mahan in 1890 considered Gardiners Bay to be one of those "points" that an enemy might seize and hold with his fleet if "intending serious operations" against the Eastern Seaboard of the United States. Here lay Admiral Arbuthnot's British fleet in 1781, keeping an eye on the French in Rhode Island. The roll call of ships was impressive: *Grand Duke*, 120 guns; *London*, 120; *Royal George*, 100; *Bedford*, 100; *Royal Oak*, 100; *Centurion*, 80; *Robust*, 74; *Culloden*, 74; and many smaller vessels. The station could be hazardous. The *Culloden*, setting forth in a rising winter gale to make contact with French ships reportedly sailing out of Newport, ran aground off Will's Point, at the east end of Fort Pond Bay near Montauk. When she couldn't be refloated, her crew unloaded cannons, gear, and stores into smaller craft and then burned her to the waterline, leaving sixteen of her

32-pounder guns to be salvaged the following summer by men from Groton, Connecticut. Will's Point was renamed Culloden Point.

In the War of 1812, Gardiners Bay was the base for Rear Admiral Hotham's fleet, which bottled up Decatur's ships in the river Thames at New London, bombarded and raided such places as Stonington and Sag Harbor, and (depending on who's telling the story) plundered cattle and timber or traded for provisions. One Shelter Islander, Lodowick Havens, recalled how the inhabitants sold "any and every-thing" to the crews of the British ships "at the highest prices for gold and silver." Some locals were more hostile: what Hardy called a "torpedo" attack was launched at his ship, the *Ramillies,* though the device—a boat loaded with explosives—missed its target and went ashore near Greenport. The British on one occasion landed on Little Gull Island and destroyed the lamps in the lighthouse. This act was well avenged, to American minds, when a British barge later ran onto Plum Island in the dark with the loss of several of its crew.

There's a thin haze this morning as *Lochinvar* runs quietly out of Three Mile with the ebb current and turns east toward Gardiners Island. Blue sky above, a shimmering sea, and a faint southerly just keeping the sails full. Half closing my eyes, I imagine the old warships lying at anchor close to the island, sails furled or hanging loose, drying out in a calm, some sunlit, some in shadow, while the gigs and cutters dance attendance on the dark high-sided hulls, Great Britain's "wooden walls," ferrying men and supplies between ships and shore.

Cherry Harbor is the name of this anchorage. It is less a harbor than a roadstead protected by the South Fork of

Long Island to the west and south and by Gardiners Island to the east. I take *Lochinvar* in close to the beach at Cherry Hill Point, the northern end of the so-called harbor. Sixteen years ago I anchored *Caliban* here and landed, in several dinghy loads, a picnic party: Margot, Rusty, and Rusty's children, Stephen and Kate. Rusty was nervous. Gardiners Island is private, and those who look after it have been known to get shirty with uninvited visitors. But it was low tide, and we restricted our invasion to the deserted beach below the high-water mark—conforming, I hoped, to common law. We had lunch, a swim, and a walk to collect shells, and were reboarding *Caliban* when a sleek black launch went past at speed with a gray-haired man at the wheel and a party of elegant-looking people. On the launch's transom it said LADY BOUNTIFUL, GARDINERS ISLAND. This had to be the Lord of the Manor. I gave the launch a wave expressive (I thought) of peaceful intent. No one waved back.

Gardiners Island has belonged to the Gardiners since 1639. It is owned by a trust whose main beneficiaries are Robert Lion Gardiner, now in his early eighties, and his niece Alexandra Gardiner Goelet. Mrs. Goelet or her children will inherit the island when Mr. Gardiner dies. For the last few years, she and her uncle have been squabbling about the future of the island: a five-square-mile chunk of woods, meadows, marsh, and beaches which has changed very little since the first Gardiner set foot on it. (It does have an eighteenth-century windmill, a grass airstrip, a boat dock, and a large brick manor house, built in the late 1940s, following a fire that destroyed the island's colonial mansion.) The woods contain many old white oaks, wild deer and wild turkeys, and ospreys or fish hawks, survivors of the DDT-using decades which endangered them. Uncle and niece each claim to have the island's environmental interests at heart, though Mr. Gardiner accuses Mrs. Goelet of wanting to develop it after he's gone; she, denying any such intention, claims to have paid ten years' worth of property taxes. A project no longer much mentioned was that of a local congressman, Representative Otis Pike, who in the 1970s wanted the island designated as a national monument and opened up to picnickers like us. I was told in East Hampton that Mr. Gardiner and Mrs. Goelet now take turns using the island, and Mr G. makes an effort to spread around some of its benefits, letting Boy Scouts camp and conducting parties of Audubon Society members through the woods and meadows.

The Montauk Indians called the island Manchonake, "the island where many had died," and perhaps were glad to unload it on Lion Gardiner, an early-seventeenth-century English army engineer. He acquired it for the then customary prices: according to one tale, for a blanket, some trinkets, a large dog, and a bottle of rum; according to another, for ten coat-lengths of trading cloth. Lion Gardiner renamed his purchase the Isle of Wight and proceeded to farm it. He got on well with the Montauketts, who paddled their war canoes out to Block Island to fight the Narragansetts there and who sometimes fought the English and Dutch intruders. By the time of his death, in 1663, the island had acquired its present name. Lion's robust grandson John Gardiner became lord of the island in 1689; he had four consecutive legitimate wives but also many native interests. He spoke the Indian language, went whaling with the Indian men, and fathered numerous children on Indian women. He died in 1738 at the age of seventy-seven after a fall from a horse in

Groton, Connecticut, where he had other estates.

In his years on the island, hostile pirates sometimes dropped by. A party of Spanish desperadoes landed in September 1728 and rifled John's house. It was also raided by a Block Island ruffian named Paul Williams. But word got around that Gardiner might be receiving these visits because he'd fallen out with former friends; it was said that he was in league with Gentleman Stede Bonnet, who had landed ill-gotten merchandise on Gardiners Island for trans-shipment to Long Island and Connecticut.

As a matter of fact, John's reputation was already tainted by his association with Captain William Kidd, New York merchant and privateer, who was proclaimed a pirate in 1699, though perhaps unjustly. It was at Gardiners Island that Kidd had unloaded an Arabian treasure; he had no intention of sharing the proceeds with the British governor of New York. Kidd had taken the treasure from a ship which was sailing with French letters of marque and was thus, since the English were then at war with the French, a legitimate prize. According to Gardiner family tradition, some was buried "in a swampy place at Cherry Harbor." Kidd was arrested, sent to England, and charged, not with piracy, since evidence was lacking, but with the killing of a sailor. Protesting his innocence to the last, Kidd was hanged. John Gardiner received a summons to cough up any treasure left on the island. He brought some to Boston, but may have kept some bales of silk and a chest of precious stones, silver, and gold cloth, together with cloves and nutmegs. However, the author Robert Payne, who has looked into these doings, says that despite much suspicion of Gardiner's ties with Kidd, "no one was ever able to prove that he kept more than a solitary uncut diamond."

Even so, "Captain Kidd's treasure" may have induced those later pirates to call on John Gardiner and has since lured many a hopeful if clandestine digger to Cherry Harbor. According to Sarah D. Gardiner, who wrote a memoir of the island in 1944, an island steward once carved the initials WK on a large boulder he wanted moved, and allowed some treasure seekers to do the work for him. As a Greenwich man, I'm delighted that some of the proceeds of the sale of the Kidd spoils brought by Gardiner to Boston in 1705 went toward the upkeep of pensioners and invalid sailors in Greenwich Hospital, now the Royal Naval College.

A century later, the then Lord of the Manor, John Lyon Gardiner, aged thirty-three, made a note to himself—"To get me a good wife"—and a few months later married young Sarah Griswold from Connecticut. J.L.G. also kept notes on the birds he saw on the island, in particular the ospreys:

> When the Fish Hawks are seen high in the air sailing around in circles it is a sign of change of weather very soon—generally of a thunder storm in two or three hours.
>
> [They] are never known to eat anything but fish—commonly eat them the head first. Are frequently seen cutting strange gambols in the air—with part of fish in their claws—with loud vociferations darting down perhaps 100 yards. They seem proud of their prey.
>
> Seldom take one from the ground when dropped.

After the bird-watcher's death in 1816, the island passed to his cousin David Gardiner, whose daughter Julia was born on the island in 1820. She grew up to be a beauty, "the Rose of Long Island," and at nineteen shocked her staid contemporaries by wearing a sunbonnet trimmed with ostrich feathers in a lithographic advertisement for a New York dry-goods store. But the scandal didn't stop Julia causing hearts to throb on a European tour and then, in Washington, D.C., winning that of the widower President John Tyler. They met on the frigate *Princeton*, on the Potomac, during a presidential naval review in 1844. A gun exploded, killing David Gardiner, a New York state senator. The President comforted the young lady, and they married later in the year. But Julia was in the White House for only a year before Tyler lost the presidency to Polk.

In the first half of this century the island was leased out much of the time to wealthy sportsmen, like Winston Guest, for the shooting. Baron von Blixen, husband of Isak Dinesen, was gamekeeper here for a while and kept a Turkish butler and a series of mistresses. Despite rumors of dire developments—a casino, a hideaway for the black evangelist Father Divine, a suburban subdivision—the only real damage to date has been done by hurricanes and the fires which destroyed the first manor house of Lion Gardiner in the eighteenth century and its replacement in 1944. This second conflagration happened on a January night; Winston Guest's caretakers, Mr. and Mrs. James Eccles, and a visiting writer named Van Campen Heilner, escaped by jumping from bedroom windows. (Heilner, also a pith-helmeted explorer and big-game hunter, took a 40-foot motorboat from New Jersey to Venezuela at the age of eighteen, befriended Ernest Hemingway, and in 1928, to prove a theory that sharks were harmless if properly approached, sailed to the Bahamas to swim in shark-infested waters. Heilner survived until 1970, dying—well away from the water—in Madrid at the age of seventy-one.)

I tack out of Cherry Harbor into Napeague Bay by way of the channel that leads south of Gardiners Island and an off-lying fragment called Cartwright Island. With the mid-morning ascent of the sun the breeze picks up; *Lochinvar* rustles along. On Hog Creek Point, off to starboard on the South Fork, is a spot named Fireplace, where various Gardiners lit bonfires to signal for an island boat to come to pick them up. (People on the island were annoyed when one mid-nineteenth-century door-to-door salesman called the boat over by using the same technique.) I spurn the shallow promises of Accabonac Harbor, a refuge bordered by marshes; at low water its entrance channel hasn't the depth that *Lochinvar* requires. I also give Cartwright Island a wide berth, remembering the time I took a shortcut and ran aground here. The tide was falling then, as it is now. An attempt to kedge off was a failure. I jumped overboard into two feet or so of water and pushed on *Caliban*'s transom while Margot hauled on the anchor line. The ebb current sluiced around my thighs. I reckoned that we might be there, sharply heeled over, for the next eight hours. But *Caliban* began to budge. She floated off. I clambered into the dinghy, and then into *Caliban*.

Another tack brings us past the fish factory at Promised Land. A strong whiff of it is borne on the south wind. Perhaps as a way of keeping in with the Almighty, many of these fishy places have biblical names: Jerusalem and Galilee, the fishing ports at Point Judith, Rhode Island, come to mind. Napeague Harbor, which is next, can wait for future investigation. It looks intriguing, surrounded by the woods and dunes of Hither Hills State Park, and I know *Lochinvar* has found her way in there under her previous owners to anchor overnight. But not now, with a falling tide and a wind sure to be on the nose in the unbuoyed entrance. Instead, I free the sheets and let *Lochinvar* reach along in absolutely smooth water a few hundred yards offshore. Once past Rocky Point I steer across Fort Pond Bay and inside the whistle buoy which warns of Culloden Point. My authority for this spot is a Swiss writer, the late Max Frisch. In a short novel called *Montauk,* which was about a brief affair between a Swiss novelist who thinks he looks like a walrus and a red-haired New York publisher's publicity woman half his age, Frisch described Culloden Point as "a flat area full of shacks, some falling down, motorboats tied to buoys, others on land awaiting repair, parking lots, gas stations, with pennants, piles of old tires, an area full of trash of all kinds, puddles, the familiar signs—FOR SALE, TEXACO, PIZZA, SHELL, BLUE RIBBON, HAMBURGER, REAL ESTATE."

Adverse wind and current force me to motor into what the chart calls Lake Montauk and is otherwise known as Great Pond or Montauk Harbor. There are jetties on each side of the entrance, and a stubby finger of land projecting from the east side that narrows the mouth of the lake. Several sportfishing boats power loudly out, making the gap seem even narrower. This is sportfishingville. The craft at the marinas are almost all powerboats, with jutting pulpits, towers on tubular legs, and outrigger fishing poles, for use in spearing, spotting, and hooking fish. Several of the marinas—which tend to call themselves yacht clubs—are on Star Island inside the harbor entrance, tethered to land by a causeway. Without this link, you feel Star Island might float north and plug the mouth of the lake. Beyond the island, and the Coast Guard station on it, the lake extends south almost to the ocean beach, with houses dotted around its low rim. Formerly a pond, fully enclosed, it was—like others on this coast—seen to offer the makings of a useful harbor; it wasn't hard to dig a channel, which dredging and the natural scouring of the currents keep navigable. But despite the secure, enclosed feeling that the harbor still gives, it is reputed to be poor holding ground, with currents that make boats wander over their anchors and even pull them loose. I therefore direct *Lochinvar* around the sandbar beyond Star Island and head toward the farthest southern reaches. There I anchor—cautiously, with both Danforth and Fisherman—in water just deep enough for *Lochinvar,* away from the churlish currents and the throb and wake of powerboats. (While in Montauk, I ought to desist from crusty sailing man's thoughts about "stinkpots." I should try to see such craft not as gas-guzzling noisemakers but as potential nice guys who someday may pull me off a shoal or tow me into harbor when my mast falls down.)

I row ashore and buy some 3-in-One oil and a jerry can of gasoline at Captains Marina. Here the dinghy and my purchases can stay for a few hours while I reconnoiter this eastern tip of Long Island. I turn my back for the moment on the motels, restaurants, and bars of Montauk, which I've seen on an earlier visit. The seven-story mock-Tudor buildings which a developer named Carl Fisher put up in the late 1920s give the place a surreal aspect. Fisher believed that Montauk, at the end of the Long Island Railroad, could become a major port for transatlantic liners. The *Berengaria* and the *Bremen* and the *Ile de France* would come into the deep waters of Fort Pond Bay and dock at the railhead. Why Fisher thought the passengers with their steamer trunks would want to transfer to the rackety railroad for a three-hour trip to the big city in lieu of disembarking at a midtown Manhattan pier is anybody's guess. The scheme petered out with the Depression, and despite occasional efforts to breathe life into his neo-Elizabethan half-timbered shops, offices, and apartments, the result still seems half-finished and half-baked.

The sailor ashore, I walk two miles east to Montauk Point. I've no burdens, no need to hitchhike, and can stride along the verge unbothered by traffic scanty at mid-week and thinning out even more near the end of the road. Along the way, several radar antennae that rear up out of the sandhills like giant mushrooms were, not long ago, ready to provide early notice of trouble from evil empires. The last landmark gives an older form of warning. This is Montauk lighthouse, a 100-foot-tall octagonal tower, painted white with a brown band, which was commissioned by George Washington, President. But no keeper climbs it now to trim the lamps; all is automatic. Modern shipping, with its loran and satellite positioning systems, is in less danger than the lighthouse itself, perched on a 60-foot-high bluff above the relentlessly encroaching sea. I clamber on the rocks below the light and then sit for a while, fully oriented, watching the gulls and terns compete for fish. They dive into the waves between the point and a bell buoy that marks Great Eastern Rock. Farther east, twelve miles distant, the cliffs of Block Island faintly interrupt the horizon.

In the 1920s, rumrunners used to dash through this broad gap with cargoes of hooch unloaded from ships outside the twelve-mile limit. In recent years drug smugglers have been sneaking in the same way. People on Cape Cod, Narragansett Bay, Fishers Island Sound, and particularly here around Montauk and Gardiners Bay, have almost become accustomed to hearing "noises in the night" and seeing in the small hours fishing craft and powerboats close to unlikely spots along the shore, engines running, with smaller boats alongside, while pickup trucks and camper vans wait on land. Summer houses are discreetly rented out-of-season for short periods. Now and then the Coast Guard, Customs Service agents, Drug Enforcement Administration investigators, and local policemen pounce; yachts and trawlers are towed into Montauk, the handcuffed suspects are led away shielding their faces, and bales are unloaded. The cargoes are generally Colombian marijuana, with (it is usually claimed) a "street-value" in the millions. The profits are so great some traffickers unload the cargo and leave the boat behind. The smugglers for some reason favor vessels registered in Colombia or the Cayman Islands, which doesn't seem like camouflage, though British yachts and craft from this coast have also been nabbed, confiscated by the U.S. government, and then sold.

Dozing on the warm rocks, breathing salt air, listening to stones grate against stones, I wonder how fruitful the cops-and-robbers approach is to this so-called epidemic. Prohibitions create their own thrills and fortunes; they engender their own bureaucracies, too. We are hooked on an inert doctrine. Marijuana, by most accounts, is no more injurious than rum, whiskey, gin, and vodka. (I'm not sure how valid the argument is that the use of hash leads inexorably to the real killers like heroin and cocaine.) Certainly the present situation, which makes it illicit to supply the tremendous demand for nirvana-inducing products, warps many lives. People increasingly resort to crime to pay for the stuff. The price gets higher, and not just in terms of money; there are hordes of victims. One Block Island man who was growing a small marijuana crop had his property confiscated. It has now been sold; in effect a $200,000 fine, with the proceeds going to the police. This is a way—and surely a corrupting one—of financing enforcement agencies.

Innocence is no guarantee for a quiet existence. Lawlessness and violence overlap our lives even at sea. One friend from Stonington sailing in the Bahamas had his 42-foot ketch hijacked; his pride and joy, it was never seen again. Another Stonington man and his wife, lying peacefully at anchor one night, were woken by searchlight beams and shouts; men carrying shotguns boarded their boat, identified themselves as lawmen to the terrified couple, and then pulled the boat inside out for several hours in search of drugs that weren't and never had been there. A tip-off had presumably gone wrong somewhere along the line. Sailing into Greenport several years ago in *Clio,* I saw a ball of orange flame. A powerboat was on fire. Later, on the dock at Preston's, one of those waterfront veterans who pass their time looking nostalgically out over the briny told me, "Oh, that's the second we've had in two weeks. Getting rid of the evidence, if you ask me."

Watching the gulls and terns squabble over the unseen fish, I think the sea is the finest addiction—if you ask me.

9

A LOVELY DAY. It starts sunny, with light airs from the east. This could mean fog, but there's no sign of it yet. *Lochinvar* slips out of Montauk at 8:00 over the last of the flood, sails full, on a broad reach. Half a dozen sportfishing boats, engines grumbling at low speed, are also making their exits, though once outside the jetties their skippers thrust forward their throttle levers and the boats racket off assertively toward Block Island. When the disturbance from their wakes has gone, I harden in the sheets a hair, let the bow come up a little into the wind, and keep an eye on the compass until the lubber line coincides with due north. My intended course is slightly east of this, but I take into account the morning current, which will set me eastward, and therefore calls for a course adjusted to the west. Fishers Island, which should be my next landfall, is out of sight twelve miles north. By 9:00 the breeze has freshened just enough. *Lochinvar* chuckles along at four and a half, sometimes five knots; the speed log is behaving nicely. I gaze around the boat at knots and shackles, fastenings and fittings, that ought not to but might give way, and "bear watching." From time to time I check the luffs of main and jib for firmness. To find if I can get more drive from the air passing over my Dacron wings, I let out the sheets until the sails start to flutter a little, then pull them slightly in.

During one of these periodic sessions of inspection and refinement I look to windward. A huge black submarine ambles along a few hundred yards off my starboard quarter, water streaming over its low flat back, on a course which surely is converging with *Lochinvar*'s. Power is meant to give way to sail—at least in open waters like these. But does anyone on this nuclear-powered monster see the lone sailor? There is not the slightest sign of human activity. The sub is evidently headed for the Race at the west end of Fishers, and its base in the Thames River. (*Lochinvar* is making for the east end of Fishers.) I take for granted that it's not some rogue Russian about to launch a sneak attack on New London. More to the point, is it going to collide with me? I'm about to take evasive action when someone (or something) on the sub comes to a decision, and the great black Leviathan accelerates, veering to starboard, until it is well clear ahead and can resume its previous course. Perhaps because submarines seem so blind, they aren't the friendliest vessels to encounter out here. I suppose we should be grateful to them for helping hold the balance of power during the long cold war, but I'm prepared to hear ill of them. One yachtsman of my acquaintance claims one came up right underneath his boat as he was sailing along between Montauk and Fishers Island and gave him the most tremendous shock and sideways shove, though no great damage was done. A few years ago an inquiry was held at the New London sub base into cans of paint, garbage, and papers marked *Confidential* that had been netted by two Montauk fishing draggers five miles northwest of Culloden Point. These items were traced to the U.S.S. *Shark,* a 251-foot nuclear attack submarine.

Apart from this, it's one of those days when nothing much happens; not that I'm unhappy about that. Occasionally the air gets damp and the distant haze looks like thickening into fog, but it never quite does. A few yachts pass ahead or astern, in from or out to Block Island Sound. I glance approvingly at those under sail and dismissively at those which are powering, sometimes with mainsails up and impotently shaking. But as always when in a self-righteous mood I need to make sure fate won't punish me for it. I slacken the main a fraction so that *Lochinvar* steers herself. Then I go below and check that the head isn't leaking and that I've remembered to turn off the stopcock under the sink. While down there I get some cheese, raisins, and an apple for a snack and pull out the chart for Fishers Island Sound, ready for when we get there.

Cerberus Shoal, halfway to Fishers, is the cue to check my pilotage. Its whistle buoy comes up close on the starboard bow. Due north remains my compass heading. After another hour, Fishers comes into view out of the haze, slowly expanding across the horizon ahead. As soon as I'm sure the current won't set me too far east of Wicopesset Passage, which will lead me into Fishers Island Sound, I bring the boat's head up a smidgeon east of north. After that, it's a matter of finding the right mansion on the shore of Fishers as a mark to steer by, so that *Lochinvar* arrives without meandering at East Point.

Between East Point on Fishers and Watch Hill Point on the mainland, there are five passages into Fishers Island Sound through a string of reefs and rocks. Wicopesset is the westernmost of these passages, fenced by rocks off East Point on the port side going in and by the eelgrass-covered boulder patch which is Wicopesset Island to starboard. The tide is running out of the Sound and the breeze seems to be inclined for a midday rest as *Lochinvar* enters the passage. She still moves purposefully through the water, but only just creeps forward over the bottom. In order to tell if she starts going backward, I line up one of the most prominent rocks with Whitecaps, the banal name for the extraordinary replica château that straddles East Point. The name Wicopesset always reminds me of my friend and neighbor, the late Peter Tripp, artist, boatbuilder, and dissident. One night, after a boozy dinner in School Street, Stonington, Peter orchestrated and tape-recorded an impromptu performance we dubbed "Seamonsters of Wicopesset," entailing the use of saucepans, a piano, empty beer bottles (struck with a spoon or blown over for hooting sounds), and the human voice (Peter's own, rumbling and booming).

A small boat inside the reefs is running slowly westward toward Wicopesset. For a moment I think, It's Peter—he's come out to meet me. But Peter died two years ago. And the boat, as it gets closer, is far more orthodox than anything Peter sailed. Peter went in for dories and Bahamian sloops, for cargo schooners with A-frame masts and Chinese junk–rigged craft with booms made of plastic drainpipes. After Yale, the merchant marine service, and several years on New York tugboats and in the Brooklyn Navy Yard, he fell further and further out of agreement with a big-spending, big-borrowing economy and took refuge in Stonington.

There he drew boats, built boats, and sailed boats, and between times fought schemes like those of the state politicians and developers who wanted to plant an international airport in the woods of southeastern Connecticut.

In those days one of Peter's boats was a 16-foot fiberglass Falcon day-sailer on which he stuck various experimental rigs and which he often sailed out here, sitting with his feet up, sketching, drinking beer, and logging the distances big-ship fashion from one buoy to the next. Peter's boat carpentry tended toward the strictly practical; yachty touches offended him; his boats had painted exterior plywood and galvanized nails rather than varnished mahogany and Monel fastenings. In his early Chinese period, the Falcon sported a sail made of blue plastic tarpaulin material stiffened by lumberyard laths and garden-center bamboo canes. And when the wind faded, Peter did not start up an infernal combustion engine but dropped a pair of extralong homemade sweeps between the thole pins and rowed sturdily home like a true seaman.

Much as I admired Peter's ability to go his own way, I didn't altogether like what he did to boats. I didn't sail with him often, though we often talked boats and helped each other with boats. When Peter did sail with me, I found it hard not to think he was surveying my craft with a view to where (if it should ever fall into his hands) he would start ripping into it with hacksaw and adze. But on occasions like this one it was always a joy to encounter him afloat, to recognize his wide straw hat under the blue plastic sail and to hail him, come close to leeward, and exchange news of our day's voyages. Peter would tell me, for example, how he had just been out to the whistle buoy 4.9 miles off Napatree on a course he'd noted on his chart as "South by

East three-quarters East." No newfangled 360-degree compass readings for him! We would sail in company for a
while and arrange a rendezvous back on the moorings or in
one or other of our kitchens, before our boats inevitably
drew apart.

The breeze just holds into Stonington harbor. I brush a
week's collection of weed off the mooring pennant as I haul
it aboard. There's a lot to do both here and ashore, but I sit
for half an hour in the cockpit, pleased to be back on
Lochinvar's mooring, even if only for a few days. Margot
arrives tomorrow. I'll give her time to recover from jet lag
and get used to the heat. But then we'll be off again.

AUGUST

10

IF GETTING AWAY from one's home port is difficult for a single sailor, it's doubly difficult for two. Lots of people want to chat with Margot. She spends an afternoon making blackcurrant jam with an old friend. She needs a morning to shop for swimming fins. Her books and watercolor paints have to be dug out of an attic and put on board. *Lochinvar*'s food lockers have to be restocked. It is amazing that Chivers Old English marmalade (without which I cannot sail) costs about the same in Westerly, Rhode Island, as it does in the old country, and (even more amazing) it doesn't cost more than it did last year. "You see, we can't afford not to come sailing here," I say. In spring, Margot has been known to suggest that we should do something different this summer, such as stay in a comfortable French hotel for a few weeks. ("You could take your own marmalade," Margot said the last time this came up, just in case I used the Gallic predilection for cherry conserves at breakfast as a reason why not.)

Like me, Margot spends her first few days here frantically socializing. But as soon as I hear her telling a friend, "No, we won't be here for the village fair," which is on the first Saturday in August, I know she's ready to sail. Once again, with checklists rechecked and fresh food stowed, *Lochinvar* makes an early-afternoon departure. We're not going far—East Harbor, Fishers Island; just far enough to break away from the enticements of Stonington and not wear out the crew with an immediate all-day sail.

East Harbor is more cove than harbor, without permanent moorings and only a few private docks, one of which belongs to the former Coast Guard station, now a house. Like West Harbor, East Harbor is open to the north and northwest, but tonight's forecast is for a light southeasterly. The harbor is partly bounded by the Fishers Island Club golf course, and players are to be glimpsed jouncing along on electric golf carts or standing with clubs swung high above the beach-plum shrubs. In the evening, sprinklers refresh the greens. As the reader will by now have suspected, my game is not golf. I was put off it in my Dayton days, perhaps because I did too much caddying; my memories are of trudging lopsidedly around an Ohio country-club course, the tedium alleviated by a ball landing excitingly in a pond, and by the final reward. One dollar bought a lot of Tootsie Rolls back then.

Lochinvar comes to rest in a fathom and a half off the former Coast Guard dock. There are only two other boats in East Harbor and one departs in the late afternoon. We row in to the little beach, where signs declare the land behind to be private property. Clumps of poison ivy reinforce its protection. We stay on the coarse sand, walking it from end to end while looking for trophies, such as golf balls; but the beach yields nothing. Margot says, "Do you think the local millionaires come down here at dawn and scout around for whatever got washed up on last night's tide?"

"I do," I reply.

Thwarted at beachcombing, we wade out and swim. Back on board, there's time to rinse, dry, and dress for cocktails in the cockpit. We have a date with Rust and Joy, who show up in their Whaler, direct from Quiambaug Cove; they've brought biscuits and cheese and their German shepherd dog, Hawk. The comestibles come aboard with Rust and Joy. Hawk stays in the Whaler, whose painter is let out to its full extent, beyond Hawk's jumping range. Joy has also brought a small gift for our cruise: a can of Chunky Chicken, ideal, she says, for quick pita-bread sandwiches.

Rust is a magazine fiction editor; we met at a literary party in New York in 1957. He and I were the only people at the function who were not trying to get introduced to the guest of honor, who was William Faulkner. Instead, we started talking to one another. It turned out that Rust lived opposite the apartment where Margot and I were then living on West Seventy-fifth Street. During the winter we played chess and I helped him build a Sunfish sailboard from a kit in his living room. Rust, divorced and single, was going out with Penney Chapin, and we spent several weekends with them at Penney's parents' house in Stonington. Many of our friendships became mutual; Yaacov and Nina, Rusty and Bob, got to know Rust and Penney, and friends of theirs became friends of ours. We decided Stonington had Manhattan well beaten as a place to live (and in my case sail) on a moderate income, and we rented the elder

Chapins' house one winter while they were in Greece. By the time they returned we had bought a run-down house of our own. Rust and Penney got married and bought the house on Quiambaug Cove (and later split up). In the early 1960s, when we had our big dory *Billy Ruffian,* Rust owned an aging, raffish 32-foot gaff sloop whose name had been in turn *Twilight* and *Typhoon,* and which Rust called *Twyphoon.*

Rust had this boat surveyed before he bought it; he also asked Yaacov and me to take a close look at it. The surveyor advised against purchase, and so did we. But Rust went ahead, taken by the old boat's characterful rig, handsome cabin appointments, and considerable speed. Sailing *Twyphoon* in a breeze was certainly exciting. As you sat below you could see daylight through the seams to windward as the pull on the chain plates lifted the topside planking apart. Judging by the amount of water that needed pumping out, the leeward seams weren't that tight, either.

Now, in *Lochinvar*'s cockpit, as the sun sinks behind the Dumplings, Rust recalls an earlier boat of his, called the *Blotto.* While living in England and teaching English literature to American airmen, he had fallen for a hearty little East Coast cutter, which also leaked. On one North Sea voyage he was towed in by a lifeboat, and later received a hefty claim for salvage from the Royal National Lifeboat Institution. Rust fled the country: he sailed *Blotto* to France and motored her through the canals to the Mediterranean. His first wife was crewing for him, but soon tired of the confines of the boat on the canals and went on by bus. By the time Rust reached the South of France, he too was tired of *Blotto.* Luckily, he managed to sell her.

"So the RNLI are still after you?" I ask Rust.

"I expect they are. It was pretty stupid. I gave the lifeboat crew a bottle of Scotch and they seemed happy. The people who ran the organization wanted more than *Blotto* was worth. They probably thought I was insured, and the insurance company would pay up."

Margot asks Joy, "Did you know what you were getting into when you married this man?"

"Oh, he's only got the Whaler now," says Joy.

At nightfall, as they are leaving, Rust pats *Lochinvar's* dark blue topsides and says, "Nice boat, Tony." But really I'm sure he's thinking that she lacks some of the inbuilt worrisomeness he likes a boat to have.

Margot and I dine on beef stew she has made, with new potatoes, zucchini, red wine, grapes, and Pepperidge Farm Nantucket cookies. When I rig the anchor light (Yaacov's repair is holding well), the breeze—though southerly as forecast—seems quite strong in the puffs, so I let out another four fathoms of scope. Lights appear on the Connecticut shore, on Mason's Island, and in Noank. Here in East Harbor we have a little world of our own: the former Coast Guard boathouse with all its windows lit and the other anchored boat, all in darkness—early to bed, it seems, for an early start tomorrow. From the nearby margin of the harbor come the squawks of several ducks. Overhead, hazy stars. As we snuggle into the fo'c'sle, I say to Margot, "I'm glad you got here."

11

THE NEXT MORNING is clear and sunny, with a light westerly. We get away at 8:30 with the ebb running, and *Eldridge* discloses that we will have it with us for another two hours. *Lochinvar* reaches out of East Harbor, her helmsman taking a shortcut. This involves extra care in order to avoid the submerged rocks off the golf-course shore. In past seasons the centerboards of *Caliban* and *Clio* have clunked over one of these, the result of trying to avoid another rock nearer the green can buoy at the harbor entrance. This shortcut saves only a few hundred yards, but it gives me the little kick that comes from putting local knowledge to work and the extra sparkle that arises from just missing trouble, for today at least. Safely through the gap, I bear away before the wind. We wing-and-wing the sails—main out one side, the jib boomed out with the spinnaker pole on the other—for the run to Watch Hill Passage. Off Napatree we are overtaken by a slightly larger yacht, under power. It comes close by, engine growling, and the bald man at the helm says to us, "Going to be a scorcher, I think." We are already wearing broad-brimmed hats. Why isn't he?

Departing through Watch Hill Passage, I make my customary attempt to memorize the buoys that mark it. There are three in all: a green can marking a shoal spot that would bother only large vessels in mid-channel; a green gong marking Watch Hill Reef to the south; and a red bell to the north signposting Gangway Rock, which is off Watch Hill Point. ("Red to right returning" is the splendid mnemonic for the American buoyage system. Going out, you have to observe the less memorable corollary, "Green to left departing.") It's the difference between a gong and a bell that always perplexes me. In a fog a *bong* sounds much like a *clang,* at least until I get close enough to distinguish the shapes of the objects producing them. Watch Hill's seaside architecture is also worth noting: the tidy brick lighthouse out on the point and, up on the bluff, the yellow clapboarded hotel with its domed roof. Here I have to decide what course to steer next. Out to Block Island on 130 degrees or due east along the Rhode Island shore?

For many years, Block Island has been our first main port of call on a cruise. Sailing the fifteen miles out to it from Watch Hill for the first time was an adventure, and each time thereafter some of the same excitement has been roused as the island has slowly loomed out of the sea. The cliffs and beaches, and finally the entrance to Great Salt Pond, become clear. In the last two decades this spacious harbor has often been jammed at the height of summer, but if we wait for the end of August, time for going back to school and college, the visiting fleet dwindles and something of the pond's old charm returns. So today we decide to save Block Island for the return voyage. We definitely have to go there; without it we would not have found *Lochinvar*.

But now the course is east. With the jib sheet trimmed until the spinnaker pole is nearly touching the starboard shrouds, I make myself comfortable for the long run. Four years ago we sailed into Great Salt Pond in *Clio* and hunted out a spot to anchor. We had in fact sold *Clio* at the end of the previous summer, intending, after many seasons of what I admitted to be a tight fit and Margot called a floating nightmare, to buy a roomier boat. But several deals to that end fell through; some boats I looked at weren't quite as sound as their owners claimed; others had skittish owners who backed off when I actually offered them money. So we had borrowed *Clio* for a short cruise from her new owners while they went to Montana. As we rowed ashore, we were hailed from a nearby sloop. A man was standing in the cockpit of a boat I recognized as a Tartan 27. He said, "Nice little boat you just came in with."

"I like yours better," I said.

"Come and have a drink later on."

"Thanks, we will."

Thus we met Carleton Granbery and his wife, Diana, both architects, from the Long Island Sound town of Guilford, Connecticut. The neat interior of their boat seemed to reflect the taste for uncluttered functionalism of many modern architects. It was well cared for, too, with metal work polished, fiberglass surfaces painted a clean white, the woodwork well varnished. Four people in the cabin sitting comfortably with drinks in their hands would have been a squeeze in *Clio;* the difference in cubic capacity between a 22-foot and a 27-foot boat can be three or four times. We talked about sailing friends we had in common and about places on the coast we enjoyed sailing to, and some of the changes we'd seen—for us in thirty years, for the Granberys in fifty. They were thinking of giving up owning boats. "Our total age is 143," said Diana Granbery, a spry, elegant lady who didn't look anything like her half of that sum. As we prepared to leave, we exchanged addresses and phone numbers, Diana gave Margot a novel she'd just finished reading, and I said that we hoped we would meet them again.

Which we did. A week after our return from our cruise in *Clio*, I called Carleton and asked him if since our meeting he and Diana had thought any more about selling their boat, which I recalled was called *Lochinvar*. No, they hadn't. Maybe in a year or so ... We exchanged brief accounts of our cruises and said goodbye. Carleton called me back an hour later. He'd talked to Diana; did I have a price in mind? Ten minutes later, the details had been worked out, and we were to take over *Lochinvar* on July 1 the following summer.

Those experienced in such transactions may be surprised to learn that almost everything went according to plan. Except that, a year after selling *Lochinvar* to us, the Granberys bought a new boat. Veteran sailors will recognize the syndrome without blinking. Ten years earlier, finding myself without a yacht in America, I'd bought in England a 1930s wooden motor cruiser, said to be one of the Dunkirk "Little Ships." Her owner talked of the heroic evacuation of British and French troops from the beaches by all sorts of vessels, including boats like his, under relentless German bombardment. But that was forty years before.

He was well into his eighties now, and he admitted, with a sigh, that it was time for him to swallow the anchor. A month or so after we had bought his boat and were on board her in Yarmouth harbor, Isle of Wight, trying (vainly) to get the engine started, a sleek new open powerboat surged by. Our boat's former owner was crouched over the wheel, grinning like a teenager. This is not to impute any deceit. At the time, our boats' previous owners no doubt felt weary of their craft and of the water. But I know from my own experience that it isn't long before not having a boat becomes more difficult than having one. After enjoying the brief euphoria in which all sorts of boats are potentially yours, you find yourself once more in the old trap.

As *Lochinvar* runs along the Rhode Island shore, Margot, hat over eyes, reclines on the cockpit seat and speculates on the equipment needed by a Chinese helmsman: a parasol, a fan, and a flyswatter. I'm not sure what has brought this up: maybe a memory of Peter and his junk-rigged boats. Off the state beach at Misquamicut, three children's silver balloons bob on the water, emblems of disappointment. I look for Herbie's restaurant, where our eldest daughter Liz worked one summer. But from this distance, half a mile offshore and ten years away, Herbie's is lost in the strip of amusements, bars, and eateries. Margot says, "And a cup of tea." Ah, yes—the Chinese helmsman.

Rhode Island is barely forty miles from west to east. The state coastline, wandering in and out of bays, rivers, and inlets big and small, is nearer four hundred. Block Island Sound confronts the western half of the Rhode Island coast, which is mostly formed (to quote the *Atlantic Coast Pilot*) "of sandy beaches which are broken by several projecting rocky points." Behind the beaches lies a series of extensive shallow ponds, with breachways navigable by small boats when conditions are calm. On some of the points, such as Watch Hill and Weekapaug, stand clusters of imposing summer houses; on other stretches, as at Quonochontaug Beach, simpler cottages acquire character and safety by standing on stiltlike pilings. The Sound itself, taking its name but little protection from Block Island, is in effect the open Atlantic. Looking south, one looks out to sea.

Today the sea is busy with yachts running east, beating west. Lobstermen are hauling their pots, and draggers are scraping the bottom for fish. A tug chuffs westward, hauling a huge barge at the end of an invisible towline. Now that Block Island has been set aside, the day's possible destinations are: Newport, tucked up into the entrance of Narragansett Bay; Sachuest and Sakonnet, on either side of the broad Sakonnet River, a bit farther east; and closest of all, Point Judith. Margot, still acclimatizing, shouldn't spend long in the sun. The unfavorable current off Charlestown in mid-morning also has to be taken into account. But this means that, although for the next hour or so we'll have a foul tide, in the narrow channel leading up into Point Judith Pond the flood current will be working for us.

Still, it's a soldier's wind all the way to Point Judith. And only when the lumpy breakwaters that form Point Judith's Harbor of Refuge appear ahead do I remove the spinnaker pole, so that *Lochinvar* has more freedom to maneuver. This manmade harbor must have been a refuge indeed in stormy weather for the packet vessels and coasting schooners of the late nineteenth century. However, for a small yacht it's by no means cozy. An immense area of uncertain holding ground, its protection is relative, proba-bly better than the open sea on a very rough night. Its three breakwater walls are built of blocks and boulders with gaps through which some waves penetrate; in one section, unfinished or damaged, the surge tumbles over it. No one is at anchor in the harbor as *Lochinvar* scoots in through the west entrance. Dodging lobster-pot buoys and keeping out of the way of a ferry heading out to Block Island, we make for the narrow breachway into the pond.

We sweep in with the current—Jerusalem to port, Galilee to starboard; the haven beyond them is our destination. This is commercial fishing territory; on both sides at state piers and private jetties there's a brash display of boats and gear, new and old, well maintained and gone absolutely to ruin. Fishermen like farmers take pride in looking after their money-making machinery up to a point. Then they often let it rust or rot to death, an offense to everyone else's eyes. Sleek steel draggers and nicely painted offshore lobster boats lie cheek by jowl with vessels in the final stages of abandonment and decomposition. NO WAKE—5 MPH is shakily painted on the decrepit flanks of one boat which will never make a wake of its own again. One boat out and about is the *Southland*, a sightseeing craft, with deafening engine exhausts and a loudspeaker system built to carry over the roar of the exhausts and announce passing attractions to the passengers: "That speedboat over there was in *Miami Vice . . .*" Between fish docks and fish-handling warehouses, small marinas cater to sportfishermen. Seafood restaurants jostle for the attentions of tourists. The whole place is a noisy, smelly, cheerful mess.

The channel runs north along the western edge of the pond for several miles. Past Jerusalem, a section called Snug Harbor has several boatyards where sailing vessels aren't despised. Some years ago on *Caliban* I spent a night tied up at one such yard, Salt Pond Marine Railway. I was alone, tired of my own cooking, and anxious to dine ashore. It meant putting up with the annoyances of lying alongside overnight with spring lines fixed to accommodate the three-foot rise and fall of tide, and fenders rigged to prevent the rub rail getting chewed up by pilings as *Caliban* rolled against the dock in the wakes of passing vessels. At 7:00 p.m. I found that the local eating facilities consisted of one snack bar, which had closed at 6:00. Back on *Caliban,* it was Hobson's choice. I opened a can of Chinese chicken with noodles. When heated, the noodles turned into a gluey paste. As I tucked into this repast, a radio program on nutrition delivered a timely warning about monosodium glutamate destroying brain cells. I didn't hear the full story because the radio voice began to fade—either the batteries going or the MSG taking effect. The best antidote seemed to be fresh air and exercise, so I took an after-dinner stroll around the neighborhood. The houses were mostly one-story vacation places, some (like the Jerusalem boats) fixed up and some neglected. The coarse grass of their gardens ran together. Few lights were on, few cars about. Though I walked with my flashlight switched on, the lack of people and the lonely little houses made me feel like a prowler. I stepped quietly in the silence, avoiding loose gravel. No dogs barked in Snug Harbor.

Going up the channel in *Lochinvar* we meet several powerboats charging out, doing far more than 5 mph and making wake. One comes right at us, though I'm hugging the starboard side of the channel. At the last moment the man driving it—a 19-foot open boat with a big outboard—twitches his wheel one way and then another, shaving past us a few feet away, doing about 25 knots and sending spray into our cockpit. Dark glasses, pursed lips. Not looking at us. My imprecations ("Cretin!" being the least insulting) are all too late. It takes a few minutes for the adrenaline to stop pumping. But the atmosphere of the pond from here on is far less stressful. A chain of coves to the left, small islands to the right, a children's summer camp on a little hill. I roll up the jib so that our speed drops to about 2 knots and we have time to look at things, and time to look at the chart for where the next buoys should be. Smelt Brook Cove, Foddering Place, Beef Island, Wheatfield Cove, Cummock Island are names to be savored. The channel narrows. Then there's a deserted, enchanted little bay, with a plateau of marsh grass at one side. Then comes a right-angle bend through The Narrows between Short Point and Wood Hill into Upper Pond.

This is the harbor of the town of Wakefield and has a goodly assortment of boatyards and marinas. For *Lochinvar*, it's the head of navigation; a low bridge carrying Route 1 across the head of the pond deters masted vessels from passing into Silver Spring Cove and the Saugatuckett River. Wakefield itself is a mile distant. *Lochinvar* flits around the moored boats and—jib unfurled and centerboard lowered— tacks back out. It's exciting work in The Narrows, tacking this way and that, slowly gaining against the tide. But then we're out in the pond again. On the foredeck Margot frees the anchor lashings. I refurl the jib and direct *Lochinvar* on a slow reach between Gardner and Beach Islands. With the main luffing, we creep into the lee of Plato Island. Here, in a small basin about seven feet deep amid the surrounding two- or three-foot shallows, the hook goes over with a splash. I stand for a moment and admire the cabin built by some philosopher or hermit under Plato Island's north-facing escarpment. The cabin's owner has the little place all to himself. As I tidy sails and ship, Plato's student Aristotle's remark drifts into mind: "The nature of everything is best seen in its smallest proportions."

We rig the awning. Feeling sun-blasted despite precautions, we have a late-afternoon cockpit nap. Then, evening behind Plato Island, with a breeze rustling the awning and making for coolness in its shadow; the resident ducks are cadging as usual. There are too few insects to be a nuisance. As the sun goes down, spectacularly, there's a great stillness. The powerboats have gone home. We are the only boat at anchor here. We hesitate to move, to get drinks, to prepare supper. But finally the big red balloon goes under. I get out the rum-and-tonic while Margot makes a spaghetti sauce. It's quite dark when I collect a bucket of pond water for rinsing the warm decks. I dip the pail into bright yellow-green blobs of phosphorescence, a million plankton glowing like subaqueous Saint Elmo's fire. And later, as I brush my teeth over the stern, it seems almost wrong to spit into the starry water.

12

DESPITE MY INITIAL shakedown cruise, Margot and I have some shaking down of our own to do. It takes us a few days to get used to being together in so restricted a space. This is so every season, and *Lochinvar* being bigger than *Caliban* and *Clio* doesn't hasten the process. On a boat, the objects you want are always underneath several strata of other objects; to get at the former involves lifting the latter off a bunk, say, and finding somewhere else to put them. Then you have to lift the bunk cushion and prop it up against something as you remove with your other hand the locker lid that forms part of the bunk top; then if you have a spare hand you can paw around in the plastic box where you keep the glue or tape or screws you're looking for. Meantime, Margot will be conducting a boatwide search of her own; cushions bump, locker lids slam, personalities collide.

I inherited Carleton Granbery's meticulous diagram showing where items should be stowed, locker by locker, shelf by shelf, around the boat. With a few agreed modifications, we've stuck to this plan. Laundry bags and carrier bags are at the forward end of my fo'c'sle shelf, unused lampshades and infrequently used fishing gear at the forward end of Margot's. Our shoes, trainers, and sandals share an under-berth locker with the collapsible plastic container which is our holding tank. For some reason, the top shelf of the hanging locker for a long time had nothing on it at all, though lately it has been given over to dish towels. Margot has a more expansive nature than I. Her boat shoes turn up in places other than the Granbery-designated and Bailey-approved footwear locker. Her swimsuits are hung up to dry overnight where they loop themselves around my head when I'm trying to read. She has her own hiding places for pots and pans, different from where I put them in July. It takes me a while to realize the legitimacy of her alter-ations—or at least for me to say, tactfully, "All right, let's keep them there." Then I have to find a new nook for the spare foghorn and winch handles that otherwise will be underneath the bloody pots and pans . . . There isn't room in a 27-foot boat for even one person to keep out of the way of somebody else who feels a sudden need for personal space or for doing things at his or her own pace. This may be why you sometimes see one member of a two-person crew sitting on the foredeck while the other is aft, behind the helm. Or why, at 8:30 this morning in Point Judith Pond, Margot is taking her time sewing up a torn shirt-sleeve and making sandwiches for lunch (easier done now at leisure than later in a bouncy sea), while I'm working off my impatience by rowing the dinghy around Plato Island in a thin fog.

The fog is thicker outside. Going out through the breach-way under power, with mainsail set in hopes of wind and the radar reflector hoisted beneath the starboard spreader, we meet a larger sloop coming back in, the helmsman sig-naling to us that you can't see very far out there. We carry on. I keep a constant watch on both depth sounder and compass until the eastern exit from the Harbor of Refuge is sighted. Once we get through that portal, the breakwater promptly vanishes astern in the thick gray air. On our port bow, the horn from the unseen lighthouse close by us on Point Judith blares every fifteen seconds. I carry on because I've so far been lucky in fog, finding my destinations with-out accidents on the way. Furthermore, today I believe the fog is going to burn off before long. And anyway, I hate giv-ing up on a venture. ("Foolhardy," "bloody-minded," and "pig-headed" are among the terms clearly passing through Margot's head. She would like to know, but is too obstinate to ask, why I was in such a hurry to come out here into this pea soup.)

We motor slowly, 3 knots being as fast as it seems safe to go in visibility under a hundred yards. I have the foghorn to hand, and squeeze out a blast every few minutes. Other ves-sels hoot back. White veils of fog shimmer, part, and then close. It's easy to see shapes of boats that aren't there. Concentration rapidly displacing early-morning grumpiness, I steer a course of 100 degrees. This I reckon balances the tide that will run out of Narragansett Bay until noon against the incoming tide that will carry us for several hours thereafter, until we are within earshot of the horn on the light tower at the entrance to Buzzards Bay. Once we're a little way southeast of Point Judith we're likely to encounter other craft on passage, which will be using the Point as a reference. Even so, I'm taken aback around 10:00 a.m., when a plaintive wail comes from ahead. We make out a big sloop heading directly for us under power. I turn *Lochinvar* sharply to starboard and there, taking form out of the fog, is another big sloop, soundlessly closing in on us from that side. As we turn again to pass between them, I call over to the damp wraith of a woman standing on the foredeck of the first boat, "I saw you but not him." She replies, "He's standing by us." It isn't clear why they need to be stood by; maybe they are cruising in company and have paused here to work out where they are or what to do next. We leave them to it. Blowing our horn at intervals, straining above the beat of our engine for every sound, we mosey on.

By mid-morning cat's-paws are ruffling the smooth surface of Rhode Island Sound; visibility improves until we can see clearly for about two hundred yards. Presently the mainsail takes shape in a light breeze from the south-southeast. I switch the motor off and unroll the jib. Blessed quiet! Or rather, blessed natural sounds of gurgle and trickle! But the bliss is short-lived. The breeze fizzles out, and after ten minutes of flopping around waiting for it to reappear, I fire up the motor again. And so it continues, a counterpoint of power and sail. Little gusts encourage us, periods of slatting and shaking irk us. I keep a watch for the big white-painted buoys that mark the U.S. Navy's torpedo range lying across our course, but don't see any. (Nor have we ever encountered any ships firing torpedoes out here; it remains unclear how the naval authorities would close off this section of sea to passing traffic.) The fog persists, though the distance we can see varies from a quarter of a mile to a boat length. Occasionally we can hear or even see a boat heading east or west, and assume we're roughly on our desired course. At one point we suddenly smell fish, pungent fish. Margot and I exchange apprehensive looks. Where is the lobster boat? Then we hear it, and a few seconds later it nonchalantly speeds across our bows before suddenly halting to haul a lobster pot. I wave to the yellow oilskinned figure, but he's too busy with line and hauler to see us. We're soon back in the invisible. The thing is to keep concentrating and not be seduced into feeling that all is unreal because unseen.

With no view of the shore, six miles north, I dig into memory for the prospect we would have if we could see it: Brenton Reef light tower presiding over the approach to the East Passage of Narragansett Bay, the Bay's deep recesses spanned by distant bridges, and the gray flanks of Newport Neck with its great summer houses planted there by nineteenth-century wealth. This stretch always consumes much of a day, whether we're running eastward for Cuttyhunk and Buzzards Bay in light airs or bucking into the breeze, which as we make westward for Block Island or Point Jude is invariably stronger and on the nose.

In the past, the voyage has been enlivened by encounters with yachts practicing for the challenge or defense of the America's Cup, the gruesome silver ewer which has come to represent supremacy in yacht racing. It was first won by the schooner *America* in Isle of Wight waters and long retained in these, until the Aussies and then the San Diegans lifted it. Riding the swells off Newport we might glimpse a tall gleaming white triangle, the sails of a Twelve Meter yacht. This splendid sight has faded with the introduction of the high-tech synthetic sail fabric Kevlar, which looks like brown wrapping paper. The Twelves, usually in pairs, would be moving at twice our speed and it was hard to approach them without getting in their way. Once in *Clio* we found ourselves ambling into the cross-fire territory of a serious duel between the two American defense contenders *Liberty* and *Intrepid.* One of the big motor yachts from the New York Yacht Club that was mothering the Twelves, and wallowing along in reflected glamour, suddenly released an agitated blast on its horn and pointed itself in our direction as if about to loose off a torpedo. I took the hint and gybed, clearly changing course away from the Twelves, though they would have passed well ahead of us in any case. A launch was dispatched to monitor our departure. It took a haughty swing past *Clio;* and as they saw our Red Ensign, and Margot photographing the Twelves slithering quickly by, we assumed that they said to themselves, "Ah, a little British spy boat." But they soon lost interest. We were too small and too obviously amateur.

Today in the fog any such imaginings are mirages of nostalgia. In the early afternoon I check the chart and compass with increasing frequency. No matter one's experience and past good fortune, a whole day of fog begins to nibble away at one's confidence. "Sakonnet must be abeam by now," I say to Margot, having done some time-and-distance figuring in my head, and hoping to rally my own faith in my navigation. But Margot, laughing aloud over a well-thumbed P. G. Wodehouse novel, appears unconcerned. The depth sounder registers 65 feet, but since the depths are uniform out here and the shore steep-to, any warning of shoaling would be the last one we'd get.

At 3:00 p.m. we begin to hear a horn. It blows two blasts every thirty seconds. It is what we want to hear: the Buzzards Bay light tower on its lofty platform with giraffe's legs. The tower replaced a lightship which sank in a hurricane in 1944 with the loss of its crew. However, the sound of the horn doesn't seem to be coming from exactly where it should. We are, in fact, too far inshore. I change course to steer slightly south of east instead of due east. And at 3:30 what I thought was going to be a consistent afternoon breeze drops away. The fog, formerly suffused with sunlight, darkens. There's a heaviness in the air, something impending. Margot and I exchange glances. Away below goes Wodehouse. Out from the port-side cockpit locker comes the canvas bag in which we keep foul-weather gear. Blue jacket, yellow trousers for her; all yellow for me. I tie a single reef in the mainsail and furl the jib. I recall the adage "If the wind before the rain, soon it will be fine again. If the rain before the wind, soon your sails you'll have to mind." Whether it's the fog condensing into solid drops or wet stuff from farther aloft, I don't know, but rain begins to fall.

It's quickly followed by thunder. A terrific clap explodes overhead, there's a sizzle of lightning, and the bottom falls out of a celestial reservoir. While we're sitting wondering if the deck and cockpit scuppers will cope, and if the dinghy is going to fill up, the reduced mainsail fills with wind and *Lochinvar* moves resolutely into the dark downpour. The thunderstorm is long and noisy. It is too immediately wet to scare us, though jagged arrows of lightning strike the sea all around. I think about the copper strip that connects the mast to a through-hull bronze fitting and wonder what would happen if a bolt hit us. But it does no good to talk about it. At one moment a big ketch under jib and jigger appears out of the cascading torrents, scudding westward, and we wave encouragingly to each other. Slowly the sky lightens to the southwest. Gradually the thunder, lightning, and rain move off. What's left of the fog disperses. On the starboard bow a part of the still murky horizon begins to solidify, take on a known shape. Cuttyhunk! Dark gray on gray. The island is still about two miles away, the first land we have seen in seven hours. With the jib unrolled *Lochinvar* reaches toward it, rainwater still dripping from the boom, the sodden dinghy tugging behind.

The stage between landfall and arrival is always longer than you think it should be. On this occasion, although we no longer have to "mind" our sails, caution keeps me from shaking out the reef in the main. And today, approaching Cuttyhunk, we have a diversion. As we come up to the red bell buoy, 2A, in the five-mile-wide mouth of Buzzards Bay, we sight something in the water to windward. At first it looks like an overturned dinghy, and as we harden up toward it I look for its crew, possibly in the water after capsizing in the thunderstorm. We have to make a short tack to reach it, and as we get nearer it seems to have ribs like the hoops of a barrel. I sail to windward of it as slowly as I can manage. We lean over the leeside. It is a large turtle, four to five feet long, buoyed up by the gases of decay. Its fat white flippers wave futilely; glassy eyes protrude from the gray head. The old armor of its shell, barnacled and weedy, has not saved its occupant from mortality.

The marine nature guide on the cabin shelf suggests that the creature is a leatherback, which like other oceangoing turtles—green, loggerhead, and ridley—drifts on the Gulf Stream from the warm seas and gets stranded in chillier northern waters. Margot, drying her hair with a towel, is excited. She was brought up on hunter-gatherer principles and seldom came home from a walk with her father without a pheasant, rabbit, or at the very least a cabbage to show for it. She wants to take the turtle in tow. "We can haul it up on the beach at Cuttyhunk," she says. "We can get the shell off. Turtleshell is valuable."

I pull rank as master of the vessel. Dead turtles *smell*. There might be a need for rubber overalls and nose pegs. What will the people on Cuttyhunk think? What about when Daisy, our springer spaniel at home in England, found a very dead, tough-skinned eel on a canal bank in Essex and would not let go of it when we tried to get it out of her clamped jaws? It took five strenuous minutes to prize it loose, by which time I was heavily splattered with the putrefying eel's internal juices. The odor was intense and ineradicable. We drove home with a disappointed dog and the car windows wide open. Besides, this turtle has a sad dignity in its forlorn state, floating in the Buzzards Bay chop. Margot concedes defeat. We abandon the turtle. It is soon hull down.

13

CUTTYHUNK, approached from the west, is the first of the seven Elizabeth Islands that are strung out toward the southwest corner of Cape Cod. They are washed on the north by the waters of Buzzards Bay. To the south is Vineyard Sound. The islands look from space (or in an atlas) like a dislocated backbone whose coccyx is Cuttyhunk; a former teacher on Cuttyhunk, Louise Haskell, called them "glacial droppings." Earth, sand, and rock were deposited here as the glacier of the last ice age was melted by the warmth of the Gulf Stream. The rounded hills of Cuttyhunk are glacier-sculpted drumlins. This afternoon, after the thunderstorm, a fitful sun highlights the western end of the two-mile-long island; the shrub-covered slopes facing on Buzzards Bay are left in shadow.

A remnant of sunlight falls on Penikese, a smaller island on our port beam. Penikese was once a leper colony and then a base for a marine biology institute, founded in 1873 by Louis Agassiz, Swiss zoologist and geologist, and later moved to Woods Hole on the less-remote Cape. It now supports a seasonal school for troubled boys; they are given vocational training in carpentry, boat handling, farming, and cooking, well away from big-city temptations. Gulls and terns are to be seen in plenty, but I haven't yet noticed anybody trying to escape by swimming across the broad channel to Cuttyhunk. This is clearly not Devils Island.

Several other boats are fetching ahead of us into Cuttyhunk's outer harbor. Getting here in the late afternoon I don't expect to find much room for anchoring in the sheltered inner harbor, the Pond. When we used to sail here on *Caliban* in the late 1960s, by the end of the day there would be no more than twenty-five boats in the pond. We could always find room to plant the hook at a comfortable distance from other craft. Since then Cuttyhunk, like Block Island, has become a staging post for everyone cruising this coast, as well as for people taking an overnight sail from one of the many yachting harbors on Buzzards Bay. Cuttyhunkers have seen the leisure-age future and made it work for them. Ranks of heavy moorings now nearly fill the dredged area of the Pond, accommodating for a fee sometimes two or three boats rafted up on a single mooring. A thin forest of pilings stands in shallower water to the west, where shoal-draft boats can tie up. There's also a small mooring-free section in the north part of the Pond where a dozen or so boats can anchor, taking care they don't swing into the more tightly tethered moored craft if the wind shifts north. Often in recent years we've spent a night at anchor in the outer harbor and then, the following morning, as the yachts leave the Pond for their next destinations, we've motored in to seize an anchoring slot before the nomads of the day crowd in. Even so, we then sit there feeling wary of and even threatened by every other boat which approaches, its skipper agonizing about whether he's got room to anchor between us and the next boat. When he does anchor, he raises further worries: Will he drag? Will he bump us? Has he dropped his anchor on top of ours?

Today we settle happily for the outer harbor. The breeze fades as we sail in, giving time for consideration. I make sure we avoid Pease's Ledge, one of whose rocks makes a handy tide gauge when visible but can puncture a boat's bottom when just below the surface. Rental moorings are out here as well, but there is still a great deal of anchoring room in the expanse bounded by the east-facing beach of Cuttyhunk, by a spit which projects from Cuttyhunk toward the next island, and by that island itself, Nashawena. We anchor between the moorings and the beach. Despite the evening sunlight the air remains humid; it has simply gone from wet to muggy. Once the Danforth is planted, I switch on the weather radio, hoping not to hear predictions of north or northeast winds, which might expose us during the night to a nasty chop from Buzzards Bay. A southeasterly is promised. We hang out the foul-weather gear and boil the kettle for cups of Earl Grey tea.

"At least you haven't asked me to go overboard and rig a new centerboard tackle," says Margot, as we sit in the cockpit surveying the outer harbor. All but one of the moorings are occupied, and there are a dozen other boats at anchor. She now has the towel wrapped around her still-damp hair, like a woman in an Ingres painting.

"And I haven't had to fix the choke cable," I reply.

Cuttyhunk seems to be the place where we always have freshly discovered problems to deal with. Maybe this time our luck is in, or am I tempting Providence by even thinking this? As we beat westward along the Elizabeth Islands several seasons ago in *Clio* the centerboard cable parted, leaving the board dangling loose under the hull. The cable could not be replaced from inside the boat. But since a similar incident with *Caliban,* and the consequent boatyard bill, our self-sufficiency has increased. We anchored here and Margot got into swimsuit, flippers, mask, and snorkel. On occasions like this I'm glad of the winter evenings she devotes to sub-aqua training at our local swimming pool. I tied a lead fishing weight to the end of a line and dropped it down the empty tube through which the pennant had passed. Margot dived under, brought the end of the line back to the surface, and handed it up to me. Then, while she took deep breaths, I waxed and whipped the end of the line. She went under again and passed the line through a hole in the top edge of the centerboard and brought it back to the surface. I tied a stopper knot in it, then pulled on the line from inside the boat. The knot held, the board was lifted up into the centerboard slot, and the knot did not jam in the slot; success!

Margot has also put her submarine skills to work in retrieving the top of the coffeepot, dropped overboard in West Falmouth, on the Cape, and in cleaning the speed-log paddle-wheel, saving the effort, anxiety, and wetness involved in doing it from within. On another occasion in Cuttyhunk, mentioned above, I pulled the engine choke-control knob and felt the choke cable snap. The repair had to await our arrival in a port where we could buy a new cable, but I learned in the course of my first and greasy investigation of the mechanism while anchored here how to operate the choke until we could get a new cable. This required having one hand on the starting key in the cockpit while leaning through the companionway and hanging down over the engine. Margot compared my contortions unfavorably with her own upside-down underwater performances beneath *Clio*.

This evening, we celebrate our safe arrival by rowing to the beach and walking along the narrow pebbly ridge that divides harbor and pond. The rest of the island will keep for tomorrow. The night comes overcast, without stars, the light wind southeast as foretold.

Our sleep is not, however, an unbroken eight hours' worth. At 4:00 a.m. I'm woken by noises, natural and man-made. The thunder roars again. The halyards rattle in the wind and rain patters heavily on the decks. Between flashes of lightning the beam of a spotlight stabs through the cabin windows. I stick my head out of the main hatch and hear shouts. Surf is crashing and grinding loudly on the Vineyard Sound beach. The night is pitch black, all the blacker for the navigation lights and spreader lights switched on by a few neighboring boats. A rough bearing taken on the flashing red beacon on the end of the jetty that protects the Pond entrance assures me that *Lochinvar* isn't dragging. Pretty soon more lights are bobbing near the beach.

A pale gray dawn reveals two boats stranded at the edge of the water: a sloop called *Thirtysomething* and a big powerboat called *Outrageous,* which were anchored near us last night. Three local craft are in attendance, professionals summoned, I imagine, by radio. They hustle about, attaching towlines to the sloop. One of these boats is the *Rawbar,* a large outboard-powered semi-inflatable which hawks seafood around the anchorage in the evenings; it has big woolly fenders and looks like a huge bedroom slipper. *Eldridge* says that high water was at 3:00 a.m., so the salvors are having to deal with a falling tide. There's a great deal of to-ing and fro-ing and shouting, though I can't hear the words. The crew of *Thirtysomething* alternate between standing on their slanting foredeck trying to help and sitting in their cockpit looking woeful. Eventually the three Cuttyhunk boats manage to haul together at the same moment and *Thirtysomething* is pulled off. One of its crew goes aboard the *Rawbar*, presumably to pay the bill. (*Outrageous*, with twin engines and twin windshield wipers, doesn't get free until later in the day.) Before I climb back into my bunk for a bit more sleep, I thank God and our anchor. It wasn't us.

The day turns out to be a good one for not sailing anywhere. More rain and far-off thunder as we have a late breakfast. I bail the dinghy, keeping some of the rainwater for washing. But by mid-morning the showers are less frequent. We row into the Pond and tie up at the dinghy float. The Cuttyhunk waterfront is not as scruffy as I first remember it, but neither is it too fixed up. Here, too, the Coast Guard have been and gone, leaving a battered dock. The *Alert II*, the ferry that runs to and from New Bedford (daily in summer, several times a week throughout the rest of the year), ties up to the adjoining wharf. There's a float to which the seaplane is tethered when it comes in from Fairhaven, several docks with slips for sportfishing boats, and a wooden jetty supporting a row of sheds where you can buy ice and fish. There's a water tap and a dumpster or skip into which we throw trash, having first done the right thing by putting cans and bottles into separate containers.

Propped up on the foreshore nearby are two long-term boat rebuilding projects, dream ships which seem year after year to be awaiting new energy from their owners and meantime gather moss. Marsh on the right hand and an apple tree which needs a boy to climb into its higher branches and throw the red-green apples down. The narrow road which leads up to the village passes the island's one crossroads junction, traversed by at the most half a dozen vehicles an hour; some wag has painted on the asphalt the words "Stop and wait for green light."

The impression Cuttyhunk gives of being an easily surveyed little chunk of coast is perhaps delusive. Dollhouse charm for some may be claustrophobia for others. The place proves to be gritty as well as pretty. Forty or so people live here year-round, and in summer this hardy core swells with amateur fishermen and vacationers who like their holiday places remote and small. The island has a one-and-a-half-room general store, a miniature post office where you can drop postcards in a slot in a wall as if they were messages in bottles, a bakery, and a hotel which serves dinner. Island institutions include a small Methodist church, a one-room school which takes the few local kids to eighth grade (after which they fly daily to the mainland for learning), and a library open two afternoons a week. The embryonic road system is far exceeded by a network of paths running between the houses and alongside dry stone walls. In recent years the prime landmark on Cuttyhunk has been a giant three-bladed windmill, similar to one on Block Island, set on a hill above the village. Put up during the first great oil crunch of the 1970s and meant to demonstrate the value of wind power, it seems not to have been integrated with the island's conventional power supply; revolving slowly or standing motionless, it was more a symbol of inertia than of conservation. It has now been taken down. The island is so small the few cars and pickup trucks seem unnecessary, apart from their use in carrying provisions from dock to store.

Margot and I walk up the damp road carrying our foul-weather jackets. A boy heading for the Pond with a crab-bing net looks us over and inquires, "You been fishing?" "No," we say, "just sailing and getting wet." I think, This would be a good place to spend a childhood summer or two. We turn right at the crossroads and walk out to West End Pond. Scrubby bushes, beach plum, wild roses, and poison ivy flourish on the unkempt hillsides, where the early settlers axed the old trees. Blue chicory flowers edge our path. In the side yard of one house a deer browses among vegetables. West End Pond has a narrow unnaviga-ble breachway to Buzzards Bay; its salty waters are well suited to oysters, grown here from seed brought from Maine and, when of an edible size, packed off to be eaten in such places as the Grand Central Oyster Bar.

On a little island in mid-pond stands a knobbly stone tower. This is the Gosnold Monument, erected in 1903. It looks like a structure thriftily created from stones found nearby and held together with thick dollops of mortar. (Of similar construction is the so-called Viking Tower in Newport, as are many gateposts for houses of the shingle era.) In May 1602, the English mariner Bartholomew Gosnold landed on Cuttyhunk from his small bark *Concord* with twenty would-be settlers and twelve seamen. Coming around the cape to the north they had been so "pestered" by fish that they had named it Cape Cod. And sailing among "many fair islands," they chose this for their fort and what was to be the first attempt at a settlement the English made in New England. Queen Elizabeth was still on the throne and Elizabeth was also Gosnold's sister's name; the island the Algonquin Indians called Poocutohhunkunnoh—Land's End—was renamed Elizabeth's Island. Gosnold and company admired the "high-timbered oaks," the cedar, beech, elm, holly, and walnut trees. They enjoyed the abundant shellfish; they traded with the apparently peaceful Indians for furs, copper, and tobacco; and they collected sassafras bark for the *Concord* to take back to England. Sassafras was then considered to have great medicinal value. Gabriel Archer, one of the *Concord*'s gentlemen, wrote: "The powder of sassafras in twelve hours cured one of our company that had taken a great surfeit by eating the bellies of dog fish, a very delicious meat." But the colonists chickened out and decided to go home with the *Concord*. It's thought by some that on his return, Gosnold—like William Shakespeare, a protégé of the Earl of Southampton—may have recounted tales of his voyage to the playwright, and that Cuttyhunk may be the foundation for Prospero's island, the location of *The Tempest,* which was first staged in 1611. (Bermuda is a better-known rival for this honor.) Nine years after that performance and eighteen years after Gosnold's landing on Cuttyhunk, the Pilgrims arrived in these parts and stayed.

In the course of the seventeenth century, the whole Elizabeth archipelago inherited the name given by Gosnold to Cuttyhunk. And for some time the most noted family at this end of the chain was that of the Slocums, who grazed their sheep on Cuttyhunk, Nashawena, and Penikese. Cuttyhunk men acquired reputations as pilots, conning ships, whalers in particular, in and out of Buzzards Bay and

Vineyard Sound. Ships in trouble with currents and reefs, possibly because they didn't have Cuttyhunk pilots on board, were often grateful for the island's volunteer lifesaving crew, who patrolled the beaches most nights and on foggy days. Just one example: in a gale in February 1893, the brig *Aquatic,* from New Brunswick, was wrecked on Sow and Pigs Reef off Cuttyhunk's western tip, and five of the six members of the island lifesaving crew drowned when their surf boat overturned near the brig. The men on the *Aquatic* managed to hang on in the foretopmast rigging, wrapped in sails, until the next day, when the seas moderated and they were rescued. Off-duty, pilots and lifesavers went shellfishing and guided parties of sportsmen who came to catch striped bass. Some New Yorkers bought part of the island in 1864 for a fishing club, which had fishing "stands" along the beaches. But the islanders successfully resisted the bid of a wool magnate from New York, William M. Wood, to buy the entire island, much as they appreciated his generous improvements to their water supply. Mr. Wood also planned a hilltop mansion and to that end had built the rather incongruous walls that line the road from the village center out to his homesite. The hilltop itself was never burdened with the promised mansion.

By now Margot and I have a Cuttyhunk routine. We feed the ducks in the pond with stale rye crisp; a female mallard fans its tail wide as it accepts the biscuit, showing a discreet electric blue marking. After some not too strenuous endeavor, like this jaunt to West End Pond, we find a spot from which to swim—for example, on the beach that faces south across the entrance of Vineyard Sound. Here you can look across at the cliffs of Gay Head on the Vineyard and find interesting bits and bobs which wash up on the stretches of sand and pebbles. The old wooden barges embedded here help hold the beach together. We walk out toward the Canapitsit channel between Cuttyhunk and Nashawena. (Near the end of the spit is a solitary low modern house whose owner has his own little airstrip.) Over the years, we've found on this beach a sponge, an onion, a towel, and an unused tube of sunblock cream. Today, we pick up a boat fender and a nice piece of mahogany—the sort of thing that "will come in useful." On *Caliban* we had an alcohol stove that, before lighting, required priming with a small measure of fuel squirted into the priming cups under the burners. Margot found on this beach the perfect device for squirting the fuel, a French's mustard plastic squeegee bottle. Ever since, she has been picking up these bottles on beaches, faded yellow as they are and scrubbed clean by the sea, *even though* Lochinvar*'s stove works on a completely different priming system.* (The vast amount of mustard consumed on the New England coast is one of the less important curiosities we've noted during our summers afloat.) We also collect thirty or forty periwinkles, whose shells, pierced with an ice pick, can be threaded on a leather thong, polished with olive oil, and hung around the crew's neck. Sometimes we find mussels for an evening meal of *moules marinières*.

Back among the houses of the village, we buy a token pastry from the bake shop, a blueberry muffin or raisin Danish, although (this is not just a Cuttyhunk problem) these are never as good to eat as they are to look at. On one occasion my rather soggy muffin had exactly one blueberry in it; but as Margot pointed out, otherwise they'd have had to call it a blueberries muffin. Things have their own seasons in Cuttyhunk. In the store we're told, "Milk won't be in till 11:45." (That's when fresh supplies from New

Bedford are brought up from the *Alert II*.) In the laundry room of the Allen House, an inn, our wash, sudsing and spinning, has to be carefully monitored, so that we don't leave it beyond its cycle and annoy other yachtspeople waiting for the machine. While there, we book a table for dinner tonight. We go back to the store to get milk, fruit, and pita bread. While picking up ice on the dock, we have a brief dialogue with a bare-chested elderly man; he is cruising alone in an 18-foot open boat with oars and sails, his belongings stowed in plastic garbage bags. "Where are you from?" we ask.

"Vermont," he says.

"Where are you heading?"

"Nantucket."

He must have had this same conversation with many strangers and we don't detain him.

Another Tartan 27, *Kittiwake*, has anchored not far from us. As we shower the salt off ourselves in *Lochinvar*'s cockpit, we watch the Cessna seaplane land and take off again soon after, its wing tips seeming to brush the masts of yachts in the pond, rooster tails of foam rising behind each float. It looks as if it is about to run out of room—the beach fast approaching—when at the last moment the wings dip from side to side and first one float and then the other frees itself from the suction of the water. The plane roars gradually aloft and heads northeast on its ten-minute flight to Fairhaven, Massachusetts. This service is, we gather, in new hands, but for twenty years the plane was piloted by an avuncular aviator named Norman Gingrass, now departed. In summer Gingrass flew as many as twenty-four flights a day, carrying islanders, tourists, schoolchildren, and fishermen. On Sundays, one passenger was the Catholic priest who comes to the island to say Mass (and was never asked to pay). Fog can halt operations, for federal regulations require a visibility of one mile. If he had any doubts, Gingrass before taking off would telephone the Cuttyhunk postmistress, Ellen Veeder, and ask her to look out her window and tell him if she could see Nashawena.

It's a close evening. Before rowing back into the pond for our Allen House dinner, we listen to the weather radio. The forecast is for southeast 10 during the night, becoming northwest 10–15. But with the wind in the northwest, we should be nicely in the lee of Copicut Neck, Cuttyhunk's northern promontory. Just as long as the wind doesn't pause in the northeast and blow from there in the course of a counterclockwise swing. However, our anchor held during last night's fracas, and has held us since. I decide that we'll be okay.

I've been looking forward to a seafood dinner in this sea-girt spot, but it turns out to be Japanese Night at the Allen House. In the face of the continued undermining of American industrial power by Toyota, Honda, Nissan, Subaru, Mitsubishi, Suzuki, Yamaha, et al., this may smack of appeasement. But like most of the Allen House customers, we eschew chauvinism, decline the fresh-caught flounder which is offered as a sop to fish addicts, and go with the stir-fry veg and chicken with ginger. Fortunately we've remembered one important Cuttyhunk characteristic: the island is dry. In the past, our shore dinners have had to be accompanied by water. Tonight we've brought along from *Lochinvar*'s wine locker a bottle of Australian white.

Our young waiter, announcing his name is Carl, puts an ice-filled wine cooler on the table for the bottle. Like most helpers in these coastal hostelries, Carl is a college student from deep inland. When he returns to take our order he says, "You folks all set?" During dinner, an icy patch of dampness makes itself felt on my trouser leg. Condensation from the wine cooler is streaming along the sheet of glass which thriftily covers the tablecloth, and then, because of the angle of heel of the Allen House dining porch, runs diagonally to the table edge and falls over, drip, drip, drip, onto me.

"Carl," I say, when he appears again, bearing more rice, "I'm not quite so all set as I was."

Carl, flustered but keeping cheerful, brings a few towels. Yachtspeople ought not to mind wetness, but no doubt we seek an impossible perfection; at least we would like to be immune from the wet while dining ashore.

As we row back through the pond, someone on one of the moored boats is giving an impromptu solo concert. The instrument sounds to me like a trombone. Margot thinks it's a kazoo. Old favorites like "Roll Out the Barrel" are rendered shakily but received with applause from most of the boats. One sourpuss, however, greets the closing notes of "Swanee River" with blasts from his foghorn, intimating "Enough! Enough!" Life afloat seems to bring out a genial exhibitionism in some. In Great Salt Pond on Block Island a bagpiper is sometimes to be heard at dusk piping a Caledonian lament on his foredeck. Carleton Granbery used to carry an electronic keyboard on *Lochinvar* for the purpose of serenading the Off Soundings fleet at its overnight anchorages. After-dark performers have the advantages of anonymity and a captive audience. While I ply the oars, Margot and I dredge up *Caliban*'s words from *The Tempest*:

Be not afeard; the isle is full of noises,
Sounds, and sweet airs, that give delight, and hurt not.
Sometimes a thousand twangling instruments
Will hum about mine ears; and sometime voices,
That, if I then had waked after long sleep,
Will make me sleep again: and then, in dreaming,
The clouds methought would open, and show riches
Ready to drop upon me; that, when I waked,
I cried to dream again.

14

I'M NOT SURE what wakes me—thunder, rain, or the tiller, which had been propped upright and must have fallen with a bang. My watch tells me it's midnight. I'm not dreaming. The storm clouds have opened again and the boat seems to be lying aslant the wind, allowing rain to blow in through the open companionway from the cockpit. The current must be holding us like this. I slot in place two of the vertical hatch slides. As I head back to my bunk, there's a sudden thump-thump-thump. *Lochinvar* is hitting the bottom. We've dragged.

In boat shoes, pajama jacket, and boxer shorts, I grab a flashlight and clamber into the cockpit, into the downpour. The boat is jolting and banging, tiller jerking as the rudder hits the bottom. Cursing, I start the engine and peer into the wet and windy murk. The beach is close off the starboard bow. On our port quarter I can just make out *Kittiwake;* she appears to have dragged, too, but is not yet bouncing on the sand. I shout, "Are you aground?" but her crew are evidently preoccupied or else can't hear; they wave perfunctorily. I'd like to know if there's enough depth of water where they are, in case I can coax *Lochinvar* off in that direction. I try to recall the state of the tide; thank God, it's high around 3:00 a.m. and therefore still rising. But putting the engine in reverse and revving it hard produces nothing except a nasty smell of hot oil from the gearbox. Switching it off, I make for the foredeck and haul in the anchor line. It comes in without trouble, and the Danforth rises heavily clogged with eelgrass. What had possessed me to use the Danforth and not the Fisherman, which held so well here last year? And yet the Danforth had done its job for a night and a day through weather much like this, though of course now the wind is blowing from the open Bay, the northeast. The waves, too, are bigger than they were last night. Had the anchor flipped when the wind changed and not dug in again? Had another boat snagged it somehow?

But there's no time for postmortems. Margot comes on deck. Clad in a black nylon nightie and an old long-sleeved plaid shirt, she is instantly soaked to the skin. While she holds the juddering tiller I pull in the dinghy and climb into it. Then I move it along to *Lochinvar*'s bow and lift in the Danforth and a hundred or so feet of anchor line. I row out to windward and, as soon as the line is taut, drop the anchor over. Back on board, with knuckles bruised and eelgrass and mud on my hands, I haul on the anchor line. The strain is taken; the anchor digs in. *Lochinvar* refuses to budge. "I better try a kedge," I shout. A kedge is a backup anchor that can be used in predicaments like this. However, the Fisherman is lying folded up in the bottom of the sail locker and has to be pulled out with its fathom of heavy chain. Margot holds the flashlight while I fit the anchor together using pliers and marlin spike on cotter pins and shackles. *Lochinvar* continues to bump on the bottom. As the tide rises, her stern is lifting higher and higher up the beach. In the streaming darkness the land looks very near—in fact, it is looming over us, like a cliff. In my head, I hear myself on the radio to the Cuttyhunk salvors, asking for assistance. Will it come to that?

When I've got a line bent onto the anchor and taken the line outside all the stanchions and shrouds and made fast to the main foredeck cleat, the procedure with the Danforth is repeated. The anchor and line go into the dinghy and I row out to windward, not quite in the same direction as before. I don't want to drop the Fisherman on top of the Danforth. So I row a bit farther out, perhaps 150 feet. The Fisherman goes over with a great splash. As the chain rattles across the dinghy transom, I lose what feels like half a finger but proves to be only some skin. The chain is no doubt taking some paint with it, but that's how kedging is: propitiations, sacrifices. It occurs to me that the thunder has stopped.

"You okay?" A voice comes out of the blackness. It's the skipper of *Kittiwake,* who has reanchored in deep water and is sitting in his dinghy offering me help. He has two hundred feet of line. He can try to haul us off with *Kittiwake* just before high water. I promise I'll take him up on this if it looks necessary. "Call on channel 9," he says kindly.

Back on *Lochinvar* I ensure the dinghy painter is made fast before going onto the foredeck and taking up a little slack which has developed in the Danforth line. This isn't the moment to let the dinghy drift off into the night. But the rain seems to be easing and *Lochinvar*'s bow is pointing not quite so directly toward the shore. We are scarcely bumping at all now. Then I haul in on the kedge line. It comes in a bit, it tightens hard—it isn't dragging. After a pause I renew the strain first on one line, then the other, gaining an inch or two each time. In a few more minutes there's a response. *Lochinvar*'s bow begins to swing out, until we are at right angles to the beach; then, the pull suddenly becoming easy, she slips free. We're off!

We motor out and search with the flashlight for the one vacant mooring. There's a mound of anchors, chains, and lines on the foredeck, entangled with mud, sand, and weed. I hardly ever remember to use the spreader lights, but this time I do. I sort out most of the mess and hurl buckets of seawater over everything. That'll do for tonight. Down below, we appreciate the wonderful drying quality of towels. Margot pours me a stiff whiskey and—unlike her—one for herself. We toast our good luck. I try to raise *Kittiwake* on the radio to report our deliverance, but there's no answer—they've probably seen us get off and gone to bed. So do we, though it takes a while before I can sleep.

At 5:30 the morning is limpid, the harbor calm, the wind light and at last in the northwest. I drop the mooring and reanchor a few hundred yards away, using the Fisherman. The Danforth is out of favor, at least in the Cuttyhunk eelgrass, and will remain so until I can acquire a longer piece of chain, say thirty feet, whose weight will keep the boat's pull on the anchor more horizontal. I abandon the mooring partly from thrift; why pay twenty dollars for barely five hours' use? Mostly I don't want to face the questions of the Cuttyhunk launch man when he comes to collect the fee: "Weren't you anchored last night? Why'd you move here?"

A tern approves our new position, perching on the bow pulpit and fishing from it for several minutes, squeaking loudly as it swoops out to catch its breakfast. Encouraged by its confidence in our reanchoring job, I go back to bed for another two hours.

Our breakfast is at 8:15 and leisurely. While the coffee water is getting hot I hang our wet clothes up to dry and sort out the foredeck chaos left from last night. Afterward I row over to *Kittiwake* and thank them for standing by. It seems they woke and, realizing they were dragging, managed not to join our kedging-off antics. We exchange a few details about our boats; they turn out to be not only sister ships but built consecutively in distant Ohio in the mid-sixties. We trade best wishes for fair passages from now on. It's surprising what a fine humor I'm in, how a small calamity averted makes me affable. I am patient with Margot and we make an unhurried late-morning departure from Cuttyhunk Harbor.

I consider briefly the southern exit from here into Vineyard Sound, the Canapitsit channel between Cuttyhunk and Nashawena. We've gone out and come in through it on several occasions when wind and current served, but it requires cool judgment. There are rocks close on either hand and often a swell cresting into surf; there's a bend in the narrow channel and a spot only four feet deep where a trough between the swells could drop you on the bottom with a hard thump. Other craft have been seen aground in Canapitsit or on its borders, and I've determined that last night's experience should be our only such predicament this summer. My caution is in any case supported by the further factor of current. According to *Eldridge,* for the next few hours the current around Cuttyhunk will be flooding clockwise, westward down Vineyard Sound and eastward up Buzzards Bay. So it is into the Bay that we first go.

In the Bay we also have a fair wind from the northwest, 15 to 20. *Lochinvar* barrels along on a very broad reach under single-reefed main and full jib a hundred yards off the north shore of Nashawena. This island has the grassy slopes and bare rock outcrops of a Welsh hill farm, or of a primitive golf course, with rough greens and rugged fairways. Its late-seventeenth-century owners, Peleg Sanford and Philip Smith, are thought to be the culprits who felled the original woods. For a long time sheep were Nashawena's main crop, more so than people. In a few informal cemeteries most graves are unmarked, though a pamphlet from Cuttyhunk tells of one stone in a little hilltop graveyard that says, with poignant precision:

HERE LIES YE BODY OF SARAH,

YE WIFE OF JOHN ROON

DIED JULY 17TH 1736

45 MINUTES AFTER 11 A CLOCK

IN YE 39TH YEAR OF HER AGE.

For John and Sarah, every minute counted.

In the 1860s the island became the retreat of a New Bedford whaling captain and candlemaker, Edward Merrill, who took to Nashawena as reading matter only the Bible and a set of Shakespeare—"enough for any man," he said. A stone monument like the Gosnold pile was erected for Captain Merrill by his six children when he died in 1884, aged eighty-four, and still forms a landmark. Yet not everyone in those days liked islands. It took Captain Merrill's heirs twenty-one years to sell Nashawena. After being considered as a possible site for a Massachusetts state prison, in 1905 it was bought by two members of the influential and in these parts now ubiquitous Forbes family, Waldo and Edward Forbes, whose descendants, as members of a family trust, take turns using the island's three houses. Sheep still safely graze on Nashawena.

There are three passages between the Elizabeth Islands from Buzzards Bay into Vineyard Sound: Canapitsit, Quicks Hole, and Robinsons Hole. A fourth passage, Woods Hole, lies between the east end of the islands and Cape Cod. Today for us it's Quicks, the quickest and easiest. We gybe at the northeast end of Nashawena around an upstanding boulder called North Rock, and with the beginnings of a fair current shoot through the three-quarters-of-a-mile-wide gap between Nashawena and the next island, Pasque. On occasion when we've had less impetus we've paused here and anchored in the concave arc of the Nashawena beach, swum, picnicked, and walked a short distance through low dunes to an idyllic pond whose service as a Second World War bombing range has almost been forgotten. The pond looks tidal, though I couldn't see where the salt water came and went. Because of the confused currents at the southern entrance to Quicks, this area was a trap for powerless sailing vessels if the wind dropped; many went ashore on the points of Nashawena and Pasque.

Today the northwesterly doesn't fail us. Across Vineyard Sound, the sandy cinnamon-colored cliffs of Cape Higgon on Martha's Vineyard draw our attention, but we aren't going that way. Instead, after giving a wide berth to South Rock, we gybe again and run along the south shore of Pasque. Like Nashawena's, Pasque's terrain is green and gray, stone-scattered moorland pasture with few trees. Like Cuttyhunk, Pasque belonged to a private fishing group in the late nineteenth century. Its members, in fact, resigned from the Cuttyhunk fraternity because of a no-women rule. On Pasque they built a big clubhouse which admitted ladies; it had an icehouse, a servants' wing, and a dinner menu listing nine soups, three fish courses, three meat dishes, ten vegetables, and six desserts. Not exactly roughing it after a day spent trying to catch striped bass. But the First World War put a crimp in the club's activities, and it didn't recover. Pasque also fell into Forbes hands in 1939, and a Forbes trust now owns it.

Lochinvar skedaddles across the southern entrance to Robinsons Hole, a gully which is narrower and consequently fiercer than Quicks. The next Elizabeth Island is the largest: Naushon. Its history is similar to that of its fellows, a place where the Indians came to fish and hunt in summer, where the early settlers farmed, and where the Forbeses now rule; in Naushon's case, the four hundred or so descendants of John Murray Forbes, a merchant in the China trade who bought the island in 1842. Naushon, unlike the other islands, has fine woods; some trees are aboriginal, though many pines, locusts, and larches were planted by J. M. Forbes. The Vineyard Sound coast of the island is faced with short cliffs and is rocky, but twice indented with mostly rock-free coves. The first we pass is small and shallow, the French Watering Place, so-called (it is said) because French privateers in the early eighteenth century landed here to fill their water casks at the pond behind the beach, drawing attention to their visits by stealing sheep. The second dent, larger and deeper, is Tarpaulin Cove. A stumpy white lighthouse stands on the headland at the southwest-

ern corner of the cove. At noon today the sight of this beacon lifts my spirits, as it always does. We have come to one
of the best of places. Rolling up the jib, we take *Lochinvar*
into the cove and, close to the beach, drop the Fisherman in
eight feet of water.

One of several cheering things about Tarpaulin Cove is
that it is rarely crowded. There are only half a dozen boats
here now. The broad semicircle is open to the south and
southeast, and a long fetch to the Vineyard enables a jab-
bing sea to build up with a wind from that quarter.
Moreover, an ocean swell rolling in and the wakes of ships
passing along the Sound can make a stay in the cove lively,
to say the least. To lie here contentedly you must accept the
partly exposed nature of the spot and take sailing for what
it is, a sport in which nothing is absolutely certain or completely relaxed, and which demands that you remain on
your toes and, if the wind changes, be prepared to get up
and go. Today, I'm as happy about anchoring here overnight
as the weather can make me. A nor'wester like this is generally good for one day if not two days. All is clear and dry.
Everything looks distinct: the old dark-green woods rim-
ming the cove, the little gray-brown cliffs on the cove's
southeastern corner, the lonely dark-shingled farmhouse
with red painted trim, the sharply sparkling waters of the
Sound. The clear air makes me feel uncluttered and jaunty.
All the same, I listen to the weather radio. Fortunately, its
forecast agrees with the feeling in my bones: the weather
will continue fine and the wind nor'westerly.

After lunch we walk along the beach from end to end.
We stroll first to the east end, where a little stream runs into
the cove and the beach is boggy; you can sink in brown
smelly ground juice up to your ankles. Nineteen Canada

geese, hove-to in a tiny subcove, ignore us. Along the beach, signs addressed to visitors prohibit dogs, guns, camping, bonfires, and any incursions beyond the strand. In recent years these admonitions have been expanded by the caveat "Beware of Ticks." On Naushon, as on the South Fork of Long Island, on the Connecticut shore, Block Island, the Vineyard, and Nantucket, Lyme disease has been doing its worst. It was identified in 1969 on Nantucket and called Nantucket fever. But it was first linked with ticks after a number of children came down with it in the mid-1970s in Lyme, Connecticut. The disease is probably not new. Fossil ticks, fifteen million years old, have been discovered. During their lifetimes these little beasties are considerably mobile: in their larval form they are hosted by mice, as adults by deer. In the intervening immature nymphal stage, from June through August, the ticks can transmit to human beings the Lyme-disease bacterium. Untreated, it can trigger arthritis, meningitis, palsy, heart trouble, miscarriages, and potentially fatal neurological problems. The ticks themselves, being pinhead size, are extremely hard to see if they have burrowed into your skin, and though the infection may produce a ring-like rash, this doesn't always appear. (Flu-like aches, pains, and chills are other symptoms.) It's not an illness to mess with; we've lost a very good friend to it. An energetic tennis player in her mid-sixties, she had had a previous attack of Lyme disease; her heart couldn't stand up to the fever the second time around. Doctors now customarily give patients with Lyme-disease symptoms a course of penicillin or tetracycline; many people with gardens near woods set up electric fences to keep out deer.

It seems like a good argument against the existence of a loving God: Why should a benevolent deity create on the

one hand places like Naushon and on the other hand creatures like ticks? On this coast now we think twice before
walking in tall grass and brush; grassy dunes and
sequestered woodlands are not as attractive as they were.
Long-sleeve shirts, trousers with cuffs tucked into socks,
shoes or sneakers are now de rigueur when off the beaten
track—no more bare arms, bare legs, bare feet. Nature
bites, burrows, and hurts, and must be kept at a proper distance. However, several counterattacks are being mounted.
A chemical preparation called Damminix has proved effective when spread on cotton, which field mice collect for
their nests: it kills the ticks but not the mice. And one
sharp-eyed Vineyard resident, reading through old scientific
papers, discovered not long ago a valuable 1937 report.
This published the findings of fieldworkers of the time who
had demonstrated on the Vineyard and Naushon that the
spread of ticks could be partly controlled by chalcid wasps.
These are even tinier than the ticks and live only a few days.
But in that period they lay eggs inside the tick larvae that
infect and kill them as they develop. Perhaps the Creator
does have the situation in hand after all. Efforts are now
being made to collect and increase the numbers of these natural foes of the tick and send them into action on the coast
and islands. Bake sales, auctions, and fund-raising drives
are being held to match state funds promised for this purpose. Meanwhile, the Forbeses' desire for privacy on their
islands is aided by an unlikely ally.

When we reach the west end of the cove, Margot suggests walking up on the bluff to look at the lighthouse.
Although the grass is fairly sparse up there, I stay below.
The lighthouse is like a pepper pot, with a circular balcony
around the lantern and a one-story rear wing with a wood-

shingled roof, presumably the keeper's quarters. The tick-free beach and water interest me more. After she returns from her walk, we swim. Margot, in mask and fins, walks backward into the water of the Sound. Now and then she surfaces to report small striped bass which come close and peer into her mask; green minnows and nearly transparent jellyfish brush past her. "You'd think anything that was going to sting you would look a bit more conspicuous," she complains, rubbing a faint rash on her leg.

We've been here on many occasions without seeing any Forbeses, but now two Naushon ladies dressed in tickproof clothes go by on big horses. They on their land, we in public water, call good afternoon to one another. A few minutes later, as we're climbing into the dinghy, a tall, slender woman hurries along the beach from the farmhouse, which, apart from the lighthouse, is the only building on the cove. She surprises us by shaking hands and introducing herself.

Her name is Lynn Danforth and she wants a ride to Nantucket, if we're going there. She's staying with a Forbes friend in the farmhouse and got here yesterday, by ferry from Nantucket to Hyannis on the Cape, by bus to Woods Hole, and by the private Forbes ferry to Hadley Harbor at the east end of Naushon. She had started walking here along the tracks through the woods with her backpack and a bag of food. Clearly the Forbeses believe in letting their guests get immediately into the swing of self-help!

However, there are Naushon wardens who look after the island's fauna and flora and maintain its privacy, and one of them gave her a lift in his pickup truck. Now it seems her friend has been called to the mainland by a family emergency. Lynn Danforth is alone in the farmhouse, which has bottled gas for cooking and oil lamps for light, and is lived in only during the long summer season. Tick inspections take place on each return to the house. She thinks she'd like to get back to Nantucket, where she runs a B&B and looks after an elderly couple. And she's hoping to find a simpler way of making the journey than the way she came.

We apologize. Nantucket is in our scheme of things, but not quite yet. "Well," she says, with a smile, "if you run into anyone else who's going that way . . ."

Catching up with odd jobs takes up the late afternoon. A section of teak rub rail that has come adrift has to be glued and clamped. I make a replacement hinge out of galvanized wire for the heel strap of one of Margot's fins. I patch the leech of the mainsail where the topping lift has been chafing it. I remember it's about time to rotate the greaser on the engine water pump. Then I sit for a while and appreciate my surroundings. About twenty boats are now here at anchor. Tarpaulin Cove often attracts vessels of character, with topsails or square sails suggestive of deep-water experience, or the look of boats that have won great ocean races. A few years ago we were here on *Clio*, and were walking along the beach when a handsome wooden sloop sailed in and anchored; it was about fifty feet long, late 1930s. "Now that's a real yacht," I said to Margot. "Looks a bit like Sparkman and Stephens." Margot nodded. She is used to my moments of nautical pedantry, and doesn't always deliver a wholehearted response. But after another glance at the big sloop, she seemed more approving.

The sloop was anchored not far beyond *Clio*, and as we rowed out, a woman on its foredeck looked our way and suddenly yelled, "Margot!" Margot looked and yelled back, "Tricia!"

On board *Karen*, which was the name of the handsome

sloop, there were hugs, handshakes, drinks. We hadn't seen our old friend Tricia Dodson for some years, though we'd kept up a correspondence. Her last letter to us had come from Sydney during the previous winter. Now here she was cruising these waters with an Englishman named Tom Fenwick, whom we'd met once before. Tricia had telephoned people in Stonington and knew our rough whereabouts. Half an hour earlier she had said to Tom, "Why don't we go into Tarpaulin Cove? I have a feeling the Baileys might be around here."

This is a love story, and a synopsis of the plot is needed. Tricia and her former husband, Johnny Dodson, son of the owner of the Stonington boatyard, had emigrated to Australia. After various triumphs and vicissitudes in the farming business, they'd got divorced but continued to live in Oz. Several of their children (one being my godson) stayed with us on visits to England. In her letter Tricia had written that she had heard from a woman friend in Cornwall concerning one Tom Fenwick, yachtsman and dairy farmer on the Isle of Wight. Tom, with a partner-manager happy to run the farm, was looking for a crew. He owned a 35-foot boat in the Mediterranean, the use of which he often swapped for that of boats in other countries. He wanted a female companion to help him cruise the West and East Coasts of the U.S.A. Tricia had told us to expect Tom Fenwick; he was going to drop in on us in Greenwich. We were to write and tell her whether she should go with him. A few days later, Tom came to Greenwich to ask us about Tricia. Should he take her on as crew?

Thus put on the spot, we said that Tricia was an attractive, energetic woman who was a good sailor but no doormat. Then we wrote to her that not only was Tom a charming bloke, he was also a competent seaman and navigator who had sailed to New Zealand and back. We thought he might be a touch old-fashioned; he had mentioned his fondness for steak and kidney pie with mashed potatoes followed up by steamed puddings, and he appeared uninterested in contemporary female liberation.

In Tarpaulin Cove, over rum-and-tonic in *Karen*'s cockpit, they told us they had listened to the good things in our descriptions and ignored the rest. After some eventful voyaging together they had become thoroughly enamored. A Force 9 storm off the harborless north California coast had ruptured a seacock in their borrowed 40-footer. The mast spreaders had jumped out of their sockets and it was a toss-up whether the boat would sink before the mast collapsed or vice versa. Trish stayed at the helm in huge seas while Tom crawled under the engine to get to the seacock to drive in a wooden plug. Then he climbed up the wildly swaying and flexing mast to secure the spreaders. It was a make-or-break test for skipper and crew, as well as for the boat, and all three had survived.

Before we returned to our own vessel, Tom gave us a tour of *Karen*. She had been designed by Henry Gruber, a German naval architect who had indeed worked for Sparkman and Stephens before the Second World War. There was an admirably unmodernized simplicity down below; in the galley, the original bronze hand pump stood beside the copper sink. Winches, blocks, and deck fittings were the real 1930s thing. As we climbed down into our dinghy, promises were made for winter reunions in Greenwich and the Isle of Wight—promises which were kept. Now we often see them between their long voyages, and feel like diffident but successful Cupids.

•

On *Lochinvar* this evening I listen in to an amiable forecast but nonetheless increase the amount of anchor line we have out. One midnight emergency is enough. The breeze is faint, mere air, still northwest, and the sun sets splashily red, pink, and purple over Cove Farm and the woods behind. Time was when the cove would have held a good number of coasting craft and privateers, waiting for the tide and exchanging letters and goods. In the seventeenth century some crews brought their vessels in here to careen them, scrape off the weed and barnacles, and tar the bottom planking. While the tar was warmed up, it might be used to renew the waterproofing of the canvas hatch covers: a process called tarpawling. One old cutthroat skipper who preyed on shipping in these waters was Thomas Pound, who off Tarpaulin Cove in the 1690s met his nemesis, Captain Samuel Pease of the sloop *Mary*. Pease had orders from the governors of the Massachusetts Bay colony to get rid of pirates, and Pound was what he was looking for: his ship was called *Pirate* and flew the Jolly Roger. In the battle which followed, the Cove echoed with gunfire and the clashing of cutlasses. The *Pirate* sank, with a hundred killed or wounded. But the *Mary*'s victory was Pyrrhic: Captain Pease died of his wounds.

During the War of Independence the British found Tarpaulin Cove handy for victualing. In Rhode Island, Colonel Mackenzie wrote in his diary on May 9, 1778: "The Transports from the Elisabeth Islands arrived last night in the Seconnet Passage. The troops have been very successful and met with no opposition. The two Transports have brought 884 Sheep and Lambs—150 of them were bought from such of the Inhabitants as were well affected and willing to sell them. The rest, being the property of noted Rebels, were taken without payment. The party has also secured about 1000 more Sheep and Lambs on a small Island under protection of the Unicorn, until the Transports can return for them. The whole were taken from Nashawn Island . . . A company of Rebels were posted upon it, but they retired upon the appearance of our fleet. Our people burnt the Barracks they had occupied and destroyed two pieces of Cannon. Captain Coore of the 54th Grenadiers commanded the party."

In the late nineteenth century an evangelist named Madison Edwards used the cove farmhouse for occasional religious meetings for ships' crews. At one, 165 mariners are said to have heard the Word; they sat on the porch, on the grass, and on the beach, I imagine.

Tonight all's quiet in Tarpaulin Cove: there are neither hymns nor gunfire. Anchor lights glow on the yachts which honor that custom, as most do; but any vessel arriving at night may just make out the dim shapes of unlit others in the faint glow of the stars.

15

ALTHOUGH WE GO afloat for independence and solitude, we now and then crave talk with other people. Sometimes we're lucky enough to come across friends such as Tom and Tricia, but more often we strike up conversations with strangers who may own similar boats or be anchored close by. This has always been the way among seafarers. Vessels hailing from New England used to meet in distant places—Shanghai, Valparaiso, or Macao—and stop for a "gam," exchanging news and letters, and sharing hoarded delicacies. Some people we meet are evidently lonely or fed up with each other's company and want to talk. "Come over and have a drink," they say, and we often do. We've had long chats with Texan retirees, an Australian scientist and his son, a New York airline pilot, a German engineer. Last year on Block Island, a couple on a big ketch from Florida saw us rowing by and immediately wanted to be friends; he insisted on towing us to the shore with his out-

board-powered Zodiac, despite my insistence that I liked
rowing. On our way back the wife came to the rail to ask
who we were and where we came from, and went on talking and finally shouting as I rowed farther and farther
away. "How rude you are," said Margot. Well, there are
moments when I want to be sociable and other moments
when I don't.

Getting under way late this morning is complicated by a
boat which sails into the almost deserted cove and, apparently desperate for companionship, anchors close ahead of
us. It's a good-looking 40-foot yawl with unusual rhubarb-
colored topsides; the name *Rhubarb* does in fact appear on
its broad transom, swinging just about over where our
anchor lies. The skies are clear, the wind brisk from the
northeast, and I'm preparing to sail, not motor, out of
Tarpaulin Cove. "Why did he plant himself there?" I mutter,
cogitating my next move. The question is soon answered.
Rhubarb's skipper hails us confidently: "Ahoy, *Lochinvar*!
This is Ben duPont. Who's aboard?"

This isn't the first time friends of the Granberys have seen
Lochinvar and expected to see them, too. As I explain that
we aren't boat thieves, I recall *Rhubarb* in the 1960 Bermuda
Race. I was crewing on an elderly Alden yawl named *Mistral;*
Rhubarb did well in the race and *Mistral* did badly. But if
Mr. duPont is disappointed now at not having a gam with
the Granberys, obviously his intention when he anchored
here, he doesn't show it. He calls back, "Well, you've got a
good boat there." I wave in reply. Then I haul slowly in on
the anchor line, so as not to shoot into *Rhubarb*'s transom.
Margot unfurls a few feet of jib and I prepare to back it
when the anchor breaks out. *Lochinvar*'s bow swings
quickly to starboard, away from the beach and the com-

pany. The Fisherman comes up with a heavy cargo of grass, mud, and shells. I wash down the foredeck as Margot sails *Lochinvar* out of the cove.

Vineyard Sound is full of sparkle again today. For two bodies of water so close together, Buzzards Bay and Vineyard Sound are curiously different in light and atmosphere. The Sound is narrower, and its shores seem higher and better defined. Moreover, it is a sound, not a bay, a through channel and not a cul-de-sac; it therefore offers greater possibilities. We have a fair tide, but there are a few hours to go before the current becomes favorable in Woods Hole, our immediate destination. So we don't mind the wind being a bit on the nose. It is a morning when one is happy just to be sailing; getting somewhere is a bonus. On the port tack, with full jib and the mainsail single-reefed, we take a long fetch over to Martha's Vineyard. It seems Bartholomew Gosnold gave this name first to the smaller island now called Nomans Land, which plays moon to the Vineyard's earth, and did so, historians say, either in honor of his daughter Martha or his mother, Martha. The name was later shifted to the larger island, supplanting the Dutch explorers' Texel. Another early name was La Soupçonneuse; the French explorer Samuel de Champlain didn't circumnavigate it completely and supposed it was joined to the mainland. Captain John Smith, who followed in Gosnold's wake, called it by its Indian name, the Isle of Capawack. The Vineyard, as most people call it nowadays, is said to have had many wild grapevines in the days of the early European settlers, though poison ivy seems to be its champion uncultivated growth today.

Some readers of the Norse sagas, seeking a truly southern location for the "Vinland the Good" which is mentioned in those texts, have been inclined to find it here, though it is a long way from L'Anse aux Meadows, in Newfoundland, where Viking habitations have been uncovered. (In *Leif Eriksson, Discoverer of America,* Edward F. Gray proposes the west end of the Vineyard for the site of a Norse settlement. He claims an arrangement of stones at Squibnocket, near Menemsha Pond, is the remains of a Norse burial place. Other writers have enthusiastically piloted the Norsemen into Cape Cod rivers, Narragansett Bay, and even Fishers Island Sound.) The German scholar-priest Adam of Bremen also mentioned Vinland in the eleventh century, as an "island discovered by many" whose wild vines "yield excellent wine." Professor Gwyn Jones discusses the difficulties of identifying Vinland in his book *The Norse Atlantic Saga.* He notes that Jacques Cartier found grapes growing on both banks of the St. Lawrence River in the 1530s and suggests that in a warm period grapes could have flourished as far north as northern Newfoundland. But Jones doesn't deny that "Vinland" might have stretched down the coast into what is now southern New England. He adds, however, that it would take a genuine archaeological discovery of bones, artifacts, weapons, or dwellings to "convert theory into fact."

The incomparable Viking ships were large open boats, low in the water amidships, their pine strakes rising high at bow and stern; they were powered by oars and a single square sail. Although these maneuverable craft lacked cannon and muskets, at close quarters they and their sword- and spear-wielding crews would have been more than a match, I believe, for the privateers and men-of-war that later sailed here. Today, we duck astern of a powerful steel fishing vessel which is making its way eastward to Georges

Bank for cod or scallops. We admire the distant sunlight falling on a big topsail schooner's lofty canvas; this is most likely the *Shenandoah* clawing her way out of Vineyard Haven with a party of fare-paying passengers. As usual, we get a little fun out of pitting *Lochinvar* against various yachts going our way. They probably don't know they are in a race.

The tide is slack as we approach Woods Hole passage. The usual current runs through it at as much as 4 knots and during spring tides, at the full and new moon, can reach 7. The main channel twists sharp and narrow around shoals, underwater ledges, and stony outcrops, one of which is named Coffin Rock. Numerous buoys mark the channel and several tributary channels in the southern half of the passage; these buoys are often laid nearly flat on their backs by the force of water rushing between the Bay and the Sound. The current is one thing to worry about here, whether it's against you, when you may need a powerful engine to push you through it, or with you, when you can barely maintain steerageway if under sail in a light wind. Another terror is the larger craft that punch their way in and out of here, ferries from Woods Hole to the islands, fishing boats, tugs, and countless yachts. Margot is fond of the perils of Woods Hole. "Why don't we go through here several times a week," she says as we ride through the passage and I sit on the edge of the cockpit coaming, waiting for signs that *Lochinvar* is about to go sideways or in circles and preparing my nerves for the sudden blast of the *Squibnocket*'s siren just behind me. The *Squibnocket* is the New Bedford–Vineyard Haven ferry, which typically at such moments is trying to get past us and in those confines looks like the *Queen Mary.* I wave coolly to the man on the

bridge. I'm as close to the rocks along my side of the channel as I dare go. I'm aware that he is just letting me know
he's there and what he's doing, in case *Lochinvar* sidles
across the swirling torrents of the channel into his path. My
wave acknowledges his warning that he is overtaking and
tells him I bear no ill will.

Today Margot rates the excitement at three out of ten.
The buoys are barely beginning to tilt as we head into
Woods Hole passage on the starboard tack, bear off a little
into the channel called Broadway, and then bear off even
more into The Strait, which leads us direct to the buoy
marking Hadley Rock. From here we steer west to the
entrance of Hadley Harbor. This is one of those rare places
that yachtsmen dream of, the marine equivalent of a happy
hunting ground, a final anchorage. Its peace and seclusion
couldn't be more different from the rough-and-tumble of
the nearby passage. Hadley's is tucked into the east end of
Naushon and given further protection from the northeast
and southeast by two small islands, Uncatena and
Nonamesset, which are connected to Naushon by little
bridges. The even smaller Bull Island divides Hadley's into
inner and outer harbors. An odd-shaped promontory called
Goats Neck butts into the inner one; intricate little channels
wander back into placid ponds and eventually "gutters,"
which trickle into Vineyard Sound. As at Cuttyhunk, you
used to be able to sail into Hadley's inner harbor and find
room to anchor. These days, not only do more and more
boats come here with this intent, but the natural expansion
of the Forbes clan has multiplied the moorings dropped for
family use. Along the in-and-out shores of the harbor, big
summer houses appear at discrete intervals, frequently with
boathouses and docks. A small private boatyard and marine

railway for hauling Forbes craft give a working edge to the waterfront without disturbing the idyll.

In *Caliban* and *Clio* we've found anchoring space in the recesses of the inner harbor, but *Lochinvar* needs a little more water. A short reconnaissance inside shows it well filled with local and visiting yachts, so we favor the greater swinging room and peace of mind in the outer harbor. I choose a spot near a substantial Forbes dock, with a pair of rocky clumps between us and the open water of Woods Hole passage to the east. Two anchors go over. Margot says, "We didn't used to drop two. And we didn't last night." I have to think before answering; how do the various demands of holding ground, exposure to wind and sea, proximity of land, other craft, and hazards like the clumps and dock bring me to the conclusion that two anchors are better than one? I try to explain. "Anyway," she says, "you're good at getting the anchor up in the morning. One more won't hurt you." Is this meant to make me feel better about my new conservatism?

We row into the sinuous backwaters behind Goats Neck. The low bridges between the islands lack only Chinese anglers to be willow pattern. Small fish are jumping and ducks make broad wakes with their plump bows. We see egrets, a heron, and a least bittern, which is like a small heron but with reddish-brown body and charcoal-tipped wings. After tucking our trousers in our socks, we land and take a walk around Bull Island, the one piece of territory in these parts on which the non-Forbeses of the world are allowed to tread. A deer, very tame, browses beside the pond which occupies much of the interior of the island, but we keep our distance.

Hadley's provokes thought about privacy and curiosity

and envy—and about ownership, privilege, and their responsibilities. It's a beautiful place and we're grateful that it doesn't have marinas, harbormasters, and onshore exploitation. As many large English country estates and numerous London squares and parks demonstrate, great landlords can create landscape or townscape that does more for the common good than property held either by numerous small owners or by anonymous public authorities. And so it seems here. All the same, I have a strong desire to know more about the Forbeses' way of life. If, as we sit in *Lochinvar*'s cockpit with late-afternoon cups of Earl Grey, a smart little launch approaches and the man at the helm says, "Mr. Forbes's compliments—would you care to join him at the house for drinks at six?" I won't say no.

As it is, an inquisitive scribe is probably the last person wanted in this Shangri-la, and not just because the second cocktail might make him bold enough to ask, "Is it true the eighteenth-century Forbeses made their money in the opium trade?" The Forbes clan, which now includes people with names like Riggs and Perkins who have married into the family, has gained immense skill at keeping a low profile. They'd prefer the wider public to believe that neither they nor their islands exist. Real-estate developers in Boston, Manhattan, and Tokyo are burning to throw hundreds of millions into leisure-age projects. There are senators, congressmen, and Park Service bureaucrats who can see mileage in developing islands like these in "the public interest"—a process which, following acquisition by eminent domain, would no doubt lead to a road bridge from the Cape, restaurants, information centers, thousands of visitors, and pollution.

I've talked in London and Boston to several members of

the extended Forbes family; they visit here, although they aren't stockholders in the privately incorporated Naushon Trust, which owns the islands, and rules on uses and constraints. We talked mainly about the desire to shun publicity and the difficulties of wise proprietorship of such domains. The trustees aren't interested in the many millions the islands would fetch. They want to keep the islands, and moreover keep them as natural as possible. They realize that any flaunting of possession could produce demands that "people" be allowed in. Family connections and friends who are invited as "house guests" or on hunting parties to shoot deer and geese are therefore asked not to make a big thing of it when talking about their visits. The Naushon Trust hopes that it has secured its lands in perpetuity against federal or state seizure by a legal agreement that the islands would revert automatically to a preservation society should such a danger become real. At the moment, there seems no great threat: bodies like the Department of the Interior and elected representatives of the people may be increasingly aware that the Forbeses do a good job of conservation. One Forbes told me, "The trustees are trying to keep the islands more or less as they were in the mid-nineteenth century. Sheep graze the pastureland and deer browse in the woods. There are many old stands of oaks and beeches. Apart from a few pickup trucks, the vehicles are horse-drawn carts and carriages. The amenities are basic. There's no splash and no show. And the sense of trust we all feel is real. The trustees regard themselves as fiduciaries for these islands, to keep them as untouched and as wonderful as can be."

I'm satisfied when in Hadley's to make do with hints and glimpses of how it is onshore. I watch the stout little steel

ferry *Cormorant* come and go between here and Woods
Hole carrying family members and their friends. This afternoon it arrives with a large chestnut horse among the deck
passengers. Ten minutes before the ferry departs for Woods
Hole, a siren hoots one long and two short blasts, presumably giving intending passengers time to foot it to the dock.
Among other island craft are a small fleet of gaff-rigged
Herreshoff 12½s, which in late afternoons are taken for
short sails by well-appointed people who could be lawyers,
bankers, corporation executives, or just couples, putting
aside their mainland cares. One evening when we were sitting at anchor in the inner harbor the sylvan silence was
demolished by a man on one shore shouting to some children on the other: "Will you pick up Will and Nan and
Uncle Mort?" The kids yelled back, "What?" The request
had to be repeated several times. Then a child shouted:
"Have you told them we're picking them up?" Further
answers and questions were lobbed over the anchored cruising yachts and their bemused crews. Finally the children set
off in a well-built skiff on their pickup errand. The
Naushoners seemed to be depending not on telephones for
message sending but on the unassisted human voice; they
felt the harbor was theirs to shout across, as if no one else
was there. *Droits des seigneurs*. Their life here as we imagine it is given faint color by a tantalizing snatch of conversation I overheard at the town dock in West Falmouth, on the
Cape, several years ago. A man who was evidently a
mechanic by day and a musician by night was describing to
a friend a Forbes wedding on Naushon, at which he had
played in the dance band: "Everybody had a great time.
Not raucous but stylish. They really know how to throw a
special party out there."

At twilight in the outer harbor, lights begin to come on in the Forbes houses, big and fairly big. Margot and I invent romantic names for these houses, like Manderley and Petronelle. It isn't so long ago that Cameron Forbes, one of the Naushon patriarchs, allowed electricity to be installed, though to begin with only in the servants' rooms; candles and oil lamps remained in use elsewhere. When electric light became general, it was treated with Scotch thrift compared to prevailing American standards: you turned off the light when you left the room. Even now, the rule appears to be early to bed on Naushon, and the lights go out in the summer mansion behind our nearby dock before the cabin lamp is snuffed on *Lochinvar*.

And what a night! Light airs from the west, clear sky, and a sliver of new moon. I call to Margot to come and see it. One of her superstitions is that it is unlucky to see the new moon through glass; but once having arranged to see it directly, you can make a wish on it. Then you mustn't speak until someone speaks to you; otherwise the wish won't come true. I don't keep Margot long in suspense. "Have you made your wish?" I ask. She nods, still careful about speaking, or else, like me, spellbound by the night. I don't ask what she wished; that would also prevent its coming true. I just hope she has wished for a completely peaceful night.

16

ONE PROBLEM with the passage through Woods Hole is that, with all the speed and excitement, you may shoot right through and miss the village. But this morning, which is hazy and hot, with a light southerly, we keep our wits about us and stay in The Strait, passing up the split-second opportunity the current allows to bear southeast into Broadway. Instead, in the slightly less fractious waters at the entrance to Great Harbor we turn north, shunning Grassy Island and its outlying rocks and dodging a ferry from the Vineyard which is about to dock.

As soon as we are out of the current, we turn the engine off and sail quietly into the top of the harbor, formed by the encircling arm of a promontory called Penzance. The moorings here are densely planted, but at least half of them never seem to have boats on them. This makes the place look as if there's more room than in fact there is; but we generally find a spot where, as now, *Lochinvar*, swinging tightly to two anchors in six or seven feet of water, just misses the empty mooring buoys or moored small craft. Big houses with private jetties rim this end of the harbor; one fancy dock has imitation owls fixed on top of its pilings, presumably to deter gulls rather than decoy owls. Mowing machines are at work on the wide lawns, grinding up ticks as well as grass, I trust, and giant Stars and Stripes flutter from lofty white-painted flagpoles. A pair of terns are squabbling for space on a nearby mooring buoy; one sounds like a car with wheel bearings about to go. The occupied moorings hold a nice variety of craft, fancy and homely, elegant and workmanlike. Some boats are tied alongside pontoons or rafts on which Huck Finn shacks have been built for storing fishing and sailing gear, and very likely for adolescent beer parties and canoodling.

But serious sailors in Woods Hole are apprenticed young. Throughout the day Cape Cod Knockabouts and Mirror dinghies are maneuvering around the harbor, racing or practicing. A small girl with an intense expression sails her boat past us, followed by a teenage lad in a Whaler who shouts, "Now come about! . . . Now let out your sheet! . . . Look out!" The red sails of the Mirrors are a friendly sight for us. I've owned several of these 11-foot pram-bow general-purpose dinghies, a design sponsored by the British *Daily Mirror* newspaper. The Mirror dinghy became perhaps the most successful do-it-yourself boat ever; its numbers are now in the seventy thousands. Our first Mirror was built from its English kit in our Stonington kitchen–living room; we stitched the plywood hull panels together with copper wire, fiberglass-taping the seams, and then, so we could get the boat outside, transformed a window into a garden door. (We had planned this in advance and wanted a new doorway.) Launched on the public beach three minutes' walk away, the Mirror, named *Cri de Coeur,* proved its worth; it was fine to row, sparkling to sail, and big enough to carry Margot and me and the Bailey children. It even towed well behind a larger craft, like *Caliban.* But it was too lightly constructed to make a good beach boat, and with *Clio* as our 22-foot flagship, the Mirror's 11-foot length made it too big for a suitable tender. *Cri de Coeur* passed into other hands.

We row ashore in our present non-sailing tender, the *L. Francis H.* A narrow beach runs west of the sailing club, where dinghies and dories are pulled up on the sand, bows pointing into a beach-plum hedge. We land and walk into the village. Woods Hole is one of those genial places where I can easily imagine myself a resident. It isn't too fixed up, and real work of a marine sort goes on. We walk by a shingle cottage where a big old comfortable sofa has been placed in the side yard—whether for the trash collector to take away or for the residents to use for siestas, it's hard to tell. Everybody seems to have a connection with the sea, and we are looked on in a friendly fashion by people we pass, not as interlopers or yachties to be fleeced and skinned. Our route takes us by the U.S. Fish & Wildlife Service. The seals are on view in their outdoor pool and we watch a young woman cutting up herrings for their midday meal. We enjoy watching the seals gliding in the water and flopping up onto the pool side, but ask ourselves, as always, do free meals make up for imprisonment? Indoors the tanks are full of conger eels, bluefish, cod, pollack, and crustaceans. Although they are just as confined, they get less sympathy, perhaps because they aren't mammals.

In the main street are the big buildings of the Woods Hole Oceanographic Institution and the Marine Biological

Laboratory. These are tanks for marine scientists, but from which—unlike the seals and fish—they sometimes escape to sea, on research vessels. The research institutions came to Woods Hole because its swift-moving waters were clean and salty. As the village's main employers, they are certainly an improvement on their nineteenth-century predecessor, the Pacific Guano Company, which from 1859 to 1889 mixed bird droppings from Howland Island in the Pacific with locally caught menhaden to make fertilizer. The resulting smells scented the air from Naushon to Nobska Point.

Past the grocery and several restaurants, we pause at Woods Holes' big mechanical attraction, the lifting road bridge. We have to stop because it's going up, the steelwork obscuring a large piece of sky. Several boats pass beneath, entering and leaving Eel Pond, a landlocked haven. The door of the little control house is open, and we watch the bridge tender pushing the buttons that close the bridge. The span is dropped into place again and the gates opened, permitting cars and pedestrians to move. The bridge tender, a burly man called Harry, tells us the old bridge is sometimes reluctant to open or close. "The hydraulics are geriatric. And then some of the boats are no help. You get some with balky motors and some going through too fast. They think I'm going to drop the bridge on their masts, though I'm not." Harry says that when Jacques Cousteau came to Woods Hole he stopped by the bridge and asked the same sort of questions. We inquire from Harry what we should blow on our horn if we ever want to come into Eel Pond.

"Two long and two short," he says. "But it may not be me opening the bridge for you. I'm only here weekends. Monday to Friday I'm out on a fishing boat, long-lining for cod."

East of the bridge you get the full effect of summer traffic. Woods Holes' other *raison d'être* is to be the mainland end of ferry lines serving Martha's Vineyard and Nantucket. As we walk by the cars full of harassed adults and hot fretful children inching toward the ticket windows and the long lines of waiting vehicles in the huge parking lot, I offer a silent thanksgiving for being able to get to these places in my own craft, even if it does mean putting out two anchors now and then or (when I neglected to do so) having to kedge off in the middle of the night. We walk as far as Little Harbor, an inlet in which we've moored in years past. This has a dinghy float to land at and a fresh water supply at the nearby Coast Guard dock. But it also has no space to anchor; the moorings are crowded and open to Vineyard Sound, unprotected by a breakwater. A stay in Little Harbor can be bouncy.

Although Woods Hole has a bake shop, an excellent bookshop, a so-so grocery, and a liquor store, it lacks one prime necessity in a civilized community: a hardware store. (Nor does it have a ship's chandler.) One summer we walked to Quissett, a small harbor several miles to the north on Buzzards Bay, hoping that the boatyard there would be able to supply us with a new stainless-steel bolt for *Clio*'s gooseneck. The surrounding terrain was all dingles and dells. Just right for a golf course, I was thinking, when an electric buggy carrying a pair of golfers and their equipment trundled across the road. The course was attached to a country club where a wedding was under way; some policemen imported for the afternoon were trying to deal with the overflow of cars parked along the verge of the road. They looked suspiciously at us as we walked by: pedestrians! I asked one where we turned off on the road to

Quissett Harbor, but it was obvious he'd never heard of the place. (He got his own back by giving the impression that even if he did know, he wouldn't dream of giving such privileged information to a person not driving a car.) It was a good thing the cops didn't hear Margot say to me, "I could do with a drink. Why don't we forget the stupid bolt and gate-crash the reception?" On the club lawn beyond a hedge, ice was being dropped in glasses and there were merry shouts and laughter; a band was playing "Strangers in the Night." When we found the right road and then the boatyard, twenty minutes later, no one was there to tell us whether a bolt was available or not. Perhaps they were all at the wedding.

After we've mailed some letters, Margot enters an old house, opposite the post office, that belongs to the Oceanographic Institution. She wants to see if they have any material on Peter Throckmorton, an underwater archaeologist and photographer whom we knew in New York in the early 1960s and who died last year in Maine. She comes out after a while with copies of obituaries from newspapers and specialist magazines. "They're all so sweet and helpful in there," she says. Whether or not they really like people just walking in and asking questions, they didn't say no to Margot. It may be that life afloat stimulates the enterprising spirit, and when we come ashore we boldly ignore the land's conventions about telephoning for an appointment. And land people—at least in Woods Hole—respond happily to this less inhibited approach.

Later, over broiled scrod in the Fishmonger's Café near the bridge, we talk by candlelight about Peter Throckmorton. He was an enthusiastic wildlife photographer when we first met him and gave us one of his pictures as a christening present for our first child, Liz. It was of an Indian elephant scratching its back with a branch torn from a tree. Margot reminds me of a series of photographs he had taken in an Asian jungle of a tiger trying to catch a butterfly, which he was unable to sell to any picture editor in New York. I remember calling on him in 1971 at his home in Piraeus, the port of Athens, but I can't recollect what we talked about. Maybe it was about caiques, the eastern Mediterranean fishing boats; he had recently converted a caique to use for his diving work on a Bronze Age wreck in the Aegean Sea. His book *The Lost Ships* has long been a part of our boat library. Now he is dead and we're sorry we left it too late to write to tell him so.

On our way back to the Great Harbor beach, where we left the dinghy, a man calls out to us from across the dark road, "Look out! There's a skunk in that hedge!" We cross the road quickly. The last ferries of the day, stacked with lights, sirens bleating, churn up the waters of Great Harbor as we row back to *Lochinvar.*

17

IN THE MORNING FOG, the big Penzance houses look two-dimensional. On the nearby dock, the replica owls seem particularly owlish. I plot compass courses on the chart and make myself familiar with the channel buoys I intend to pass. Our first visit to these waters was in 1960 on *Mistral*, returning from Nantucket on a foggy night. *Mistral*'s owner not unreasonably became confused by the bizarre Woods Hole buoyage system and took us first into Little Harbor instead of Great Harbor. The chart still shows two red nun buoys, both marked "6," separated by a few hundred yards and a green can buoy (which used to be black) marked "7." If you leave the easternmost nun "6" close to starboard, you avoid the rocky shore above Nobska Point and gain entry to Little Harbor. If you leave the westernmost nun "6" close to starboard, you avoid Juniper Point and enter Great Harbor. We spent some time in *Mistral* off one or another of these buoys, at sixes and sevens.

The fog is thin enough as we motor out, main set, so that we can just see a buoy appearing as we shoot past its predecessor. We trust the ferries can see us. The flume of the current speeds us southeast into Vineyard Sound, more or less the direction we want to go. The Vineyard itself is invisible. I steer a course that takes account of the east-setting flood and assumes that our destination hasn't disappeared in an overnight cataclysm.

The gateposts of Vineyard Haven are East Chop and West Chop, the bluffs on each side of the entrance to the long, V-shaped inlet. "Chop" is an old word which one informant tells me used to mean a division of land, another gives as the name for the jaws of an animal, and yet another says was a term for the side of a vise, which seems appropriate here, though the Chops are wide apart and there's no need to squeeze between them. Ruffled water marks the east end of the shoal called Middle Ground, and soon the foghorn blares from the lighthouse on West Chop. Here the breeze fills and the fog thins out as we tack slowly into the haven. Once this was Holmes Hole, where Sir Robert Holmes paused with his squadron while on the way to wrest Nieuw Amsterdam from the Dutch (or—as with "chop"—an alternative story, where one John Holmes, a blacksmith who crossed on the *Mayflower,* was an early settler).

What first catches the eye is a group of bulky gray oil tanks like those you expect to see in a serious port. As we approach the breakwater and reduce sail, we look for space in the anchorage north of the breakwater in case there's no vacant mooring in the protected area south of it. (The anchorage north of the breakwater is not only exposed to north winds but gets a good deal of wake from ferries rushing in and out of the haven; they don't seem to slow down until they're inside the breakwater.) In our pre-VHF radio days, I'd sometimes pick up an empty mooring if I could find one, and then row into the dock at the foot of the town park, which slopes up the hillside. Here I would get directions from Don King, the chubby harbormaster, whose mobile office is his pickup truck. Today, however, I reach him on Channel 16, switch as directed to Channel 9, and follow his instructions to pick up a mooring well inshore. The moorings in Vineyard Haven are closely arranged; the man aboard the boat ahead of the one we take hospitably pulls in his dinghy a foot so that it clears *Lochinvar*'s stem. The moorings are also rented for a reasonable price (compared to some New England harbors) and this adds to the sense of welcome.

High on our Vineyard Haven agenda are getting the laundry done and visiting good friends. Chore and visit can be fitted together, though we aren't quite as ruthless about this as might appear. Our friend Al lives year-round in a small summer house between Vineyard Haven and Oak Bluffs. Now eighty, a native of Pittsburgh, Al was a counter-intelligence officer during the Second World War and thereafter worked in real estate in New York City; but his house, which in fact is an expanded cabin, seems closer to Walden Pond than Manhattan. We've got to know him through our friend Janet, who teaches English at an upstate New York university and (in what I hope they won't mind me describing as a June-December relationship) lives with Al during vacations. We'd call on Al and Janet early on in any event, but the fact that Al has transcended his Walden period to the point of installing a bathroom is a plus at this stage in our voyage. We phone, and while we wait for them to come to collect us, we climb the grassy slope of William Barry

Owen Park. This has big trees, a small bandstand, marigolds around the base of the ship's mast with topmast which is the town flagpole, and a war memorial plaque to local men who died for their country and the Vineyard. Al and Janet roll up in Al's fifteen-year-old Honda, and after the hugs and handshakes, Janet—blond and smiling—asks, "First showers or first laundry?" We always do need a shower after sitting in a laundromat, and Margot and I say together, "Laundry first."

Doing your laundry on the Vineyard brings you face-to-face with a basic fact of Vineyard life: there are a lot of people here in summer. Many of the motorists who were snarling up Woods Hole are cruising around the island's skimpy road system, driving to and from the ferries, stopping and starting along Vineyard Haven's main street, and facing each other down at a Vineyard Haven road junction quaintly named Five Corners. Here any sane municipality would have built a rotary or roundabout to make the traffic flow more easily. Vineyard Haven in its insular wisdom (or perhaps from a touching trust that the automobile will soon disappear) goes on allowing five busy roads to come together without signals to give any precedence. Drivers are either polite and patient or frantic and pushy; mostly the latter. When I remark that a little traffic engineering might help grease the wheels of civilization at this spot, Al, an islander, says, "We get on well enough here out of season." He negotiates the intersection with veteran coolness and a casual wave to his baffled or outraged competitors, who are held up on the other four roads. We take the one that leads over the Lagoon bridge, past Al's house, and into Oak Bluffs. This cheerful little resort is known for the Victorian cottages with wooden gingerbread trim that replaced the tents of participants in Methodist summer camp meetings. In Ocean Park, the Civil War monument for some reason features a soldier in Confederate uniform, but this hasn't prevented Oak Bluffs from being particularly popular with black vacationers.

In the Oak Bluffs laundromat, sticky on a humid afternoon, other washdays on other cruises come to mind— occasions often purgatorial and always celebratory; on a small boat in warm weather, clean clothes make us feel richly renewed. In Osterville, on the south shore of the Cape, the laundromat management for a small but worthwhile extra charge washed, dried, and folded our things while we walked around the town. In Provincetown, we did our wash in a laundromat but returned to our friend Paul's house in North Truro to hang it out to dry on the clotheslines around his vegetable patch. Once, landing at the west end of the Vineyard, where Jan in those days had a cabin overlooking Menemsha Pond, we went to the laundromat behind Alley's General Store, a nineteenth-century time warp of a shop, mid-island, selling just about everything. The laundromat, however, was strictly coin-operated twentieth-century; it was also full and hot. We took our turn, waiting for a machine. The system seemed to be that you stood next to one, reserving it by keeping a proprietorial hand on the trembling top. When our chosen machine came to a halt and no one claimed its contents, we lifted out the wet wash and put it in a basket. Our own laundry had no sooner been shut inside the machine and the coin tray pushed in when an irate woman arrived and said she intended to wash a second load. A girl at the next machine took our side in the ensuing argument, saying to the woman, as if it were the accepted rule of engagement, "You gotta be here when the machine stops."

Anyway, to be in possession counts; our clothes were by now whirling in a blur of suds. We held the field. In Oak Bluffs today, while machines grind and whine in the steamy air, we commit several sins, using empty baskets which we assume to be for public use but are in fact those of other customers, and barging what turns out to be a line to use the driers. But most people tolerate us; we are evidently new folks here.

Margot and I take turns sitting on the steps in the less tropical air outside to read the *Vineyard Gazette*. This coast is well served by local newspapers, but the *Gazette*, appearing twice weekly in summer, is a paragon of its kind, a handsome broadsheet with fine photography and good writing, which holds a mirror to the warts, wrinkles, and beauties of island life. Yet a skim through this issue of the paper also suggests that normal life goes on here: houses are built, bought, and sold; children are born, old people die; banks lend money and foreclose on properties; schools search for superintendents; doctors practice child and adult psychiatry; ladies stitch quilts by hand; victims of crisis are counseled; cats are lost and found; yard sales are held; the local AA meets; visiting celebrities speak; a woman murders her former lover. Perhaps more particular to the Vineyard are two advertisements, one seeking a lost futon (how and where we are not told) and another saying, "Desperate: ferry ticket sought—Labor Day weekend. Call collect. Will pay premium."

Leaving the warm and fragrant laundry at Al's house and postponing our showers until we dress for dinner, Margot and I tour the high spots of Vineyard Haven: Mad Martha's, for ice cream; the Bunch of Grapes bookstore (once we've finished the ice cream); and the thrift shop. In most stores I go along with Socrates, who in the Athens market exclaimed, "How many things are here that I do not want!" But in thrift shops cupidity is encouraged by cheapness. Today, our customary covetousness in the presence of other people's castoff clothes, utensils, toys, and books going for charity is fairly restrained. We remember (or at least I remember) that our present home is only a boat. But we agree on buying a bright yellow Lucite tumbler, just right for rum-and-tonic, and a stainless-steel lid which will fit last summer's lidless saucepan from the thrift shop in Wellfleet, on the Cape. They might have been made for one another. There is no swimsuit, however, to fit Margot, so we walk off up the street to the Old School House Museum, where several rooms of similar household items are on display, except that they are even older. The elderly soft-spoken custodian tells us that he and his wife retired to the island twenty years ago and he loves his job here. Among the exhibits is an eye-catching late-eighteenth-century portrait of a little girl, naïvely painted. She wears a green frock over white pantaloons, folds her hands in her lap, and smiles broadly—the smile reflected in her widely spaced dark eyes. "Done by an itinerant painter," says the custodian. In the back room hangs an early photograph of a young woman in a long white dress, also smiling, and with features very like those of the child in green; maybe they were related. Other objects we notice are a 200-year-old demilune for slicing vegetables, a spinning wheel, a revolver, a doll, and some slippers. In many another small coastal museum like this, the proximity of the past has been all the more tangible for being conveyed by the homespun and homely. In Stonington's museum, for example, in the old lighthouse, not only are the usual whaling items, ships' logs, scrimshaw, and baleen corset stays on show, but so are inkwells and quill pens used for writing up the logs, and the shoes which were buried in the walls of houses for good luck.

Memories and lapses of memory. Dining out in Vineyard Haven you need to keep in mind that, despite its name, the town is "dry." As in Cuttyhunk, we have forgotten this in the past and had to eat *sans vin*. Once, so forlorn were we that a compassionate restaurateur wafted to our table a bottle of his own in the necessary brown paper bag and whispered, "Say notting. You brought thees in wit you." Tonight, remembering these weird regulations which don't in fact prohibit drinking, simply the selling of wines and spirits on the premises, we have brought along to the Tisbury Inn Café a bottle of Napa Valley's best, bought in Woods Hole. Al is celebrating his eightieth birthday, Margot and I our wedding anniversary, the thirty-fourth. When my mother was alive she used to send us a card of congratulations just in time to remind me of it. Left to ourselves we have once or twice forgotten it altogether. We have even disputed which squally August day it was that we were married, but have recently agreed it must have been the tenth. Now in my logbook I inscribe it in advance, "the famous tenth," so that the proper observances are made. Tonight, after we've had an exchange of toasts with Al and Jan, Margot fingers her periwinkle necklace as if the shells were pearls. She asks me, "What in fact have you given me for an anniversary present?"

"Well," I say, "there was that saucepan lid from the thrift shop. And tomorrow I'm buying you a new swimsuit, if you can find one. And"—the supreme gesture—"I shall do the grocery shopping tomorrow morning at the A & P."

Back on board *Lochinvar* I sit in the open companionway, a nocturnal dram in hand, savoring the night. The harbor is not quite so noisy as it is during the day. Vehicles are being chivvied off and on the last ferry of the evening by stern loudspeaker voices, but these soon fade. On a nearby 30-foot sloop named *Speedy Gonzalez* some young men are having a party with radio music turned up loud, but when a firework is let off a crisp voice from another moored boat snaps, "Cool it, you guys!" and a surprising calm reigns. Haze obscures moon and stars. Margot, reading *The Rover* in her fo'c'sle berth, calls quietly: "What's it like out there?"

"Peaceful."

A few days ago, prompted by something I've forgotten, she mentioned "a state of happiness in which you aren't conscious that you are happy." That is the way I am most of the time when afloat. But right now I am conscious of being happy. Which state is better?

18

DON KING, the harbormaster, accepts my twenty dollars for another day and night on the mooring. I say, "We always find it hard to leave Vineyard Haven," and he nods amiably; he must have heard this from other yachtspeople. I hope he's aware that he is part of the reason we and others like this harbor. In his late fifties, round-faced, stocky, even a bit paunchy, he used to work on the ferries to Woods Hole; a red rose tattoo on his left forearm is a salty memento of those days. For twenty-one years he has been the harbormaster and shellfish constable for Vineyard Haven, Lagoon Pond, and Lake Tashmoo, just beyond West Chop. He wears a khaki uniform, carries a hand-held marine radio, and from his launch *Roving Eye* or his parked Toyota pickup truck (the town hasn't yet got around to giving him an office) exercises a benevolent sway over the Haven. Unlike many harbormasters, Don seems to be helpful by nature. He also recognizes people who've been

here before, even if it's just a day or so in a previous summer. When I say to him, "I think we're on the same mooring you put us on last year," he replies, "No, Cap, you were
on that one over there, with the black powerboat on it."
But he isn't only an attentive provider of moorings. One
couple who were anchored outside the breakwater when a
vicious nor'easter hit in 1989 credit Don with rescuing
them as their 37-foot cutter, on its third and last anchor,
headed for the rocks. Another boating couple, according to
Don, were at the terminal stage of marital bust-up after
being stuck in the harbor for several days in fog, but he
talked them out of it.

Among the summer inhabitants of the inner harbor is an
osprey. It perches on a nearby mast top, a big bird with
hunched shoulders, wings that bend abruptly at the elbows
when stretched out a little, and a keen, eagle-like head, which
it now and then twists from side to side. Our cabin bookshelf
bird guide calls the osprey "worldwide" but also "uncom-
mon." The big bird is unfazed by the harbor noises or the
wakes from the ferries that rock its perch. It has sensibly
picked the flat, wooden mast cap of a big gaff-rigged cutter,
with none of the high-tech gear most modern boats have on
their mast tops—spearlike radio antennae or whirling wind-
speed indicators. I assume the osprey also prefers the relative
silence of a wooden mast, with no jangling wire halyards, as
it rests between its flights to catch fish.

Vineyard Haven always harbors a few interesting craft,
like the big schooners *Shenandoah* and *Ernestina,* and
admirable old yachts whose designers I make a stab at
guessing, as I did with *Karen.* "That's a Starling Burgess," I
say, or, "A Laurent Giles, I believe." Margot grimaces; but
part of the crew's burden is putting up with prattle of this

sort from the skipper while trying to look as though you don't think the poor fellow is several sails short of a full suit. Onshore, other boats draw my eye. In a large shed near Five Corners an antique Scottish fishing vessel of the type called a Zulu, once worked by sail, is being rebuilt. You can look in through the doorway at her stem, bare of planks on one side for some way aft, the ribs exposed, an anatomy lesson in bright orange primer paint. In a small building behind the Black Dog restaurant, Robert Douglas has the headquarters for his *Shenandoah;* Douglas is the man who more or less founded the modern business of taking people sailing for a day or so on historic vessels, or replicas thereof. In the nearby boatyard of Gannon and Benjamin, risen from the ashes of the previous year's fire, I talk with one of the partners about the wooden boats they design and build. Like many people who have fiberglass boats, I am a wooden-boat owner manqué, a lover of oak and elm, ash and larch, teak and African mahogany, copper nails and bronze straps, and would own one again if I could juggle the finances and geography, either living near the boat so that I could work on it during the winters or (better yet) becoming rich enough to buy a boatyard like Gannon and Benjamin's.

Lying at their dock is a large wooden motor vessel with an upstanding funnel and a spacious back porch. I recognize her as the former Chesapeake Bay oyster buy boat, the *Coastal Queen,* on which I once cruised with her then-owner Slade Dale up the inland waterway from Florida to Virginia. "She had a run-in with a fishing boat in Vineyard Sound and lost her bowsprit," says my informant in G. & B.'s yard. Two shipwrights, dark black and barefoot, are fitting the new bowsprit and chatting to each other with lilting Bahamian accents. It strikes me that Slade Dale, a New

Jersey boatyard owner who had an encompassing love of the entire Eastern Seaboard, would have been happy watching this repair work. Dale for several years ran the *Queen* as a miniature passenger liner (crew two or three, passengers three or four) up and down the waterway, but her present owner apparently uses her for purely private cruising. (He flies a Stars and Stripes as big as a king-size bedsheet.) One other boat in the harbor interests me. This is a narrow blue-gray cutter named *Trade Winds,* maybe 26 feet overall, flying like us a Red Duster, small and faded. *Trade Winds* has the look of a boat which has recently crossed the Atlantic. Rowing past her with a block of ice in our tender, we hail a man who is climbing into an inflatable dinghy. "Nice-looking boat," I say, thinking to myself it might be a Harrison Butler design. "Nice of you to say so," replies the mariner in a British accent, but not really giving us much of a glance and certainly not acknowledging *my* British accent. Oceans, I imagine, can put a distance between those who sail them and those who poke along coasts, like us.

In the afternoon, Jan is working on an academic paper, so Al drives us to the South Beach. Access to much of this splendid strand facing the open Atlantic is by way of dirt lanes running through private land. Al, in a smart real-estate move some years back, sold a section of such land which has beach rights, but kept the right to use a lane and the key to a padlocked gate which bars intruders. At the gate, by pre-arrangement, we are met by Al's daughter Margaret and his eleven-year-old granddaughter, Cory; Margaret's friend Marcia and her daughters, Cleo and a baby, are with them. Al delegates to me the seigneurial job of opening the gate with his key, letting the cars through, and locking the gate again. From a sandy parking area we walk fast through the sole-singeing dunes and then to a section of fairly empty beach where, Al tells us, bathing suits aren't needed. Marcia's baby, in sunhat and singlet, is parked in the shade of a beach umbrella. Al, in the altogether, looking remarkably like one of the seals at Woods Hole, slowly wades into the low surf. Margaret and Cory lie in the yellow sand, bare to the sun. Marcia wears blue shorts but no top. Like Margot and me, Cleo, aged five, wears a swimsuit. Margot, not satisfied with what Vineyard Haven's stores have to offer, is in last year's model, a black one-piece, in which she looks stunning. (My ancient bathing shorts are aqua-green and baggy.) Everyone is happy. I go through life without taking a stand on many of the Great Issues of our time: Is Yeltsin a demagogue? Should the United States adopt the prime-ministerial form of government? Is the Royal Family superfluous? I admit to enjoying the sight of the unclad female form, especially in the living flesh. Human nakedness is familiar enough in privacy and I would think that what really matters when people go around starkers on beaches is whether the weather is warm enough. Yet, as a rule in a public setting, I prefer the human form when it has a few clothes on. The makers of sunblock and moisturizing creams must, of course, be hoping I am out of touch with prevalent opinion in this respect.

After swimming, Margot and I take a stroll. Soon a dog is following us. It has obviously sussed us out as serious beach walkers and deserted its no doubt sunbathing master—all man's-best-friend loyalty thrown over for the chance of a walk. This pooch is a black-and-gray spaniel and is excellent company. By this stage in our annual voyage we are almost always missing Daisy, our springer spaniel, who is kept in Greenwich by British anti-rabies regulations. We don't want to subject her to six traumatic months in quarantine on returning from any trips abroad. So we pine after other people's dogs as they stand watch in the prows of dinghies or ride the narrow decks of windsurfing sailboards with happy confidence. Most dogs immediately recognize us as dog-deprived and are glad to give us some of their valuable time. This Vineyard spaniel dodges in and out of the water, hoping we will throw a few sticks into the sea for it to fetch. We are well trained and obliging. The dog accompanies us on our return to Al and party, and then leads us across the dunes to the parking area. We say goodbye. The last we see of the spaniel, it is greeting a newly arrived car; the people in the car don't know it, but they are about to go for a long walk.

The following morning comes gray with a fresh southeaster and the possibility of rain. Not a day for Nantucket, thirty miles farther out to sea to the southeast. After topping up the water tank at the dock, we reach out of Vineyard Haven and harden up around East Chop. From there, it's a thrash to windward across the big bay lying between Oak Bluffs and Cape Poge, the northern tip of Chappaquiddick Island—which, by the way, is not always an island; often the shallow breachway from Katama Bay into the Atlantic that separates the main part of the Vineyard from Chappaquiddick silts up and becomes part of a continuous beach. The seas within the Bay are fortunately moderate. We tack first toward Oak Bluffs, then toward Cape Poge, and then into the embrace of the Bay. *Lochinvar* now and then plants her nose in one of the steep little combers and we duck, the spray flying over our backs. The fourth time the lee rail dips under is when a reef in the

mainsail is in order. Reefing involves a step-by-step procedure which may seem complicated and even exhausting to
the novice but, properly done, is satisfying, particularly
since you're often accomplishing it at a difficult angle of
heel. The drill is to ease the mainsheet slightly, hoist up the
topping lift a bit, loosen the main halyard and drop the
mainsail several feet, bouse down the luff tackle now
attached to the first reef cringle, haul down the first reef
cringle on the leech, take up the halyard, let off the topping
lift, haul in the mainsheet, and then tidy up the bight of the
sail and tie in the reef points. Still with me? Thus snugged
down, *Lochinvar* heels less, makes less fuss in the water,
and goes better to windward. A line of rocks runs roughly
northward on the west side of the approaches to Edgartown
Harbor, to which we are bound, so we favor the eastern
shore. The tide is with us. This makes the entry into
Edgartown's zigzag channel a little easier, though as it is
we're fully exercised, first hard on the wind, then running
free, hard on the wind again, and even forced to make a
quick tack to avoid the Chappaquiddick ferry, a fast-moving open barge with three or four cars that darts across the
narrow channel to the town on the west side of the harbor.

I have mixed feelings about Edgartown. A correct and
pretty place, its properness seems unmitigated by civility. For a
start, there's little room to anchor near the town itself. Some
years ago in *Clio* we found a spot, too shallow for most
yachts, between two posh private docks on the western shore,
where we braved the haughty stares of the people who lived in
the summer mansions to which the docks were appendages.
We rowed to a dinghy float at the Harborside Inn and walked
to buy groceries. The town has charming brick sidewalks, but
these were crowded; a youth came brusquely out of a shop

and shouldered Margot into the street. There was no apology. All over Edgartown people seemed to be standing aggressively on their rights—protecting their "space" against intruders with bull-like glares or gull-like raucousness.

After circling for some minutes with sputtering outboard the busy float in the harbor at which fuel is sold and water dispensed, waiting our turn, we picked up a nearby mooring, meaning to hold on until there was room at the float. From the shore came a shout. An irate man was walking down a dock in our direction. He shouted again: "That's my mooring!"

"Right you are," I called back. "We'll be here just a minute, if you don't mind."

He turned on his heel, snorting and fuming.

The Edgartown rental moorings cost fifty dollars a night, which is more than half of what we spend each week on groceries. So *Lochinvar* keeps going southward past the docks, through the moorings, and along the harbor channel until it opens out in Katama Bay. This bay is really a huge pond and much of it is very shallow. But between Long Point, on Chappaquiddick, and Katama Point, on the main of the Vineyard, there's a spot with elbow room and depth enough for us to anchor. A few other cruising yachts are here, including a gaff-rigged high-sided boat with the look of a Baltic fishing vessel, flying the Swedish flag.

My mistake today was neglecting to close the seacock on the drain under the galley sink before we sailed. Consequently, when we were heeled on the port tack, a lot of seawater came in and flooded the storage area behind the sink: all our coffee filter papers are soaked. Thrifty to the last, I sponge them with fresh water and spread them on the cockpit seats to dry. In the late afternoon the wind falls, the sun almost appears, but the air remains humid; damp salty filter papers may be with us for some time. However, a rum-and-tonic in the cockpit at the cocktail hour improves my mood. The grumpiness Edgartown induces seeps away. The evening is benign, our surroundings attractive. But Margot has a theory that if I say—or even if, as now, I am about to say—"This is a marvelous spot. I could spend a fortnight here!" a minute later something irritating will happen. Sure enough, two loud motorboats appear, towing waterskiers. They roar by, the boats rocking us with their wakes, one of the skiers slaloming close to us as he passes at great speed, showering us with spray and missing our anchor line by inches. Surprised, furious, I cup my hands and shout after them, "Bloody fools!" And immediately I wish I hadn't; the ineffective words echo in my head; a stoic silence the best defense.

Of course, a few days later I'll forget my good advice to myself when a huge gas-guzzling powerboat of the Cigarette type passes us sounding like a squadron of Flying Fortresses taking off to bomb the Third Reich. I ostentatiously stick my fingers in my ears. The powerboat driver returns this salute with two fingers of his own. One has to suppose that waterskiers and powerboaters go on in this way because they are bored and find taunting the blow boaters an easy thrill. But let me end this catalogue of spleen: the loathsome jet ski. Public-relations advisers to the manufacturers of these monotonously noisy toys have been attempting to present them as "personal watercraft," as if they were in the same league as canoes or coracles, whereas your true sailor knows they are the marine equivalent of Hells Angel motorbikes, controlled (if that is the word) by beer-swilling boneheads. In the despotic ideal world I sometimes conjure up for myself when afloat, these inane things will be banned.

19

SOME SUMMERS we don't reach Nantucket. Time and weather conspire against us. But a year or so's absence stokes up our need to get there again. Melville, in *Moby Dick,* described the island as "away offshore, more lonely than the Eddystone lighthouse. Look at it—a mere hillock, and elbow of sand; all beach, without a background. There is more sand there than you would use in twenty years as a substitute for blotting paper." Offshore Nantucket certainly is; the Indian name may have meant "the faraway place." But you can't really call it off-soundings. Shoals litter Nantucket Sound, south of Cape Cod. There's a one-foot spot I've circled on our chart with a red pen, which helps highlight it and, amid a confusing welter of depth indications, may keep us from landing on it. There are also quite a few two-foot and three-foot spots where *Lochinvar* could bump. Nantucket itself is low, little more than a large shoal which has so far managed to keep its broad shoulders above water. In one famous old yarn, the skipper of a coasting schooner was presented with a tallowed lead to which his crew had for a joke stuck Nantucket sand. You can see why he thought the island had sunk and, in thick weather, while he slept, that his vessel had passed over it.

On our first voyage to the island on our own, in *Clio*, we were boarded by a small bird. We were crossing Tuckernuck Shoal when it fluttered down on the cabin top, apparently exhausted, and sat with its eyes clamped shut. It was yellowish-brown, with two white stripes on each wing. The bird guide suggested that it was a pine warbler. After ten minutes, it opened its eyes, seemed to take a deep breath, and skimmed over the water toward the Cape. We had been going in the wrong direction for it, but it had needed the rest.

Today the only birds we see are gulls, scouting the shoals where the tide rips make the water popple. Once we're past Cape Poge, at 10:00 a.m., a dandy breeze blows from the northeast and *Lochinvar* romps along on a close reach. From time to time little waves break against the dipping bow; a fine glistening spray of warm droplets shoots aft. We mean to take a non-rhumb-line route, circling east of the shallower bits, but the wind slowly heads us—it veers southeast and forces us to sail hard on it. This is now a course that does indeed take us near the real shallows and, if we survive them, will bring us in on the Nantucket shore well west of the harbor entrance. A big yawl is following us, apparently unaware that we draw less water than she does. Margot says, "Do you remember Dollman, in the *Cormorant*, luring the *Dulcibella* into danger on the Scharnhorn?" But we aren't given the chance to emulate the villain of *The Riddle of the Sands*. The yawl must have checked her depth sounder; she tacks eastward into safer water. We have to take our chances alone.

With all the good feeling induced by the lovely morning, well out of sight of land, I reckon the chances of hitting a one-, two-, or three-foot spot as remote, but nevertheless keep an eye on the changing colors of the water. If it looks really sandy, we'll tack. But my foolhardiness isn't punished by a grounding. We gain the Nantucket shore a good way west toward Madaket.

The breeze lightens, the current turns foul, as we tack eastward along the edge of the shallows that extend far out from the beach. A water standpipe and a church tower in Nantucket town provide landmarks for our slow progress. Just before 3:00 p.m. we reach the harbor entrance. The chart doesn't emphasize the perils of this: much of the eastern breakwater and the seaward end of the western breakwater are below the surface; one shouldn't treat the buoys marking the entrance channel high-handedly. And once in the busy channel, a sailing vessel shouldn't insist on its rights. We hang on, pinching and luffing, at the western edge until a large ferry makes its impressive exit, and then we take a quick tack across the channel to make a gain to windward before tacking in again. The small shingled lighthouse on Brant Point, at the inner end of the entrance, lets us know we've arrived.

The last time I picked up a rental mooring in Nantucket harbor the charge was forty dollars, which I thought steep. The launch operator who collected the fee said apologetically, "We've got a very short season out here." In other words, the plunder has to be maximized while the victims flock in. From the victim's point of view, the problem is that the alternative, anchoring, isn't easy here. Although the harbor seems large, the town end of it has moorings planted in most of the good water. Central parts are extremely shoal, and what looks like a reasonable spot in the area just north of the center is swept by fierce tidal currents, rushing to and from a connected series of harbors extending five miles to the northeast.

We've anchored in the past on the northern edge of the moorings and in a strong wind against strong tide found *Lochinvar* sheering around madly on her long anchor rode, dangerously close to craft tethered on mooring chains and riding differently, for reasons of hull shape and windage. A heavy Colin Archer–type cutter nearly sawed our dinghy in two with its chain bobstay and mooring chain one wild night, though at the time we anchored I was sure that we were at least a hundred feet distant and would stay well clear. Not a bit of it. Having reanchored with difficulty, I kept an anchor watch for four nervous hours until the tide turned. Fortunately for us, the last few years of recession and Nantucket's pre-recession prices have meant more empty moorings, and today we find a niche in the southern part of the harbor, close to two such untenanted moorings. Although the currents are less in this position, we aren't altogether free of anxiety: at dead low water, *Lochinvar* may touch bottom. It shouldn't be serious, unless she drops on the fluke of an ancient anchor.

After changing into our shoregoing clothes, we splash out by hailing a launch to take us into town. The fare is $2.50 per person. The launch driver is a young woman and our fellow passengers are four cheerful men, red of nose and cheek, who appear to have been celebrating at length their successful arrival here under sail. One of them tells us, "We get together to charter a boat every year. We have a blast."

"When did you get here?" I ask.

"I think it was yesterday."

Their jovial attempts to reward the launch girl with embraces as well as dollars are good-naturedly but firmly resisted.

Onshore, I'm not sure at first if I really want to be here. Nantucket town in mid-August is Manhattan-by-the-Sea. Throngs of tourists pour on and off the ferries and crowd the quaint, uneven brick sidewalks. Longer-stay summer folk are getting the utmost out of their vacation investments by gridlocking the quaint cobbled streets in their four-wheel-drive sports wagons, sailboards on the roofs, mountain bikes on the backs, and picnic gear, fishing equipment, and obstreperous children crammed inside. Recession or not, shoppers pack the resort-clothing boutiques and galleries selling you pictures-to-go-with-your-decorating-mood. A long queue snakes around the interior of The Hub, the newspaper shop; people are waiting to buy *Vogue, The New York Times,* or, in our case, the Nantucket *Inquirer and Mirror,* which is a broadsheet like the *Vineyard Gazette* but comes out once a week. Nantucket's citizens have pioneered merchandising as well as whaling: R. H. Macy came from this island to plant his store in Herald Square, New York, and much of the town's waterfront has been more recently redeveloped by William Beinecke, once the S & H Green Stamps magnate, into a quasi-historic district of summer cottages, art galleries, knickknack stores, and cafés, in which the cuteness quotient is as high as the prices. Close by are the wharves of the Nantucket Boat Basin, where million-dollar yachts are tied up head to toe and paid hands in white uniforms coiffure the lines, buff the decks, and polish the topsides. We peek from the dock through the saloon windows of one such vessel; the table is already set for dinner with fingerbowls at each of the ten place settings. (Lobster again tonight, I'm afraid.) A disadvantage of this basin is its proximity to the Nantucket Power Company, which, as it generates the island's electricity, sounds and smells like a busy express-way. But many of these big yachts are air-conditioned and presumably their occupants neither hear the din nor smell the fumes. (I'm not envious. I'm content with my breeze-driven, naturally ventilated boat which two of us can sail, or get into trouble with, all by ourselves. I'd hate having to manage a paid crew, even if I could afford one. But clearly some people want to reproduce on the water the overorga-nized insulated luxury they enjoy onshore.)

It takes me a while to get into the swing of things. A promenade through some of the quieter back streets helps, past houses with gray shingles and white trim, and with hollyhocks around the doors and roses climbing garden trel-lises. We visit the Whaling Museum, a former factory for refining spermaceti oil and turning the resulting wax into candles. We admire the giant oil press, a whaleboat, the col-lection of scrimshaw and ships' logs, the portraits of ships' captains and their wives, and the mighty 43-foot skeleton of a finback whale; we admire the men who made those often three-year voyages and the women who waited for them. Lives with apparently simple aim but large scale!

At a small bakery we buy what look, feel, and smell like fine croissants for breakfast and a real loaf for lunches. We sit with drinks in the Atlantic Café and salute our fellow launch passengers, whose celebration is continuing boister-ously at a nearby table. We read *The Inquirer and Mirror* and approve the cool eye it casts on new developments, town officials, the awarding of contracts, and the increasing numbers of tourists. One leisure-age argument, unleashed in the *I. & M.*'s correspondence columns, has to do with the use of beaches by sunbathers and dune buggies. A driver of one of these vehicles describes it as a conflict between sloth-ridden, "zoned-out" sun groupies and high-tech adventurers, and gives the impression that the former are lucky not to get squashed by the latter. But Nantucket has so far done a thoughtful job of coping with the desire of so many new-comers to build on the island. In 1983, its town meeting agreed to a 2 percent tax on all property transactions, and these funds have gone to establish a land bank of open space; currently, about a third of Nantucket's twenty-five square miles are set aside for conservation and public use. Because this policy has made the remaining land more valu-able and put property beyond the reach of many islanders, another half of one percent was added to the tax in 1987, with the proceeds going toward affordable housing. Right now, we gather from the paper, houses are cheaper than for some time, and over seven hundred are for sale.

Our next step is to find an affordable dinner. Chic restaurants abound where mingy portions of nouvelle cui-sine can be had for conspicuous amounts of money; but we're interested in something more "down home." On South Water Street, a high-ceilinged bar-and-grill seems to fit the bill. Margot has seafood marinara and Greek salad. I have chowder, meat loaf, and mash. The meat loaf arrives a bit tepid, and when I ask our waitress if it can be warmed up, she brings me a second glass of house red on the house to keep my spirits up. So two content customers of the Rose and Crown Saloon wend their way back to the launch dock, where we find the charter-party yachtsmen once again.

"We are fated to travel together," says one to Margot.

Another breaks into song: "Some Enchanted Evening," more or less.

A man is operating the launch now; he asks them where they are going and what the name of their yacht is, but gets no answer. They can't remember its name and are vague about its location.

"Well, I'd better take these folks to their boat first," says the launchman, nodding at us. On the way out, I ask the charterers about the color and rig of their craft, and manage to elicit that it is (probably) a white ketch and they may have left the masthead light switched on from the night before. "The name's on the tip of my tongue," says one of the group, with a blissful smile. Dropping us on *Lochinvar*, the launch steams off to survey the dark harbor.

If *Lochinvar* touches bottom during the night, we aren't aware of it. In the morning, which is gray, we row to the town pier and from the parking lot near Steamboat Dock catch a bus to Sconset. This is what everyone on Nantucket calls Siasconset, a village out on the southeastern elbow of the island. Our conveyance, run by the Bartlett Company, is a white-painted ex-school bus; the fare is five dollars return, we are the only passengers, and our driver is a young Australian, with an orthopedic strap around one wrist, it seems because of a surfing accident.

"You from Down Under, too?" he asks.

"No," I reply. "Up Above." And since this doesn't seem to register, I add, "Regular Pommies."

He doesn't hold this against us. As we bounce along the highway, which crosses a scrubby moorland, he tells us that Nantucket is "a grite plice to spend the summer." Off duty, he surfs and bikes and meets girls.

Sconset is a picturesque mixture of old small shingled cottages and newer large shingled houses. It was a fishing settlement—the land behind the village beach, where the dory men used to land their catches from long-lining, is still called Codfish Park. The former fishermen's huts were eventually taken over by squatters and are now highly prized summer residences, with trellises supporting vines and rambler roses on their low roofs as well as against their walls and fences. Margot and I walk a mile or so up the beach toward Sankaty Head, where a lighthouse sits on top of the sandy cliff, alerting transatlantic shipping to the beginnings of America. The beach sand is a bit soft for easy walking. A light rain starts to fall. The wind is onshore, from the east, and we decide not to swim. As we climb aboard the return bus, our Aussie driver says, "Pretty plice, eh? But didn't you find it a bit quiet?"

Back in the hubbub of Nantucket town we go provisioning: groceries from the A & P, ice from the boat basin, and a freshly caught bluefish from a charter fishing boat. For three dollars we get the big gleaming fish, and for two dollars more it is filleted and cleaned by a skillful Jamaican woman, like our Australian a summer resident and apparently eager for small jobs like this. Our bargain fish makes the high island grocery prices easier to bear. As we load the dinghy at the town pier, a man in a tan uniform stands looking out at the moored ranks of yachts through sunglasses and binoculars. His shoulder badge says *Environmental Police* and there is a holstered gun on his hip. What violations is he looking for? And what else does he see? As we row out, a launch carrying two similarly kitted-out individuals speeds past on what appears to be big-brotherly business. I imagine a drug bust or ("My God, the horror of it," says Margot) a pollution bust, the suspected boat swaying as the officers jump aboard, the lone yachtsman in the privacy of his head with his trousers down cringing at the clump of studded boots on the cabin sole, the authoritative rap on the head door, and the command "Open up in there!" Quick: the valves, the stopcock levers. Too late; the door is smashed open . . . It's time for us to exchange the attractions and distractions of Nantucket town for the Head of the Harbor.

This is such an unspoiled place that I hesitate for a moment before writing about it. On the other hand, why will words of mine cause people to flock to a congenial spot from which until now they've stayed away? However, their reasons for doing so are surely curious. The voyage to the Head of the Harbor isn't difficult, though the channel winds through shallows. The sail is somewhat challenging in that we have to pick out the miniature and very spaced-apart buoys that mark the route. There are some sharp bends and some easy turns, and we keep an eye on the depth sounder, so that we know if a shortcut we're taking on the rising tide makes sense. We sail five miles on this irregular course, the damp wind gentle, the flood with us. To the west, on our portside, the inner shore of Coatue Neck, the long spit dividing Nantucket Harbor from Nantucket Sound, is scalloped into five shallow bays. To the east lies the main bulk of the island. After we round the sand cliffs of Pocomo Head to starboard and leave Bass Point on Coatue to port, we're in the huge body of sheltered water which is the Head of the Harbor. A few skiffs are out fishing, a small catboat and a dinghy are under sail, but not one boat is at anchor here. With a fading breeze and a forecast for a calm night, we head for the northwest corner of the harbor and tuck ourselves in fairly close to Coatue, a few hundred yards above Wyers Point and the shoal that extends out from it.

One reason for people to avoid the Head of the Harbor is that it may be hard to leave. We generally stay several days. Last year, over a weekend, two other boats appeared and anchored in the same area, but by no means close; the herd instinct doesn't bring people here and it doesn't seem to operate with those that come. We walk on Coatue, on both its inner and outer beaches. We row up into Coskata Pond and cross the short stretch of land to the east-facing beach, on the open sea, that runs eight miles from Sconset and Sankaty to Great Point at the northern tip of the island. If the wind looks as if it will blow from the east, we sail over to the eastern side of the harbor and anchor in the lee of the beach there. But otherwise we enjoy being on *Lochinvar* with no fretful need to get somewhere. We lunch late. We swim, Margot in mask and flippers. We hang out laundry washed in rainwater and air the sleeping bags. I do small jobs, calking the seams in the teak-planked lazaret hatch, gluing a pair of Margot's sunglasses. Margot paints a watercolor and we both read more than usual. Because *Lochinvar* is more or less at rest for a period, Margot makes little arrangements on the cabin shelves and table of the kind one has on domestic mantelpieces: fragments of fern, beach foliage, bayberry (which smells a bit like marjoram), a tiny moplike cluster of codium, a sponge seaweed; soap-colored shells; a small piece of bleached and sanded and water-worn wood. We lie in the sun and at night sit mesmerized by the stars. It is a holiday within a holiday.

By now we are accustomed to being together in a small space. We take better care not to step on each other, though we aren't always tolerant of every little quirk and whim.

My stowage of certain items goes on annoying Margot. Margot, from my point of view, is an innately sandy person; she can't come aboard without bringing a large amount of beach in her sneakers or on their soles. My repeated request that she get into the dinghy or the cockpit in bare feet isn't welcomed. Her moods and mine in their ups and downs do not always coincide. But much of the time the harmony is even greater than it is onshore.

One late afternoon a few years ago we took a long walk on Coatue. A sandy road running its length is crossed occasionally by other tracks. Poison ivy grows in the verges, together with bayberry bushes and pink-and-white beach roses. Some shrubs are in fact low trees, wind-formed to hug the ground. We saw the skeleton of a deer. As we reached the Sound beach, a fleet of yachts came beating down the shore into a smoky sou'wester. It was the annual race for wooden yachts for the Nantucket Opera House trophy. I thought I recognized one big schooner, and as it got closer, I said to Margot, "Yes, it's the *Nina*!" The *Nina* is one of the most beautiful yachts of this century. Designed by Starling Burgess, built at Monument Beach at the head of Buzzards Bay, her short-ended 60-foot hull has proportions perfectly matched by her tall, powerful rig. It was a thrill to watch her standing in toward the beach close-hauled on the starboard tack and then come about and stand out again. But something wasn't right. It became clear that *Nina* was luffing up for too long, then bearing off too far; tacking out but then tacking in again too soon, before she had built up the right momentum. And then, once more on the starboard tack, she seemed to be coming in much too close to the beach for such a deep-draft boat. Was the skipper trying to cheat the foul current? Suddenly she stopped moving forward. Her bow swung inshore and the tall masts tilted toward us. She was hard aground.

We stood on the beach about a hundred yards away and watched, unable to help. Her crew seemed in complete disarray. It was some minutes before they began to lower and furl their sails. Nobody was to be seen putting an anchor out. The tide was falling, but she was fast on a lee shore. I felt miserable. This was the yacht that had sailed the Atlantic in 1928 and gone on to win the Fastnet Race against the best British ocean racers. It was embarrassing, like watching a hero undergo squalid disgrace. Frustrated, I walked down the beach for a way, hoping to find picnickers with a boat; but the beach was empty. Evening drew on, with low clouds and sullen yellow-gray light, and the sou'wester blew as hard as ever. Nasty short waves crashed on the beach. *Nina*'s masts leaned at an even sharper angle of heel. Eventually there was no point in watching any longer. On the walk back across Coatue, we flagged down a beach buggy and asked the driver to report *Nina*'s grounding, though surely the skipper must have radioed for help. That night, as we sat in our quiet, protected anchorage, we thought of *Nina* heeled over on the exposed shore, waiting for the tide's slow withdrawal and return. High water was at 4:00 a.m. Would she float off? Next morning, when we looked for her spars over the scrubby sand hills of Coatue, there was no sign of them. *Nina* had vanished during the night. It was as though I'd dreamed it all.

This time, on the day after arriving at the Head of the Harbor, we explore Coskata Pond. It's a perfect morning, light airs and sun, the temperature soon in the high seventies. We row up the creek which winds north from the harbor, a tiny creek with deeps and shallows of its own. Little sand cliffs overhang it where the current rushes transparently, and there are broad muddy flats where we have to step out of the boat into four inches of water and push as armies of fiddler crabs scurry away from our toes. At the head of the creek the pond broadens out, housing egrets, herons, and ospreys; these last nest on poles erected specially for them in a marshy area called the Glades. Our copy of *The Inquirer and Mirror* has told us that the first Forster's tern of the season has been seen here, as have sixteen whimbrels, two families of American oystercatchers (eight birds in all), three ruddy turnstones, a spotted sandpiper, and various plovers. We see some oystercatchers and plovers but haven't yet learned how to identify a ruddy turnstone. We poke the dinghy into several side creeks banked with grass-crowned hummocks of mud. Such places are wonderfully regressive. I could be rowing myself back into a primordial womb where our amphibian ancestors were at home.

At the end of this mid-August morning in the late twentieth century, we anchor the dinghy at the top end of Coskata Pond and take to the Nantucket land again. A short hike up a sandy track and a quick step through the hot dunes brings us to the ocean. Half a dozen beach vehicles cruise slowly along the sand, apparently not trying to squash sunbathers. We are the only people on the beach apart from those in the vehicles. The beach shelves rapidly into deep water and we swim close to the shore. Not far out, large fish are breaking the surface with great silver splashes.

Margot and I are practiced at being foils for one another. We are by turns practical and contemplative. Today, feeling housewifely, she lists for me some of the foods we should depend on when we give up supporting the New England ice industry: Genoa salami, dried fruit, iceberg lettuce, cheese . . . She says, "I don't want to die out here of salmonella and have people find our whitened bones years later, like that deer." She thinks that the United States needs UHT: Ultra-Heat-Treated milk of the kind obtainable in Europe, which comes in cartons and until opened keeps without refrigeration. If there was UHT milk on board, I could have muesli for breakfast. Of course, we'll have to start catching our own fish. I match these suggestions with a passage I've just come across in Boswell's *Tour to the Hebrides*. Dr. Johnson—who elsewhere says notably that a man who is tired of London is tired of life—declares ponderously, "It would require great resignation to live in one of these islands." Boswell replies, "I don't know, sir; I have felt myself at times in a state of almost mere physical existence, satisfied to eat, drink, and sleep, and walk about, and enjoy my own thoughts; and I can figure a continuation of this."

With a mind to our continued physical existence at the Head of the Harbor, I check the weather forecast on our second afternoon and, hearing nothing untoward, shift *Lochinvar* over to the eastern shore. We anchor off the Wauwinet Inn, largest of the few buildings in the harbor's one inhabited corner. Tonight, it seems to me, we should celebrate being once more at the Head of the Harbor. Margot, more to the point, says, "You mean I don't have to cook dinner?" In shore dress, credit card ready, we row to the inn's floating dock. The Wauwinet has been a casino or club and later a family hostelry. Now it seems to have gone as far upmarket as an island inn can go, with elegant rooms and elegant-looking guests, but also a cordial welcome for boatpeople like us who row ashore for dinner, sea-dazed mariners scrambling onto the beach of a tropical paradise. The inn's chic restaurant, Topper's, has a subdued tartan motif expressed in table mats, chair upholstery, and the skirts of its waitresses. The food is also a bit "designer-arranged" and with too much ginger in it for me. Even so, the meal has the sense of being an occasion, and the shock of the bill will be cushioned by time. As we walk back to the dinghy across the lush damp lawn, rabbits freeze in the beam of our flashlight, like children playing Statues. *Lochinvar*'s anchor light is burning helpfully not far off the dock.

20

IF I HAD BOTHERED to listen to the weather radio again before turning in, my worries about the day to come might have ruffled my sleep; the morning forecast is unfriendly. The wind is expected to blow from the northeast at 18 to 20 knots. Northeast is where we want to go. But at 7:00 a.m., it is flat calm and foggy. Wauwinet can't be seen. Picking out the little buoys marking the devious channel won't be easy, but with chart at the ready and depth sounder switched on we motor down harbor. The engine is just ticking over, but all the same driving us along at three and a half knots. I'd rather be going more slowly in such places as the bar off Pocomo Head. I put the gear lever in neutral so that we coast along, the depth sounder showing 4 feet, 4, 3!, 3!, thank heaven 4. But we don't ground or even bounce, and the fog begins to lift as we approach First Point. We can see the moored yachts and the town and hear police or firetruck sirens for the first time in several days.

The breeze rises as we go out through the breakwaters. The main is already set; we unfurl the jib, shaking loose a spider, which swiftly lowers itself and skitters away across the deck to hide under a cleat. On the tried and trusted principle that one should take the long tack first, we stand forth on the starboard tack, heeling gently and chuckling along at 4 knots. Our intention is to reach Chatham today. If we keep to this course, just west of north, it will bring us to land about halfway along the south shore of the Cape. Before that, it will take us again close to some of the shoaler bits of Tuckernuck Shoal.

During the morning the fog thickens and thins, but we don't ever have more than half a mile's visibility. Once we're away from the route of the ferries, we sail in our own little world. Because the sun pierces the haze above us more effectively than it burns off the vapor at water level, I rub sunscreen ointment on Margot's back. This operation causes *Lochinvar* to veer a long way off course, but no one's watching! On unstrenuous passages we exercise our wits with self-imposed challenges: for example, how many words can we get out of the letters that make up the name *Lochinvar*—which is helpfully painted in an inverted U on the stern rail life buoy. Or what common terms and usages can we think of that have a nautical origin? We try to add to those we've previously come up with, including "toe the line," "son of a gun," "peter out," "end of the tether," "bitter end," "under the weather," "beam ends," "pipe down," "showing the flag," "three sheets to the wind," and "one over the eight." This morning we add "groggy," "all at sea," "clear the decks," "shipshape," "true colors" (as in "He's showing his true colors"), "chockful," and "taken aback." When we've run out of these, and I'm pondering whether I should reef the main, Margot starts pretending she's on a cruise ship and tells me about her day. This begins with a swim before breakfast in the pool on the Lido Deck. For breakfast there would be fruit, porridge with treacle, kippers, and coffee. More swimming, letter writing in the library, more eating and drinking at lunch (lobster thermidor and vegetarian *blanquette de veau*), and tea brought to her while she lies wrapped in a rug in a deck chair. She is now lounging on the leeward cockpit seat, and with the wind so far peaking at about 15 the lee rail remains just out of the water, a few inches from her elbow. She anticipates champagne cocktails before dinner; the entrée will be duck with apricots. And then of course lots of dancing.

A few minutes later, Margot says, "I wonder where they are now." She is no longer on the cruise ship; she is wondering where the charter yachtsmen have got to.

Me: "You don't see many gentlemen drinkers these days."

M.: "One of them definitely was a gentleman. He handed me down into the launch."

Me, jealous: "I bet he does that with all the women. Didn't you see him give the launch girl a big hug?"

The wind never becomes unfriendly, though it remains on the nose. The little billows stay constant. When land appears in early afternoon, we're not sure exactly how far away it is or where exactly on the Cape we've got to; although the fog has lifted, the light is haze-filled and inscrutable. There is what looks like a huge white billboard on shore, which can only be a drive-in movie screen, and judging from where this screen is marked on the chart as a landmark near South Yarmouth, I conclude that the bluff on our port bow is Point Gammon, which stands out from the shore below Hyannis. Just as well I'd worked this out, for there's a reef ahead, the Bishop and Clerks, which needs to be avoided. We come about and stand along the Cape eastward, with the current against us and wind going fluky.

Nearer the elbow of the Cape, the 8-mile-long sandspit which is Monomoy Island makes a darker line along the horizon to starboard. The nor'easter has kept us well away from its southern tip today, which is to the good, as it is a place known for fearsome fog and terrific tide rips. We still have to miss the fish traps which stretch out from Monomoy over the shallows of Common Flat, a good place for scallops and quahogs. The island itself is less than two hundred years old; formed by sand drifting from the great beaches on the east shore of the Cape, it dangles like the hour hand of a clock that has stopped between 6:00 and 7:00. Monomoy once supported several fishing settlements, a lighthouse, a Coast Guard station, and a shelter for ship-wrecked sailors. It is now deserted and officially a National Wilderness. Birds, migrating north or south along the Atlantic flyway, use it as a stopover. But the creature I asso-ciate with Monomoy is portrayed in a painting called *The Lair of the Sea Serpent*, by Elihu Vedder, which hangs in the Boston Museum of Fine Arts. The monster is snaked down in the dunes, waiting to strike.

Chatham, to which we're headed, also has a reputation for fog. Thoreau, here in the mid-nineteenth century, said that the people of Chatham made do with fog instead of trees for shade. The town has two main harbors, each with subsidiary ponds and coves. Stage Harbor, our destination, is on the underside of the Cape's elbow. Chatham Harbor is just above the elbow on the raised lower arm of the Cape, and can be entered—preferably, one's told, with the help of a local pilot—through a break in the outer barrier of Nauset Beach created in a northeast storm in January 1987. (This replaced a former entrance farther south around the top end of Monomoy.) The two harbors are connected by a devious channel only just navigable by shoal-draft boats, and the entrances to both harbors have sandbars, with the one at the mouth of Stage Harbor being less bothersome; it is also in more sheltered water, though a stiff sou'wester heaping up Nantucket Sound seas might make it seem less so.

Today, there are no such problems. But we are wary of the starboard edge of the 75-foot-wide channel, beyond which the water suddenly shoals to a scanty single foot at low tide. To port, featureless low dunes lie behind Harding Beach, but culminate at a splendid landmark, a lighthouse with keeper's house attached. It has been out of commission for the last sixty years. In the misty afternoon light it looks to me more than ever like that in a painting by Edward Hopper called *The Long Leg*. Sun and shadow pick out the lighthouse in the painting; sun and shadow define the sails of the yacht, which beats down the channel past it. Both building and boat are lonely, as almost all Hopper's subjects are. The light wind is coming straight at us down the channel, and as we furl the sails and motor in and Margot kneels on the foredeck, readying a bow line, I reflect on Hopper's misfortune: he had to give up sailing, which he loved, because it made his wife nervous.

At Stage Harbor Marine, a boatyard situated by the small bascule bridge over the Mitchell River, we come alongside the fuel dock and ask about moorings. The youth in charge tells us the owner has gone home and as far as he knows there aren't any vacant moorings, though we can take a look for ourselves. The Monomoy Yacht Club has its simple headquarters here, and a member, getting out of his tender, makes a more hospitable impression by saying we can tie up our dinghy at the yacht club float if we want to come ashore after we've found somewhere to park. But when we return down the channel to the little boat-packed cove north of Stage Island, the only empty moorings we can find appear to be private. There's just room to anchor between moorings and mud, and water enough to float in at low tide.

After we're sure *Lochinvar* is snug, we go exploring in the dinghy. I sometimes think this is the best part of cruising, the low-key, small-scale expeditions of the watery locality we find ourselves in at the end of a day getting somewhere. Each pond and creek is different, though many of the elements are the same. We row upriver, under the bridge (it takes a call to Chatham Police Department to open it), and into Mill Pond and its farthest extension, Little Mill Pond, the head of navigation of this branch of Stage Harbor. There are bosky stretches along the banks; a solitary clammer standing up to his waist; a few moored boats and a small boatyard; and in Little Mill Pond, a public wharf from which it's a short walk into the center of town. Chatham figured in my life a long time ago, and I want to recapture the feeling of it. But now the evening is closing in, we have a return row against the flood current, and there will be time tomorrow. On *Lochinvar* again, I contemplate our part of Stage Harbor over a drink in my Vineyard Haven thrift shop beaker. White cedars grow in the wet margins of Morris Island to the south of us. The sunset is flamboyant. Samuel de Champlain, the French navigator, came here in 1606 and called the place Port Fortune. He was unaware Gosnold had been in these parts four years previously, also dispensing names. Champlain named Gosnold's Cape Cod Cap Blanc, which didn't stick. Another celebrated personage who visited Chatham was Squanto, the native guide who helped the Plymouth Pilgrims. He died in Stage Harbor in 1622, on a sailing vessel named the *Swan*, and is commemorated on a stone memorial near Mill Pond.

I wake in the small hours to the sharp fragments of a complicated dream. I'd been at the helm of a boat being towed by a horse on dry land, heading toward a field fenced off as a mooring or parking area, jammed full of other moored boats. My crew is my late friend Peter Tripp, and he is furious about my failure to find a place to moor. I finally abandon the horse outside the fence and find a mooring. Peter, calming down, opens a couple of bottles of beer.

It has the makings of a hot day. We row up to the bridge and, leaving the dinghy at the yacht club float, walk eastward on the road that leads to Chatham Harbor. On the way, houses set at suburban distances gradually get closer together and older. Opposite the lighthouse—this one still functioning—the 1987 inlet to the harbor seems to be full of surf, and not an easy way of getting in or out. The road north alongside the harbor brings us past the Chatham Beach Club; unlike several houses along here it was not washed away in the 1987 storm. Children are noisily splashing in the swimming area. It is nearly fifty years since I was here last, making my eight-year-old's share of noise with the Spaeth children in the summer of 1941. I wonder if my father still has the cup I won at the beach club that summer; it used to be in his trophy cupboard, alongside all the silverware he won at athletics championships. My cup was inscribed: *Best Beginner in Junior Swimming, 1941.*

Not much farther along the road are two gray-shingled two-story cottages, with wide porches and red-brick foundations, built on a lawn that slopes down to the harbor; one cottage, next to the road, one below. I remember coming out of the back door of the top cottage, where we children lived in the care of Miss Sjolin, our Swedish governess, and running down the grassy slope to Eloise and Otto's cottage with a message. There were foggy days when we couldn't see Nauset Beach across the harbor, and the lower cottage—gray shingles suspended in gray air—seemed far away. I remember Fourth of July fireworks, and swimming in the tide pools on Nauset Beach, which we reached by skiff, and winning a dog-paddle race at the beach club, and going fishing with some older boys and getting drenched. This is where I, a young fugitive from Hitler's bombs, first encountered the sun, sand, salt water, and even fog of this coast. No wonder I was marked once and for all.

I'm standing here with Margot, brooding about these things, when the front screen door of the top cottage opens and a man comes out, gives us a brief but penetrating glance, and begins fussing unnecessarily with the plants in a flower bed. Then, with another wary look ("Why are you giving these houses such an intent once-over?") he goes back indoors. I suppose I could have said, "I lived here for two months one summer during the war." But I don't really need to look inside; memories will do. Oddly I'd forgotten how close the cottages were to the lighthouse, only a hundred yards or so down the road. Surely the loom of its light must have been visible in the dark from our bedroom window, as Tony Spaeth and I whispered to each other instead of going to sleep as ordered, the beam of light swinging across Nauset Beach and way out to sea, where the convoys sailed and the submarines stalked . . .

"Had enough?" says Margot, who was evacuated only as far as Northumberland and thinks I had an overprivileged war. "It's time to buy pita bread and salami if you want lunch today."

On the way back, with me carrying the shopping in my small nylon backpack, we walk out onto the rippled sand in front of the lighthouse and head south. A little boatyard, surrounded by rental cottages, harbors skiffs and small powerboats. Since I hanker one day to explore Chatham Harbor and its farther reaches called Pleasant Bay (the Head of the Harbor of these parts), I ask a man about using the channel that winds around from the Stage Harbor entrance to here, passing between the top of Monomoy and Morris Island. "It can be done, depending on what you draw," he says. "There are markers, orange balls and stakes with metal radar reflectors on them. I'd say you might have two feet, three feet, at high water, most of the way. But the channel never stays long in one place, and the shallow bits move around, too. We're waiting to see if the breakthrough in the beach out there has a long-term effect. There used to be talk of the Army Engineers digging a proper channel connecting the two harbors, but I reckon that plan is dead. We can rent you a skiff right here. Might be the best way."

Going back to the dinghy, we pick blackberries in a wild patch near the Mitchell River bridge. The difficult thing, as always, is to keep more than you eat on the spot. "Miss Sjolin made the most wonderful blackberry jam which we used to have on pancakes," I say, licking my purple-stained fingertips.

21

THERE ARE TWO WAYS around the Cape to Wellfleet and Provincetown and we choose the slightly longer and—I hope—less chancy west-about route, which takes us first along the south shore of the Cape. We're not going down to the tip of Monomoy, through Pollock Rip, north up the long Back Shore, and around Race Point. I might do it with three or four in my crew, prepared to keep regular watches, in settled weather with no strong easterly to dump us on the beach Thoreau recognized could be "a vast morgue." The south shore has a number of tight little harbors and river mouths west of Chatham, but they are a bit too close at hand to make worthy destinations for an afternoon's sail. Maybe we're missing some compact pleasures in Harwich Port's Saquatucket, Wychmere, and Allen Harbors, though Duncan and Ware assure the cruising yachtsman that these inlets offer little anchoring room. This afternoon, with a warm southerly on our port beam, we romp past them, and also spurn the narrow openings of the Herring River, the Bass River, and an even tinier creek called Parkers River, despite the giant movie screen we'd seen before and which serves it as a landmark. You'd need a very shallow-draft boat for crossing Dogfish Shoal at the entrance of Parkers River, and a movie schedule might be useful before you decided the three-quarters of a mile run up the squiggly Parkers was worthwhile.

What we have in mind today is Hyannis. At 4:00 p.m. we round Point Gammon with caution because of its dangerous rock-studded approaches, and run in toward Hyannis, watching out for the marks that warn of Gazelle Rock, Halftide Rock, and Great Rock. We dip behind the rather ruined-looking breakwater on the west side of the outer harbor, scoot through the moorings of the small yacht club, note the walls of the Kennedy compound set among other large houses, and decide that there's not much shelter here if the wind continues from the south. In the eighteenth century this was known as Hyannis Roads, and "harbor" is a modern euphemism. We turn east toward Lewis Bay, a much more enclosed body of water, with the town of Hyannis on its north shore. The entrance channel to the bay hugs Dunbar Point to port. We sail in.

Here my wits desert me. It's a fine clear afternoon, the breeze still a perfect strength. I concentrate on the channel as we go in and am aware of shallows on both sides. Hyannis is the Cape's big town and busiest resort, but this is one of those days when I have not the slightest wish to go through the business of getting cleaned up, finding my wallet, and rowing ashore. Lewis Bay offers several seductive anchorages in its lower reaches, behind and tucked within Great Island, whose southern tip is Point Gammon. Perhaps these are in the front of my mind. The chart shows, on the starboard side of the entrance channel, a blob of land called Egg Island, but I fail to recognize Egg Island itself. It might be that, over there to the south. Perhaps I think we've gone farther into Lewis Bay than we in fact have gone. The strong late-afternoon light often plays tricks with substance and distance. I also fail to take into account that the chart I'm using dates from the early seventies and that Egg Island was never the most substantial of land masses. The time is 5:30, getting on for high water.

Margot is not deceived. "I think those people are clamming," she says, pointing forward.

"We've got lots of water between here and Egg Island," I reply.

"Those seagulls ahead of us are standing up, not floating," Margot says, undeflected.

I am scanning the chart again when there's a slithering sound and then silence. No more friendly chuckle of water from the moving hull. One of the gulls, standing in a few inches of water a boat length away, stares at us haughtily. What I had thought was Egg Island is actually Great Island, farther south; Egg Island—it has finally dawned on me—is invisible at high tide.

"Egg Island!" I exclaim. "It's not an island—it's a focking sandbar!" (Since we have read *The Last Grain Race*, Eric Newby's mirthful account of his sailing apprenticeship on a Swedish square-rigged ship, the swearing we do on *Lochinvar* has been mainly in the idiom of Newby's Scandinavian crewmates.)

According to *Eldridge*, if we're lucky we have another half hour of rising tide. On the other hand, since the tides are on their way from springs to neaps, rising less at each high tide, we could be stuck here for a week. Still, it's daylight this time, with no thunder and rain. I row out the Danforth into what I hope is deep water off our port quarter. A downward stab with an oar finds over a fathom. Then, back on board, I sheet in the sails in order to induce *Lochinvar* to heel. Margot, holding on to the port shrouds, leans outward. *Lochinvar* duly heels to port. On the foredeck, I bring in the anchor cable inch by inch. There's a long period when nothing happens, except sweat and swearing. But with painful slowness the bows begin to pivot. At last, in complete silence, *Lochinvar* floats off.

After this, caution's side is what we err on. Two of the secluded Lewis Bay anchorages, in Uncle Roberts Cove and behind Pine Island, look enticing on the chart, but a thorough reconnaissance of their approaches would be advisable before plunging in. Instead, we drop the Danforth again in about eight feet of water off the south end of the still unseen Egg Island. The north shore of Great Island is a hundred yards to our south. We row to the beach here and swim before supper, getting rid of the day's stickiness and the aches from recent exertions. A dip after a day's sailing is prized by us—and one reason we haven't yet made tracks for the chill waters of Maine. A few mosquitoes home in after dark, but they are lethargic, neither buzzing nor biting much. To our north, Hyannis's metropolitan glow, enhanced by floodlights at a baseball ground, makes the sky too bright for stargazing. Low overhead the landing lights of planes approaching the Hyannis-Barnstable airport probe the air above Lewis Bay.

In the morning, which is less humid, with a light northerly, we row into Uncle Roberts Cove. There are rocks on both sides of the convoluted entrance and then a narrow creek into the tree-encircled cove; half a dozen boats are on moorings, and a high-class yawl is tied up to a substantial private dock. It has the attraction of a place that, but for the chart, you wouldn't suspect is there. Rowing in, we encounter a big ketch going out, apparently a stranger, with two of her crew in an inflatable leading the way, one sounding with a boat hook. "We've only grounded twice so far," says the skipper of the ketch, as he cons his vessel slowly past us. Who were the nephews and nieces who christened this secluded cove? Perhaps they found their uncle here hard aground on the top of a spring tide, and by the time he was hauled off he'd decided to buy Great Island and make the cove his own. I put this theory to Margot, but she is more interested in the failure of the National Ocean Survey people to put an apostrophe before the "s" of Roberts on the chart. "Maybe there are two or even three Uncle Roberts," she says, and pays no attention to the look I give her, which stands for "That doesn't help."

The light northerly becomes variable. We get under way soon after 10 and tack out around Egg Island, now beginning to lift its long sandy spine above water. Then we head westward for Osterville. It's one of those hot mornings when the wind poops out for ten minutes at a time and, rocked by the dying wake of a far-off powerboat, *Lochinvar*'s sails slat, the jib sheet blocks clatter against the toe rail, and the dinghy dangles impatiently astern, awaiting the pull from the mother ship that will give it impetus and direction. Margot searches out the shade cast by the sails. I drape my old beach towel, a Wheaties breakfast cereal promotion found on a beach, over my knees, shins, and ankles. We resist the temptation of the motor. This is as short a day's voyage as we ever make and we are in no hurry. Half a mile north the undramatic south shore of the Cape is further muted by heat haze. We drift by the entrance to East Harbor and the shallow Centerville River, around Osterville Point and along Wianno Beach, before turning in toward the hard-to-see entrance to West Bay. Duncan and Ware say that the starboard-hand breakwater lies immediately to the west of a row of beach cottages, and they are right. A brief flourish of sweet southerly breeze gives us way over the ebb current in the narrow entrance of the bay, though by now we have the engine going, just in case. We slide gently in. Numerous little rivers, creeks, and crannies pierce the rim of the bay, but we hew to the narrow channel northward. In the bay's northeast corner numerous moorings have been dropped for the Wianno Yacht Club, and the boats proclaim their owners' discernment; many of the craft are Wianno Senior one-designs, 25-foot wooden gaff-rigged centerboard sloops with little cabins. Their raked-forward masts may be compensating for an inherent weather-helm problem, one suspects. From their first launching in 1914, the Wianno Seniors have spread from here all along the Massachusetts coast; one of them, *Victura,* owned by the Kennedys, was occasionally raced by J.F.K., and helped preserve the ex-PT boat commander's salty wind-tousled image. Beyond the moorings, the bascule bridge appears, providing access to the big summer houses on Little Island and Grand Island. (Little Island, half a mile broad, is only little in comparison with its big brother, Grand Island, to which it is also attached.) We hoot, one long, one short. Then we wait, on the usual tenterhooks: is the bridge tender awake, having a snack, on holiday? But the response is delightfully rapid. Bells ring, lights flash, road gates come down, and the bridge goes up. *Lochinvar* passes through, her crew saluting.

At anchor in North Bay, sheltered by Little Island to the south, I examine my feeling of well-being. This is such a good spot. Why don't we come here every summer? Can a place be too good? Perhaps our absences have to do with the different priorities held by captain and crew. I like what Americans call gunkholing and the British call ditch crawling. I like these harbors that have many islands, inner channels, and snaky passages to semisecret ponds. Margot prefers wide beaches and deep sparkling water, where she can skin-dive or body-surf in the waves. But coming to Osterville from Stage Harbor by way of Hyannis's Lewis Bay may seem as if I'm favoring my own likings, and I attempt to redress things with the suggestion "How about dinner ashore tonight?" Then, while Margot paints and reads a history of royal intrigues in eighteenth-century Naples, I row the dinghy across North Bay to explore the marshy intricacies of Isham Pond. Sixteen Canada geese are using it as their summer residence but show no signs of resenting my intrusion.

In the evening we row back toward the bascule bridge. To the north of it are several boatyards with the Crosby name, though only one still belongs to a member of the Crosby family. (As with Dodson's, in Stonington, it is a tribute to the character of the previous owner and the goodwill attached thereto that new owners keep the old name when they take over a boatyard.) The Crosbys have built and maintained boats in Osterville for 150 years, and at one point had five boatyards. Their fame arose particularly from their catboats, single-sail fishing craft which worked Nantucket Sound and were the progenitors of many other wooden boats, working or pleasure, among them the Wiannos. A "Crosby catboat" was in its time a term like a "Ford car" or a "Kleenex tissue"—a brand that encapsulated an age as well as a genre.

We leave the dinghy at the town dock, a venerable heap of granite and pilings. Dusty signs forbid the visitor to tie up for more than thirty minutes, but nobody is going to tick me off for doing so. We take the twenty-minute walk into the town center along a road still warm from the day's sun. Osterville is a comfortable rather than characterful small town. We dine in a restaurant called Wimpy's. This is a name which for Brits has a downmarket flavor; in the mother country Wimpy is the name of a fast-food chain that sells an eponymous hamburger. But Wimpy's of Osterville is of a higher gastronomic order. The fish is excellent. I don't find the house white *comme il faut*, but our motherly waitress quickly replaces it with what she calls blank de blank. Danny, the proprietor, puts a friendly seal on the proceedings by asking, "Where you folks from?" and when he learns that we are "from" our boat, he drives us back to the town dock.

A few summers ago we sailed into the entrance of West Bay in *Clio* and immediately took a left turn into the Seapuit River. This in fact is not a river but a channel connecting West Bay to Cotuit Bay and in the process separating the Sound-side barrier island of Dead Neck from Grand Island. We ran along the Seapuit past plush houses and then gybed in order to run up Cotuit Bay past Noisy Point. Here, local legend has it, a woman fatefully called Hannah Screecham surprised Captain Kidd and his crew, who were at it again, burying a treasure chest, possibly one left over from the Gardiners Island booty. The bloodthirsty pirates are said to have slain the poor woman and buried her along with the chest. Hannah's ghost goes on screeching in protest to this day. Just beyond here, on the west side of Grand Island, is Tims Cove, where we anchored. On the lawn of a coveside club a cookout was in progress and the smell of broiling meat was wafted to us on the evening breeze, together with the braying of alcohol-exaggerated merriment.

"You'd think, seeing us out here, they'd invite us in," I said to Margot.

"If they did, you wouldn't want to go," she replied, stirring our spaghetti sauce.

"Don't be so sure. I like those slightly drunken stand-arounds, the men rashly giving you stock tips for new electronic firms, the women who look so self-possessed on the tennis courts getting so confessional over the hot dogs . . ." Here I paused, as Margot lifted the loaded wooden spoon from the pan. *Clio*'s cabin was very small.

On that visit, we were held over in Osterville for another day by a strenuous westerly. It's often hard to leave these cozy harbors with entrances that present you immediately with rough seas outside. But in the calmer late afternoon we took the chance to explore the top end of North Bay. Weekend clammers were working the shores of one cove. So was a shellfish warden, who was making the clammers produce their permits and show him the size of the clams they'd tonged. The permits were supposed to be pinned to their shirts, but some bare-chested clammers claimed to have left their permits with their wives on the shore. A lot of yelling back and forth went on. It was quieter in Prince Cove. This has two arms, and in the western one I decided that here was the perfect hurricane hole, where we could lie safe in the shelter of the encircling woods while the storm raged.

"Even so, it'd be boring to stay on board," said Margot. "I think I'd rather sit out a hurricane onshore, among friends."

"I'll try to arrange that," I said.

22

BREEZY NEXT DAY from the southwest, and overcast.
Before leaving the shelter of West Bay we pull down a single
reef in the main and drag on our foul-weather gear. Our
morning is occupied in getting to windward. Although the
current is with us, this adds to the green-gray chop that
Lochinvar buckets into. A bit late, I wrap a small towel
around my neck to prevent the waters of Nantucket Sound
trickling down my chest and back. *Lochinvar* goes to windward best when she isn't sailing on her ear; now in the puffs
her lee rail goes under. I let the mainsheet traveler all the
way down to leeward and sometimes let out the sheet as
well, so that the forward third of the mainsail is aback
while the after part continues to drive her. We beat several
miles out from the shore and then come about, Margot on
the winch handle and me tailing the jib sheet, steering with
my leg against the tiller. We crank in the jib until the leech is
almost against the tip of the lee spreader, then stand west-

ward on the port tack for half an hour or so, slowly closing with the shore. We repeat the procedure, out and in. It takes a while for the cliffs of Succonnesset Point—more shoulder than point—to come broad off the starboard bow, and we ascertain that we have the bell buoy at the east end of Succonnesset Shoal on the port bow before we drive through the slot between shoal and point. Although the water is by no means deep in this inshore passage, the seas are kinder, the energy of the waves sapped by Succonnesset Shoal and its partner to the south, L'Hommedieu Shoal, which in this breeze serve as underwater breakwaters. The Vineyard is now in view to the south and Vineyard Haven tempts us as always. But the current urges us on. It's with us in Woods Hole, and we're through in a trice. In Buzzards Bay we turn north and run wing-and-wing up the Bay shore of the Cape, past the little harbors of Quissett and West Falmouth.

Quissett is a tight and pretty cove with big summer houses set around it on the low hillsides. It has no facilities other than the boatyard we walked to from Woods Hole seeking the bolt for *Clio*'s gooseneck. I anchored *Caliban* there once close to a varnished clinker-planked Folkboat, which still serves as a reference point for Quissett in the sea of memory. John McVitty, a retired architect who befriended us in our early days in Stonington, used to talk of his childhood summers in Quissett, where he learned to sail. Macky gave us brilliant, unpaid advice on how to rebuild our house. He was a perfectionist who couldn't handle the imperfect world of contractors and clients, but fortunately had the wherewithal to retreat from it, to sail his elegantly simple L. Francis Herreshoff sloop *Broomstick,* and painstakingly record one aspect of New World maritime history by taking off the lines of West Indian beach boats. When we heard of his death in August several years ago, we sailed *Lochinvar* into Quissett and after some searching found a spot to anchor. One big house had every room lit up after dark; it could have been, we imagined, the old McVitty place, honoring its departed. We held our own memorial service, recalling Macky's love of boats, his impatience with things as they are, and odds and ends he had given us over the years we knew him: a plywood dinghy, which became the tender for the *Billy Ruffian;* a stand-up pyramidal toaster for *Clio;* two green canvas zip-up bags for boat clothes, used on *Lochinvar;* and a volume of E. E. Cummings's poems he had bought while a student at Harvard. "What if a much of a which of a wind . . ."

West Falmouth, a few miles north, is associated in my mind with the friendliness of complete strangers. In *Clio* once we ran aground attempting to anchor in the second cove on the left going in. A helpful man in an outboard-powered skiff watched over us as we pushed off and then piloted us into the inner reaches of the harbor and introduced us to the elderly assistant harbormaster. This gentleman, who sat in a hut on the town dock and sold gasoline, gave us a mooring for the night (and received a tip from me for his generosity). We in fact stayed two nights, rent-free, weatherbound. A local yachtsman who changed his mind about going out rowed over to give us a block of ice. On a second occasion, several years later, the harbormaster was a different man and gas was no longer dispensed. But a man we asked about fuel took our empty jerry can to a roadside gas station a few miles away and filled it up for us. Despite these instances of good fellowship, there was no real village in West Falmouth, though plenty of houses and an old

Quaker graveyard to which we walked while the wind blew on Buzzards Bay. There we admired the plain, uniform gravestones, which displayed no pomp but absolute equality in death. Memorable, too, was the little inner harbor at nightfall, when the wind had died and we could hear the sounds of fish jumping and of fishing reels being let out and wound in by men on the town dock.

Today, to get the best from the wind and be in a good jumping-off place for tomorrow's passage through the Cape Cod Canal, we press on up Buzzards Bay. Past Wild Harbor ("Wide open to the usual southwest breeze," caution Duncan and Ware), Silver Beach, Megansett, Fiddlers Cove, and Squeteague Harbor. Past Cleveland Ledge lighthouse, standing like a white enamel coffeepot out in the middle of the Bay. The west shore of Cape Cod is more emphatic than that of the south: the land is higher and there are more trees. We round the wooded promontory of Scraggy Neck, taking care to avoid several off-lying rocky ledges. Then, in the deep bay to the north of the Neck, well in the lee of the land, we round up and furl the sails. Here we have to decide whether to make our way into Red Brook Harbor by going north or south around Bassetts Island.

Bassetts is shaped like a wonky Y. We choose to pass southward around the island's bent lower limb. We entered this way two years ago, after coming south through the canal and meeting fierce wind against tide at the head of the bay. This seemed a good place to duck into, though it was dark as we followed the narrow channel into Red Brook Harbor and Margot stood on the foredeck seeking the next channel buoy with the flashlight. In darkness, when you need them most, the marks seem particularly far apart. But whatever the weather, Red Brook Harbor is a fine refuge.

We've anchored in the past in its southernmost reaches, though the greater number of moorings now makes this more difficult. (One spot we found was several boat lengths from a sign saying ROCK, helpfully nailed to a stake, around which there was not unreasonably room to anchor.) This afternoon we hail the Parker's Boatyard launch and are led to a vacant mooring. Twenty-one dollars gets us the mooring, launch service, and showers ashore. The boating custom in Red Brook is divided by Parker's and another yard, Kingman's. Kingman's is more of a marina, with many powerboats at floating slips and a dockside restaurant. Boatyards have personalities, and like some people some attract quick judgment, to be or not to be confirmed by work done and bills received. Many yards nowadays are mere cogs in the consumer economy and might as well be servicing cars and washing machines or peddling condos and time-share apartments. But there are still some where an obsession with boats is evidently an integral part of making enough money to keep the yard in business. One gets the feeling that the owner and his work force actually sail boats of their own. Dodson's in Stonington is such a place, and so Parker's would seem to be, though I speak only as a transient $21 customer. It has a pair of workmanlike docks, a slipway, and usually several wooden boats being attended to. I often find one or two necessities in the chandlery. We get rid of our garbage in the boatyard dumpster and obtain a block of ice from the freezer and water from the tap on the dock. Not least is the blessing of the hot water in the showers.

Like many of its fellow harbors on the Buzzards Bay side of the Cape, Red Brook is a backwater. There's no commercial center. We have gone out looking for groceries there but had a long walk of it, northward along quiet roads as far as the so-called convenience store in the village of Pocasset. There was no bread for sale worth eating, and no fresh vegetables. We bought synthetic lemonade and a newspaper and trudged back to Red Brook. (The brook itself runs down to the harbor via a pond, and enters between Kingman's and Parker's.) But in fact we appreciate the backwaterness while we're lounging in *Lochinvar*'s cockpit, rum-and-tonics in hand, the sky clearing and the wind dropping at sunset. A train hoots and the lit passenger cars rumble between the trees on the hillside behind Parker's. This is part of the old Plymouth-Hyannis-Chatham line, on which I rode in the last stage of the trip from Dayton, Ohio, in 1941, and which has a resuscitated summer service. It is odd to think that fifty years ago I could have looked out of a railroad carriage at the boats moored in this harbor and had not the slightest inkling that one day I would be out there on a boat looking in at the passing train.

We're ready to depart at 8:00 next morning for the canal. As I fire up the engine a 35-foot sloop motors close by us, heading straight for Parker's slipway; the man at the wheel calls, "Say—I can get out this way, can't I? Haven't been here for a few years." I answer, "No—you can't!" He is heading for solid Cape, not to mention a railroad. I point a rough heading to the buoyed channel south around Bassetts Island. A woman is in the cockpit with him. He may be suffering from an acute case of Egg Island syndrome, but I wonder: Does he have charts? If so, can he read them? Has he just stolen the boat?

We take the north-about route around the top of Bassetts

and sail along the south shore of Wings Neck. The sky is gray and the wind is a light southeasterly. On the tip of Wings Neck stands a neat lighthouse, an attached keeper's house with a pale green shingled roof, and a set of traffic lights on a tall steel framework. These control the passage of large ships proceeding north to the canal and don't affect small craft like *Lochinvar.* What does affect us is current. This flows through the canal at up to 5 knots, so it is crucial to have it with us. The current runs so fast partly because the tidal rise and fall is much greater in Cape Cod Bay than in Buzzards Bay. North of the Cape the tides go up and down over a ten-foot range compared to four feet or so to the south. Moreover, the times of the tide are three hours apart in the two bays, so the level in Buzzards is going up while in Cape Cod Bay it is going down; at extremes, there can be a nine-foot difference between the two. In the canal, which links the two bays, the water squeezes back and forth in five- or six-hour bursts in a perpetual attempt to equalize the levels.

We reach the entrance channel just after 9:00, when the current has already been running for an hour from Buzzards Bay toward Cape Cod Bay and building up speed. We foam past the starboard-hand buoys and the beacons placed on stone cairns. The channel proceeds past Onset, whose harbor opens north of us, and past a mooring basin for large ships adjacent to the channel to the south; but we're not about to stop in either. The current concentrates a helmsman's mind. Powerboats, fishing boats, even fair-sized tankers, with enough power to run over the adverse current, are coming the other way, and we're swept toward them at fearsome speed. We have the engine running again and the jib furled as we flash past the wharves of the

Massachusetts Maritime Academy, the training school for young seafarers, whose former cargo ship, the *Patriot State,* is tied up at right angles to the mouth of the canal. A large sign here (there's one at the other end, too) says AUXILIARY POWER MANDATORY. In the past, I've read this to mean that all boats passing through must have an engine. Qualifying in that respect, we've sailed merrily through, feeling pretty smart about it, though there are places where the high banks of the canal may flatten the wind and places where powerful eddies and whirlpools may compete for control over one's boat. A sailing vessel could lose steerageway and get sufficiently out of hand to impede a vessel proceeding properly under power. The signs mean use your engine.

We found this out a few years ago when running with the wind free and no engine on. Suddenly, amplified through a loudspeaker, a mighty voice from astern bellowed: "Skipper of that yacht! Your engine must be running!" A chocolate-brown patrol craft of the Army Corps of Engineers, which controls the canal, had sneaked up behind us. It was not to be messed with. "Right you are," I shouted. There was little chance they could hear me over their engines, so I added an acknowledging wave. In record time, our engine was on, too, and the cooling water frothing from the exhaust pipe was confirming this to the beady-eyed Engineers.

Their land-based colleagues are also keeping watch on canal traffic by way of television cameras mounted along the banks, with (one is told) "zoom lenses and image intensifiers" to detect vessels anchoring, dawdling, or behaving in a deviant fashion. (Another regulation to be heeded is that boats heading into the current must give way to those impelled by it.) The Engineers have their base at this Buzzards Bay end of the canal and they tend to be out and about here because of the Bourne railroad bridge. This reminds me of a giant Erector or Meccano set version of London's Tower Bridge—or, on less optimistic occasions, like an immense guillotine. The span is generally kept raised, but when it is down there are only seven feet to spare, the perfect height for slicing off *Lochinvar*'s mast just above the boom. The Engineers patrol this section of the canal in order to keep passing craft at a safe distance as the bridge span starts to descend. They're also ready to put a towline on any vessel that looks as if it might be swept into the bridge by the current. We've approached on several occasions to find the bridge coming down and had to turn into the current. Once, in *Clio,* with the outboard scarcely allowing us to hold our own, we crabbed over to the edge of the canal and were nudged out of danger by the back eddy close to the bank. Today, no trains due, the bridge is up and we shoot underneath.

The canal is seven miles long, a roughly west-east cut through the shoulder of the Cape. One of the first people to think of digging such a ditch was Myles Standish, who in 1623 came down from Plymouth and took note of a small river, the Manomet, flowing into Buzzards Bay. He observed that the Manomet's headwaters were divided by a mere three-quarters of a mile of sandy ground from the top of a creek off Cape Cod Bay. A few years later the Pilgrims established a trading post on the Manomet, at a place called Aptucxet, not far from the present railroad bridge, so that they could barter with the New Amsterdam Dutch and the local Indians for furs, sugar, tobacco, and cloth. During the Revolutionary War, according to the Cape historian Jeremiah Digges, Continental Army generals decided a canal would be useful and a survey was made that reckoned the cost (to the last penny) at thirty-two thousand one hundred and forty-eight pounds, one shilling, and eightpence. In the nineteenth century, further proposals for a canal were made, at this and other locations on the Cape, in order to cut the time needed to sail around the outside of the Cape and reduce the dangers of wrecked ships and lost lives and cargoes. (Stagecoach operators, fearing the competition of sailing packets, lobbied the Massachusetts legislature to vote such projects down.) The first attempt to dig a canal started in 1880, but soon ran out of cash. August Belmont, a New York financier, backed the second effort, which succeeded over six years (1909–14) in excavating a 25-foot-deep and 100-foot-wide canal, at a cost of over $13 million. The trouble with Belmont's canal was that it wasn't big enough. Neither did it have locks; the currents ran much too fast, and big ships couldn't pass safely through. In the end the tolls collected weren't enough to keep the canal company solvent. The United States government took it over and gradually widened and deepened it; by 1940 it was 540 feet wide. The tolls were done away with. Big ships and small alike go through for free.

I'm always excited by the canal passage. Although the banks against which the canal waters wash are faced with stone riprap, there are grassy slopes above. The green landscape is interrupted now and then by campsites, trailer parks, and stretches of highway. Joggers, cyclists, and walkers move along the canalside tracks, sometimes waving to us. Phlegmatic small boys hold fishing lines. Old men stand on the banks and watch the boats go by. Doing 8 knots, 4 of our own, 4 from the current, we overtake the joggers, but one lad furiously pedaling a mountain bike keeps ahead of us. The canal's sinuous bends hide the coming stretches from us. Apart from the railroad, two highways cross the canal on spans which are high enough for a full-rigged sailing ship to pass under. We lose air as we pass under the bridges. Then the wind comes in from a new direction and we gybe the mainsail. The cresting wakes of passing motor yachts rock us severely. After being shaken by several of these, we learn our lesson and present our stern or bow to the wake, to lessen the rolling. Here and there overfalls form, and *Lochinvar* plunges through these waves heaped up by the bustling current. One comber breaks over our stem and pours back over deck and cabin top as far as the main hatch. One big motor yacht called *Excellence* toots its siren as it overtakes us; no false modesty there. On some wakes and waves the dinghy picks itself up and surfs forward, overtaking us, and once crashes bluntly into *Lochinvar*'s transom.

We know we're approaching the east end of the canal and the end of our sleigh ride when the tall smokestack of a huge electricity generating plant appears on the Cape side. Just beyond the power plant there's a brief gap in the stone bank: the entrance to a small and crowded boat basin. Margot asks, "Why don't we ever go in here?" She asks me that question every year. The main reason is as usual momentum; we are whisked right by. Moreover, our day's destination is still a long way off, and this basin—officially referred to as the Sandwich Harbor of Refuge—is known for the smells from its commercial fishhouses and the surge rolling in from canal traffic. She should also recall the experience of our good friends Buell and Margaret. Buell is an ardent sailor, Margaret less so. One evening, as they made their way from Boston to their home port in Buzzards Bay, they decided to moor overnight in the basin here rather than face a contrary current in the canal. According to Buell, the reek of fish was intense, the canal surge discomforting, and to cap it all, an air-cleaning device at the summit of the power station's 300-foot chimney sent a hideous rattlesnake-like noise over the basin every fifteen minutes. At one point in the small hours, Margaret, unable to sleep, tearfully told Buell that she would never set foot on a boat again. She has broken this resolve, but Buell ever since has called the Sandwich Harbor of Refuge the marina of tears.

23

CAPE COD BAY has its own weather this morning. The sun is out, the wind is a firm southeasterly, and the seas—at least to start with, in the lee of the Cape—aren't large. *Lochinvar* lollops blithely along. A happy man is at the tiller as the crew brings lunch and joins him in the cockpit. I've been wondering whether to go first to Wellfleet or to Provincetown, but the wind decides for me: the course to Wellfleet, leaving Billingsgate Shoal safely to port, would be hard to windward today; that to Provincetown will be a broad reach. The tall stack of Sandwich power plant recedes behind us. Our next landmark, all going well, should be the Pilgrim monument in P'town, to be seen in four or five hours. Numerous sportfishing boats are out and about, and several small planes make slow circles overhead, spotting for swordfish and tuna and radioing their sightings to the boats. One bluefin tuna is big money. At $20 a pound, the price a prime fish may fetch if it passes the meticulous survey of the white-coated buyers on Cape fish docks, a 500-pound bluefin represents $10,000. It can be swimming in the Bay one morning, be at Logan Airport that evening, and find itself in a Tokyo sushi bar next day.

Although the waves increase as we get farther out into the Bay, they're on the beam and *Lochinvar*'s motion remains unexcited. "Wake me up if you see anything interesting," says Margot, from her customary siesta position on the leeside of the cockpit. "Particularly fish." Half an hour later she sits up to tell me the dream she has just had: An old man, wearing faded red shorts and a ragged coat, was walking over the tops of the waves and looked at us disapprovingly as we sailed past him. God in faded red shorts?

"And did you see any fish yet?" she asks.

"It's you who's been seeing the exciting things," I reply.

Provincetown is the farthest north we've so far sailed, and we get there, breeze fading, in the late afternoon. Approaching Provincetown Harbor we duck around Long Point, which depends like bent arthritic fingers from the hand of Race Point. Provincetown itself, spreading along the beach inside the harbor, tricks you into thinking it lies on a north-south axis, facing west, but this tip of the Cape is so curled in on itself that the town in fact faces southeast. Getting oriented in P'town isn't simple. Captain John Smith, who was here before the Pilgrims, called this harbor Milford Haven, after the large natural harbor in southwest Wales, but that name is long gone. It is the monument put up to his successors, the Pilgrims, that helps guide us in. Dedicated in 1910, this is a square-sectioned granite shaft about 250 feet high, standing on a 100-foot sandhill, and it is the sole high structure on the skyline apart from an immense aqua-green water storage tank or standpipe. The monument seems to have as much relation with English religious dissent in the seventeenth century as the Eiffel Tower. It is said to be a close copy of the Mangia tower in Siena—one of those crenellated edifices that fourteenth-century Italian nobles erected to defend their families from hostile clans. The Mangia tower was popular with New England architects around the turn of this century as an inspiration for railroad stations and fire departments. However, the dour gray stone used here may express a mood closer to the puritanical Pilgrim Fathers than to quattrocento Catholic Italians. And it does of course serve to remind those who associate the Pilgrims with Plymouth, on the main shore of Massachusetts, that their ship *Mayflower* first called here in mid-November 1620. The Pilgrims spent five chilly weeks in these parts, facing up to their New World. Here Peregrine White came into the world, the first English child born in New England, and here was lost—drowned in the harbor—Dorothy Bradford, wife of William Bradford, the colony's first leader.

Lochinvar comes to anchor in eight feet of water southwest of the main wharves of the town and with the twenty-year-old, nearly half-mile-long breakwater at our backs providing some protection from the swell which habitually rolls in around Long Point. Many moorings have been planted here by entrepreneurs hoping for rental income, but few have boats on them. Provincetown is very much a commercial fishing port and seems to be regarded by most cruising yachtsmen in the manner that the Pilgrims came to regard it; that is, as out of the way and uncomfortable. We rig the awning against the hot late-afternoon sun and put off to the morrow a trip ashore. Party fishing boats and whale-watching boats come in, rocking us with their wakes.

Margot swats flies and I serve drinks in the cockpit. At 7:45 the sun goes down in the northwest behind the town. The shingle and clapboard houses that stand shoulder-to-shoulder along the harbor edge merge in a gray band, their roofs in bumpy silhouette. We dine on linguine with spinach and Parmesan sauce, accompanied by sardine, tomato, and onion salad—"Very fine" is my verdict.

"That would have cost you forty dollars in a restaurant," says Margot.

After dark, the Pilgrim monument is floridly floodlit. With a red beacon light glowing on top, it seems less a commemoration of the Pilgrims' oceanic achievements than a most unpuritan priapic emblem.

In the morning—calm, foggy, and promising heat again—we row ashore. Finding a place to haul out the dinghy takes a while, but we eventually choose a spot near the Coast Guard pier, where an alley passes from the beach between buildings to the street behind. (We drag the dinghy above the tideline and turn it over.) Time was when Provincetown looked as if it were blowing out to sea or were being buried by sand. The settlers who eventually succeeded the Pilgrims chopped down the old woods of pine, oak, juniper, and sassafras, and released the dunes. By Thoreau's day sand was everywhere; the main street was a boardwalk laid on the beach. "The sand drifts like snow, and sometimes the lower story of a house is concealed by it," he wrote in his book *Cape Cod*. "There was a schoolhouse . . . filled with sand up to the tops of the desks and of course the masters and scholars had fled." But beach grass and pitch pines have since moored the marauding sand hills. The grass seed came—as did the Pilgrims, indirectly— from Holland, where they know a thing or two about holding on to land from the assaults of wind, sand, and sea.

Although sand no longer gets into everything in Provincetown, the dunes are close behind the town. Provincetown looks large from the water, but it is merely wide and thin. The streets are now paved with asphalt and many of the houses are antique. The place has lasted long enough to have traditions on two counts, fishing and the arts. For many decades, when whaling ships docked here and a hundred Provincetown schooners trawled and long-lined for haddock, mackerel, flounder, and cod, the town's working language was Portuguese. And then, from roughly the beginning of the First World War, the emigrants from the Azores were joined by theater folk, literary types, and painters. The Provincetown Players spawned Eugene O'Neill. Writers such as John Dos Passos settled, and others like Tennessee Williams and Norman Mailer visited frequently and flamboyantly. Beginning with Charles Hawthorne, a long roll call can be made of the artists who have found the P'town air and light congenial, even inspiring. And as is often the case in attractive bohemian places, the workers and the artists were soon accompanied by camp followers and tourists. Gardens that once were covered with flakes of drying fish flaunt contemporary statuary. Fish-freezer plants have become summer apartments.

By mid-morning the place is beginning to come to life. Shops and eateries tend to keep Mediterranean hours, opening late and closing late. The main streets, two deep, are quickly gridlocked with the cars of sightseers, who have gone as far as they can go on the Cape and now are looking for a parking spot. Some are also just looking. Like Key West at the end of the road south, and San Francisco at the end of the road west, P'town is a sanctuary for the unorthodox and therefore a raree show for the staid. Two women sit kissing on a front porch in full view of the street. Men walk hand in hand. "Alternative lifestyles" seem almost regular. The town has an annual Gay Carnival Week—which we are several days too soon for. We therefore have to imagine the "Fairies and Fantasies" parade and what goes on at theatrical performances with names like *Vampire Lesbians of Sodom*. There are weekly meetings for Sexual Compulsives Anonymous. The local churches are often packed these days at memorial services for AIDS victims. It is a long 370 years since William and Dorothy Bradford were here, but one awaits, without relish, the phase which must soon be upon us, the New Puritanism.

Margot and I make our way down to the main wharf, which is named after the Arctic explorer Admiral Donald MacMillan, a local hero. Here the ferry from Boston comes in, and fishing boats and sightseeing boats tie up. Among them are half a dozen large steel craft which take passengers whale watching and provide for P'town mariners an altogether less onerous and bloody occupation than that which their forefathers practiced. Similar boats go on pacific hunting trips out of Barnstable on the Cape, Gloucester north of Boston, Nantucket, and Vineyard Haven. We have bought tickets for the *Dolphin V*, as have roughly a hundred other people. Its radar scanner revolving, the boat powers out through the dispersing fog, around Long Point, Race Point, and the unnamed northernmost round tip of the Cape. We are heading north for the Stellwagen Bank, a huge underwater shoal of sand and gravel whose southern edge is about five miles away, where whales hang out at this time of the year. But we still have the hazy Cape in sight when *Dolphin V* slows down. Whales ho!

I'm glad we're not doing this on *Lochinvar*. *Dolphin V*'s size and steel construction give confidence. As we line the rails, a young woman from the Provincetown Center for Coastal Studies talks over the loudspeaker system, telling us passengers about the differences between humpback whales, fin whales, right whales, and minke whales. The pair of 40-foot-long marine mammals which have just surfaced here—from hundred foot depths that presumably don't seem so deep when you're that size—are humpbacks. They have been feeding on schools of small fish. They have stubby dorsal fins, white markings on the flukes of their tails, and move around in couples, our informant tells us, "just like people." As they come to the surface in the gentle swell, materializing in such great bulk, they bring forth from all of us watching a spontaneous chorus of *oohs* and *aahs*. When not exclaiming, most of us are smiling. There is polite competition to be the first to see one of the whales rise, and get to a spot on the rail close to it before one's fellow watchers crowd to the same side, causing the *Dolphin V* to list. The humpbacks browse unconcernedly nearby, now and then twisting and making a sort of kayak roll, showing their flippers. Then they snort out jets of water and steamy air, arching their backs, before suddenly diving again with a vehement flick of their tails. They leave big pools of smooth water where they've submerged. In a few hours, we see eight humpbacks, four of the smaller minkes, and six of the more streamlined and less approachable finbacks, which swim at a great yet somehow unhurried speed, with less cavorting than the humpbacks, and with their fins piercing the surface now and then. Many of the whales come back to the Stellwagen Bank summer after summer and, having marks by which the professional whale watchers identify them, have been given names such as Ibis and Mallard (not particularly suitable names, you might think, but also not Disneyish or anthropomorphic).

It seems to Margot and me wonderfully trusting that the humpbacks come so close to human beings and human artifacts. The skipper of the *Dolphin V* doesn't have much to do to bring us and keep us in their vicinity. He stops the engines because it appears the whales prefer us not to be noisy. I would have thought whales would have developed a sense of man as enemy. Isn't Ahab part of their race memory? How is it this couple know we haven't got a Norwegian harpooner on board, or a crew of Japanese sharpening their flensing tools for work on their blubber? Do they suspect that, on the contrary, we are moved by their immense yet ever surprising presence? For a while we share the surface of the sea with them—air breathers like us, sucklers of their young like us, but true denizens of the liquid element. And suddenly it's over: they submerge and don't reappear. On the way back toward P'town we make donations to save whales from our fellow men. We buy T-shirts and badges and sign petitions. We land at McMillan Wharf with the happily bemused look of an audience coming out of the theater after a really good film or play.

We depart next morning for Wellfleet, halfway down the inside of the forearm of the Cape. Light and fluky airs from the northwest. We don't sail close to the shore because we have to allow for the shallowest parts of Billingsgate Shoal, sticking out from the land on the west side of the entrance to Wellfleet Harbor. As we run past the mouth of the Pamet River, the one creek that breaks into the Bay, I scan the horizon; my friend Paul keeps an outboard skiff in the Pamet and may well be out here, seeking bluefish. Among the houses in the dunes near the entrance is one which belonged to Edward Hopper. The Pilgrims sent a scouting party down this shore soon after they arrived in Provincetown harbor and raided Indian caches of corn they found. Corn Hill is the name of the hundred-foot-high dune just north of the Pamet. The sky is cloudless today, the sun hot, but the mainsail gives us shade until midday, when the sun moves west of our course. What breeze there is comes in flurries, ruffling some patches of water and leaving others a shiny calm. We run across Billingsgate in about eight feet of water, according to the depth sounder—though when we look over the side through clear water to the bottom, it seems closer than that. Billingsgate might have been named for the London fish market because it was prolific in fish. Indeed, sportfishing boats and small draggers are busy today, and the tuna-spotting planes have been joined by a small airship or blimp, which looks like a portly silver fish five hundred feet out of place. Following a circuitous route into the southern approaches of Wellfleet Harbor and tacking up the narrow channel between Billingsgate Island and the bar off Lieutenant Island, we snuggle into the lee of Billingsgate Island and drop the hook. This "island," now a sandbank which is completely covered at high tide, was a place of habitation in the seventeenth and eighteenth centuries; until 1875 a lighthouse stood here. It is just after low water now, and we row the dinghy into a little gully between the sandy hump of Billingsgate and the end of Jeremy Point, to the north, where a few other small boats are pulled up. Little offshoots of the incoming tide run between the furrows of the sand. We swim in the tropic warmth of our miniature harbor, then eat our picnic lunch. Perfect pleasures.

Here as elsewhere I compare today's with earlier arrivals of ours. On other occasions we've sailed directly from the canal to Wellfleet. This has sometimes meant fetching in here in the late afternoon. With the sun behind us and falling directly on the west-facing shore of the Cape, Jeremy Point and its northern neighbor Great Island on the west side of Wellfleet Harbor appear to merge with the shores of Eastham, which run down from the east side of the harbor to the inner elbow of the Cape and are in fact several miles east of Jeremy Point and Great Island. The best seamark then is the wreck of the *General James E. Longstreet,* a Victory ship from the Second World War; it was grounded here as a bombing target, like the Gardiners Bay Ruins or Nomans Land off Martha's Vineyard, for navy reserve pilots to keep in practice with. The chart marks a "prohibited area" around the black, broken hulk, but in a northeasterly we've tacked close to it without getting strafed by diving jets. Once you're in the neighborhood of the *Longstreet,* the lie of the land becomes clear. The broad and deep expanse of Wellfleet Harbor, in fact a bay, opens up to the north. And then it is always a surprisingly long last leg upharbor to Wellfleet itself.

We arrived here in *Clio* one evening in fading light and decided against trying to find a mooring in the inner harbor of Wellfleet in the dark. In the great outer harbor behind Great Island, counting on the forecast "light southwesterly" for a settled night, we anchored in what I expected would be about six feet of water at low tide. I took account in my calculations of the greater rise-and-fall north of the canal. But my reckoning must have been out. In the small hours I was woken by a bump. *Clio* had hit the bottom. I checked my watch—only half an hour till low water, and no need to panic. *Clio* didn't assume a great angle of heel and pitch the crew member on the upside, which was me, out of bed. We were nicely afloat when I woke again in the morning and gave thanks for the miracle of tides.

On several other occasions we've been forced to beat up the harbor against a strong headwind—a long day lengthened. The sun setting behind the dark shape of Great Island, the almost horizontal shafts of light illuminating the shores of Lieutenant Island and Indian Neck on the eastern side of the harbor, and the buoys distant enough from one another to make them hard to spot. The penalty for straying too far from the channel is an involuntary and possibly lengthy grounding. Today, however, in the full light of early afternoon, in the light northwesterly and with the flood under us, *Lochinvar* has no such problems. We furl sails not far from the breakwater and motor slowly into the small basin off the town dock. A toot on our horn brings forth the launch of Wellfleet Marine. The family who run this firm are a taciturn lot; you might mistake their attitude for surliness, and they don't seem particularly glad to be in the business they're in, renting moorings and boats. But after five or six years of coming here I've decided they are Cape types, shy of summer folk. They give the impression today of almost recognizing us. We actually get a smile from the ginger-haired lad who runs the launch, and after a few minutes' negotiation and the passing of sundry dollars, we have a mooring for two, maybe three, nights.

24

PAUL LIVES a few miles from Wellfleet at North Truro and is our mainstay on the Cape. I met him in the late 1950s, when we were both young writers on *The New Yorker,* and we've been encouragers, critics, and sounding boards for each other ever since. In the past when we've been pushed for time Paul has driven to pick us up at Woods Hole or Osterville or Chatham. But since our visits to him last two or three days and I fret at leaving a boat anchored in unfamiliar and rather distant harbors, we now try to get as close to North Truro as possible, and that brings us agreeably to Wellfleet. Sorting out our gear for these days ashore is less agreeable; we argue about what food we should take to Paul that won't keep in our ice box or in the nets slung for provisions. Paul by now expects (and dreads) gifts that range from damp salami to lettuce going black at the edges. As well as a kit bag of laundry, we pack clothes for who knows what social occasions, indoors and out. Frayed tempers are best avoided in a hot cabin, and so, while Margot is deciding which dress and which pair of swimming fins to take ashore, I row in to the telephone at the town dock to tell Paul we've got here.

A few years ago, as we sat on the Wellfleet dockside with our smelly bags of laundry and food, waiting for Paul, a very long black Cadillac limousine of the early 1970s tailfin variety pulled up. The driver, wearing dark glasses, leaned from his window and said to Margot, "Lady, I'm here for the Baileys." Thinking Paul had done us proud by sending such a vehicle for us, even if it was hired from the local Mafia, we climbed in the capacious back with our bags and admired the blue velvet upholstery, the jump seats and cigar lighters, and the silk blinds with little gold tassels. We were halfway to North Truro along Route 6 before we discovered that our chauffeur was dining with us that night at Paul's. His name was Charles Zender. A noted architect, he had designed Paul's house; he had a passion for big old cars and had amused himself by letting us assume he was a chauffeur. "I'm still waiting for my tip," he said that evening, when we met again.

Paul's house is a concrete-and-glass tower whose third-floor living room rises above the topmost branches of the surrounding scrubby woods. The house is a lookout and at night looks like an up-to-date lighthouse. It has splendid views northwestward to P'town and across Cape Cod Bay, and northeastward to two warning devices of different eras, like those at Montauk: the Highland Light (built in 1857 on the site of an earlier lighthouse), which warned coastal shipping of the proximity of the Cape, and half a mile down the beach the huge white radar dome at the former North Truro Air Force Station (motto: "Potent Defense.

Permanent Peace"), which until the end of the Cold War scanned the skies for incoming enemy aircraft. From Paul's third-floor balcony the scrub forest is a knobbly green carpet flecked with the black of branches and shadow. The small trees seem Oriental, gnarled and twisted by salt in the air and the sandy ground. Next to the house Paul has cleared a patch out of the scrub, planted it with vegetables and fruit bushes, and wrapped it in a wire-and-plastic-mesh fence and canopy to keep out hungry rabbits, squirrels, chipmunks, raccoons, and birds. As for the hornworm caterpillars which eat his tomatoes, Paul hopes their natural predator, the braconid wasp, will make an appearance. Meanwhile he stays vigilant.

Soon after our arrival Paul's new washing machine has done its job and our wash is drying on clotheslines he has stretched between the trees. Margot parades our shirts, shorts, sheets, and socks in a pleasingly ordered way, enjoying the free drying power of the sun. The other natural resource we exploit is fresh water. Making up for shipboard privation in that respect, we take lots of showers at Paul's house. His water comes from a well and one summer while we were here it ran dry. By the next year, he had had a deeper well drilled and a new pump installed. "Having you to stay last summer cost me three thousand dollars," Paul told us with a grin.

At Paul's for several days we see the land again from the land; we lead a sort of land life while remaining boat people. "The Baileys are here on their annual cruise," says Paul, explaining us to his friends. From time to time, I can't help thinking about *Lochinvar*. But I also compare Paul's surroundings now with what they used to be. The once plentiful land and fresh water of North Truro are being depleted. Development houses are mushrooming in the woods to the west of Paul's house, whose solitude he has cherished. The number of people living on the Cape has been rising in recent years at six times the rate of population increase in the United States. People want to live near the sea, and who can blame them? Driving to and from Wellfleet, we have to use Route 6, the one main highway in this part of the Cape. It leads to P'town, and it seems to channel and intensify the obsessive need of everyone on it to get somewhere as fast as possible. It can be a lethal need. The road is ill designed for the amount of traffic it carries, with frequent minor junctions and access points at which impatient drivers try to break into the constant stream of vehicles. Two years after he gave us a ride to Paul's, Charles Zender was killed on Route 6 by a pickup truck which hit him head-on when its young driver reached down to change a music casette. Paul releases his fury at those overtaking in the wrong places or turning abruptly without signaling by shouting "Turkeys!" "No-necks!" and "Imbeciles!" By the time we get back to *Lochinvar,* the perils of the sea appear relatively tame.

If it is what Paul calls "a good beach day," we may drive a mile or so on a back road to Coast Guard Beach on the Atlantic shore. The land hereabouts is all National Seashore, part of the 27,000 acres of the Cape protected from future development, though with scattered houses that predate the takeover by the National Park Service in 1961. This great beach stretches unbroken all the way south to Nauset Inlet and it is easy when walking or sunbathing on it to think of it purely as a seashore on which we gratefully stretch our limbs and lungs, rather than as a leeshore on which hundreds of vessels and their crews lost their lives in the centuries of sail. Battered corpses and wrecked cargoes have strewn the sands at the water's edge where we splash and paddle. But the benefits of this beach don't always include clear water for swimming. August brings the red tide of mung, a seaweed also known as monk's hair. Swimming through it is like floundering through stewed rhubarb.

If the backshore is thick with mung, we head for the Bay. We drive to the Pamet River with a cooler full of lunch things and Paul's fishing rod strapped to the car roof rack. At the Pamet there's a basic parking lot and a small harbormaster's shed overlooking a shallow harbor and a creek winding through marshes into the low hills. The Pamet once harbored (and built) fishing schooners, but it gradually became a haven most suitable for dinghies. Dredged twenty years ago, the channel from Cape Cod Bay into the harbor has again silted up so that only canoes and light skiffs can get in and out at low tide, though a few day sailers and larger powerboats moor here and make their exits and entrances when the tide serves. The river itself nearly cuts through the Cape. It rises no more than a hundred yards from the Atlantic and in several past northeasterly storms, in 1896 and 1936, helped by coincidentally high tides, the ocean broke through the intervening dunes to flood the Truro cranberry bogs and threatened to turn the north end of the Cape into an island. A Coast Guard station on the ocean beach nearby was abandoned in 1933 because of the Atlantic's obstinate advance. When Thoreau came by the Pamet the story was the same. "One who lives near its source told us that in high tides the sea leaked through," he wrote. My book of local names says of the Pamet: "The name may come from [the Algonquin] *pum-*

moh 'the sea' *andut* 'at'"—therefore, meaning "at the sea."
A dike has now been constructed at a mid-point to keep
the salt waters of Bay and sea apart and the fragile Cape in
one piece between them.

Paul takes us in his aluminum skiff down the harbor. I sit
in the bow as lookout, trying to spot the deepest water. But
in several places Paul and I get out and walk shin-deep,
pushing the skiff and Margot in it over the sandy shallows.
Motoring out between the little breakwaters at the Pamet
mouth we turn south and then immediately into the beach
to land and unload. This beach—which is named Fisher
Beach—is less striking than that on the Atlantic side. No
steep sand cliffs overhang it, no surf rolls in. But there's no
mung either, and you can walk out a fair distance into the
Bay before you come to water deep enough for swimming.
It seems to be more for local families than Cape tourists.
Some enterprising adults and children are digging for sand
eels to use as bait. While Paul goes out in the skiff to hunt
bluefish, Margot and I swim among thousands of fat minnows; these are baby sea perch, according to an eleven-
year-old boy who is pursuing them with a net and bucket.
We walk the beach looking for trophies. There are many
flat stones, just right for skipping. The day is clear; the
heights of Manomet, south of Plymouth, can be seen
twenty miles away across the Bay. When our fisherman
returns, we can tell from his abstracted expression that he
hasn't hooked a fish; but there are plenty of recently caught
blues in his freezer, and we will be all right for dinner
tonight.

Some people don't like reading about food. The authors
of accounts like this are expected by some reviewers to be
abstemious, ascetic individuals, interested in landscape and

past and present happenings but not in the materials which fuel movement and observation. I think the food along the way is often worth recording. I like its local variations. I like reading about meals enjoyed in the past by people such as the diarists Samuel Pepys and James Woodforde, and I sometimes regret that other writers—William Cobbett, for instance—didn't tell us more about what they ate on their travels. On this coast, the summer bounty of land and sea includes bluefish, striped bass, swordfish, scrod, lobsters, oysters, mussels, clams, corn (particularly the white-and-yellow sort that is straight from the field), and blueberries. Chez Paul we have a host who is not only a trenchant reporter and novelist but a skilled cook. Our sandwiches on the beach are pockets of pita bread crammed with his seafood salad. Tonight, the bluefish is grilled on a charcoal stove on the top-floor balcony and is served with rice, fried zucchini blossoms, and tomatoes from the garden. Then come blueberries (from New Jersey) and ice cream (from Vermont). The white wine is Australian.

Paul has a transcontinental second marriage; his wife, Milane, runs a bookstore near San Diego, where he spends much of the winter. She may or may not be there when we sail into Wellfleet. But we generally encounter at his house architects, poets, artists, and members of the much maligned legal profession. Paul's writing has brought him in contact with lawyers dealing with what the legal trade calls "toxic torts," particularly those who have been fighting for the rights of workers injured by asbestos and radiation. One night at Paul's a small plane buzzed the house. "That's Jack Harper!" exclaimed Paul, and we rushed to the balcony and waved to a circling Piper Cherokee. Forty minutes later, after driving to P'town airport, Paul returned with the pilot, who had just flown in from Helena, Montana, by way of Camden, Maine. Jack Harper had been a surgeon, but when in middle age his fingers ceased to function well enough for surgery he studied law, took bar exams, and became a lawyer. It was a different form of rescue work. Many of his cases were on behalf of men injured in copper mining. He was an ebullient, chubby man, with a small suitcase, a fishing rod, and a leather bookbag which contained a magnum bottle of Chivas Regal. His landing in Maine had been to buy lobsters, which he now produced for Paul to put in the pot for dinner. While we were eating, a thunderstorm arrived. It hung low over the house, lightning crackling all around us and the thunder growling. High up as we were in the charged air, our nerves weren't soothed when Paul mentioned that his house had been hit by lightning before, splitting the ceiling above where we now sat at the dining table. Jack Harper carried on, tucking into his lobster, and talked about fishing.

One evening at Paul's we met George Shafnacker for the first time. He came to dinner bringing a bluefish he had caught that afternoon in the Bay. George and Paul are rivals in fishing, but they also operate an excellent mutual-aid system, supplying each other with fish when the sea hasn't been fruitful. George is a sound recordist for a company that makes natural history films, and he is a local resident when he isn't in a South American jungle, on the Antarctic ice sheet, or on an East African mountain range. His mother has a summer cottage behind Fisher Beach near the Pamet. One of his brothers runs a tuna-fishing boat out of P'town. George has a house in Wellfleet. On several voyages we've spent the last day or so of our stay in these parts at George's, while waiting for storms to blow past; this has enabled us to get to know Wellfleet a little and enjoy George's living arrangements, which, despite his similar interest in fishing and gardening, aren't at all like Paul's.

This year George puts us up for a night. After checking *Lochinvar* in mid-morning, we drive George's car out to Great Island. This is the second "Great Island" we've encountered on the Cape, the first being at Hyannis, enclosing Uncle Roberts Cove, though in fact both chunks of land are promontories rather than islands. ("Herring River" and "Gull Pond" are other common Cape names.) We walk first on the Wellfleet Harbor side of this Great Island and, after a solitary mile, encounter another couple. He is wading waist-deep in the water, casting for fish; she is sitting on the beach. As we approach, she starts talking; she has long red fingernails and numerous rings on her fingers and clearly needs a listener. In short order we learn how they left western Massachusetts at 2:00 this morning in their camper truck and got here at 6:30. They do this most weekends. Her husband is a policeman. They've left the dogs at home, but the neighbors will look in on them . . . She jangles on, now and then glancing at the back of the fishing policeman, who is fifty feet away, concentrating on his sport, oblivious. She makes the best of us, fearing that if we leave she'll have no one else to talk to all day long. We hear about the house, and more about the dogs, and about the camper van, which is an improvement over the one they used to have, and how you get used to getting up at 2:00 and driving in the night, when there's hardly any traffic, even when you come over the Canal and hit the Cape. How that man loves fishing! It's a break from the police, not that there's a lot of crime where they live, just the usual car crash and break-in and barroom fight . . . Her bottle of Dusky Carmine is at the ready on the sand beside her. The policeman lifts his rod and makes a long cast. We say goodbye.

We cut through the pine woods and dunes to the Bay side of Great Island. (This, too, is part of the National Seashore, and the Park Service maintains trails and fencing to prevent people encroaching on the places where human erosion may be a problem.) As we head north up the beach, we come on a dead sand shark, about four feet long, a minor version of the killers of the deep. Margot points out the sand-speckled body of the fish to some passing children, anxious for them not to miss it. They are in advance of their parents, and they crowd around shouting, "A shark! A shark!" They dare each other to pick it up. The grownups decide to bury it.

On one stay with George he suggested that we go to swim not at a beach but in the woods east of Wellfleet. On a glaring hot day the seven ponds hidden in these woods are seven jewels—clear crystal—that cool you even as you admire them. A town resident's permit was needed, which George possessed, and a knowledge of how to get to them from where we left his car. We walked along sandy paths through thin mysterious woods and saw a small plant, which George said was wintergreen, whose little white berries could be eaten. The leaves when crushed released the smell familiar from Life Savers candy and chewing gum. We came to Dyer's Pond. Only one house was to be seen, perhaps the successor to a Walden-like cabin put up by a man called Dyer, but it was set tactfully back from the pond's edge and screened by trees. With the place entirely to ourselves, we scrambled down a sandy bank, startling a frog, and plunged into the clear yellow-green water. We could have been swimming in a glass of drinking water, though in this case it was a glass with sand at the bottom and shelving, sandy sides. We looked for arrowheads or other treasures but saw only a few small stones. The water was less buoyant than the sea, which should have caused us to expend more energy, but the pond made for repose.

Today rain sets in after midday when we return from Great Island. George has a young nephew he has promised to take to the movies, but to ensure that Margot and I aren't bored, he programs his video machinery so that we can watch a Fred Astaire film. In fact, it's not possible to be bored in George's house. It is a clapboard cottage of the late eighteenth or early nineteenth century, of the style that is now called Cape Cod. It has five rooms on the ground floor and several more, with dormer windows, squeezed up under the roof. It is crammed with artifacts that span two hundred years and spring from several hemispheres; some came with the house, some were acquired on George's travels. The house is only partly fixed up. A few rooms are clean and freshly painted; others have peeling wallpaper and damp-stained ceilings. One side porch or summer pantry has a sloping ceiling made of old fence pickets and cupboard doors. The washing machine, set on another enclosed porch, functions with the help of twenty feet of garden hose that can be connected to a tap on the kitchen sink, while George holds the downstream end of the hose in the machine. Several rooms are full of sound equipment in black trunks and boxes, so full, in one of the rooms, that you have to walk over the boxes to get to the far side. On the walls of the living room hang bows and spears made by Yanomami Indians in the jungle fastnesses along the upper Orinoco. Some of the spear points were once poisoned. One room, its faded blinds pulled down, is stuffed with dark old furniture, pictures, bookcases, an upright piano, dust, and cobwebs; one expects to see the Wellfleet Miss Havisham. There's a front door which is never used and has shrubbery growing against it.

Where Charlie Zender designed Paul's house to climb upward to peer over the treetops, George's house flows horizontally and naturally in various directions and through several doors into a wild garden of flowers and vegetables. The doors always seem to be open, at least in summer, but insects for some reason don't intrude. An orange female cat called Bill patrols the exits and entrances, mistress of the entire sweet disorder. Tea cannot be found in George's kitchen. Finally, in a cupboard containing fishing lures and electrical fittings, we uncover a packet of tea leaves that George brought back from China ten years ago. The cups are old earthenware jars that once contained Keiller's Dundee Marmalade. The tea tastes a bit dusty, but we don't complain. While the rain patters on the roof, we sprawl on George's bed upstairs, eat salami grinders, and watch *Shall We Dance?*

How George came by this house is the stuff of Wellfleet gossip, though his method happened to follow a long-established Cape and Islands custom. Thoreau wrote of houses built on lots in Provincetown to which titles were first obtained "by possession and improvement." The cottages in Sconset, as mentioned, were once taken over by squatters. George's house was lived in by a reclusive old man and his nephew, who (in the town's opinion) was a bit soft in the head. The old man died, and a few years later, so did the nephew. George often walked by the empty house, which already had roses growing in through the windows. He began to make inquiries: it seemed there were no known heirs; no one apparently owned the house; property taxes were long unpaid. George moved in. The town of Wellfleet decided that it would take over the house and refused George's payment of the back taxes. However, after five years of legal tussling, the town relented: George's possession was acknowledged by the courts and he is now the owner of the house.

In the late afternoon, Fred and Ginger over, the rain easing, Margot and I walk to Isabel Avellar's little house a mile away, on the road to the harbor. I swish along in my foul-weather gear, singing (quietly) "Won't you change partners and dance with me?" Isabel has lived in Wellfleet for many years; her older brother Ray is staying with her. He is now in his mid-eighties and used to live in Stonington; we've known him since we first went to live there. Over more cups of tea, now abetted by rainy-day drams of Myers's rum, we resume old times. Ray talks about his and Isabel's parents, who came from the Azores to New England when they were eighteen. They met on the sailing barque that brought them over and several years later they married. Ray and Isabel were born and grew up in Provincetown; he went to college at Dartmouth but dropped out after a year for lack of money. His first job was as a reporter for the Provincetown *Advocate,* which is still a weekly paper on this part of the Cape. In Provincetown Ray met his future wife, Katherine, a New York Art Students League pupil, when she came up one summer on a painting course. Ray worked toward the journalistic big time by way of suburban newspapers and eventually broke into New York, where he became a features writer on the *World-Telegram.*

When we first met Ray and Katherine in the early 1960s, they had just retired to Stonington and lived in the big 1840 Trumbull house on Cannon Square, looking out to the har-

bor over the guns which had held off the British in 1814.
They had no children, but Katherine and Ray used to give
candies to my small daughters when they went trick-or-
treating at Halloween. Among many kindnesses, Ray often
lent me his 15-foot Falcon to race at the local club. Today he
recalls the many newspapers New York once had: apart
from the *Times, News,* and *Post,* there were also the *World,*
the *Telegram,* the *Journal-American,* the *Mirror,* the *Sun,* the
Herald, the *Tribune,* and *PM.* Mergers for some only post-
poned doom. Talking of boats, he lists those he has owned,
including his first, a 19-foot day boat. At one time he had a
32-foot Alden cruising sloop which drew six feet and which
he ran aground in 1947 here in Wellfleet; the harbormaster
was on board directing him to a mooring and put Ray's boat
on a sandbank. Then there was *Sunflower,* a big Grand
Banks motor yacht, in which he and Katherine and then,
after Katherine's death, he alone used to cruise down the
waterway to Florida each fall and back to Stonington in the
spring. He has sold *Sunflower* but still hankers after a boat.
His residence now is an apartment in Jacksonville, but he
isn't all that keen on it. He is passing this summer with
Isabel, who is widowed, but he thinks the Cape is spoiled.
It's the problem with living in good places: they change. Too
many people find them good, but what can you do?

"And another thing," he adds, "the Cape has too many
memories for me."

I'm still young enough to think, Why should one mind
remembering? But I don't say this aloud, and on reflection
am glad I didn't.

As we leave, Isabel (who so far hasn't managed to get a
word in) says happily, "I haven't heard Ray talk that much
for ages."

•

Walking back through the village, we find the thrift shop has closed for the day, depriving us of bargains. But the fish market is still open; we buy flounder for dinner, waited on by a sixteen-year-old named Caleb Gilbert, whose summer job this is. Caleb is outspokenly curious about us. "Just got to town?" he asks.

"We sailed in a couple of days ago," I reply. "We're staying tonight with George Shafnacker."

"George!" exclaims Caleb. "He's teaching me the guitar."

Caleb asks what sort of boat we have and where we're going next. He also wants to know about the English school system and what I do for a living. A line of potential customers is piling up behind us and listening to our conversation with interest. I think we're undercharged for the flounder.

George and his friend Annie cook dinner: the flounder, linguine, and snowpeas. Annie is an actress who keeps afloat between stage engagements by baking bread, cakes, and pies at the Flying Fish restaurant half a mile away. She has brought a Key Lime pie for dessert and a baguette loaf for us to take to *Lochinvar* in the morning. George always strikes me as the mildest of men, but his film work takes him to dangerous places. In Rwanda he was once held captive by rebels for three days while filming a story about gorillas. Together with his producer-cameraman, he spent six weeks in Antarctic waters on a 45-foot ketch with an eccentric family which had agreed to take part in making a film but suddenly turned uncooperative somewhere south of Cape Horn. The French skipper refused to speak "on camera." One of the children, a five-year-old, harbored apparently murderous instincts toward George and his mates, and one night told George, with absolute conviction, "I'm going to stick a dagger in you while you sleep." ("We had another month to go before we could get off the boat," says George. "I had trouble closing my eyes.")

His most recent trip took him up the Orinoco to visit the Yanomami Indians, a more or less Stone Age lot who live on the border of Brazil and Venezuela. George shows us photographs of the expedition. In one, several of the Yanomami, who have no body hair, are to be seen touching George's hairy chest and smiling thoughtfully, while George looks as if he's being tickled. He brings forth a set of hand-carved points for spears and arrows, with barbs varied to suit different sorts of prey, such as birds and wild pigs. He acquired these, he says, in exchange for a Swiss army knife; the Indian who made the trade did so rather reluctantly, thinking, it seems, that George was getting the best of the deal. The Indian may have been wondering how useful the knife (and its associated implements: corkscrew, screwdriver, nail clippers, extractor of stones from horses' hoofs, etc.) would be in the jungle combat the Yanomami go in for. They live in small and internally quite peaceful groups of thirty or forty people, but have to keep an eye peeled for hostile members of other groups or ex-members of their own, thrown out for infractions of one kind or other, who may ambush them fatally while they are hunting or have just stepped out of camp to perform their bodily functions.

25

ONE OF THE LADS at the Wellfleet Marine float is hosing down the guano-encrusted decks, cabin top, and cockpit of a 30-foot sloop as we embark in the launch for *Lochinvar* in the late morning. He is still at it, using just the hose, without a scrubbing brush, forty minutes later when we depart from Wellfleet. Cormorants are the culprits. Drying their wings or admiring the view, they rest on the mast spreaders and radar scanners of the bigger boats. On some craft, if there are no radio antennae or burgee poles to tickle their tails, they stand on the very mastheads, like the Vineyard Haven osprey. One boat owner, I notice, has hung four fenders from halyards, with downhauls attached, so that the fenders dangle at spreader height and keep the birds at bay. But this doesn't stop one cheeky Wellfleet cormorant from calmly perching at the outboard end of a spreader, just out of range of a swaying fender, even though there's no room for wing stretching. We have only a few crap marks on our deck. The bird which may be responsible lands briefly on a spreader, but takes off again when it realizes we are making ready for sea. We put away our clean clothes and tie to a cabin-top handrail a short fishing rod Paul has given us. He can't understand how we can spend all August on a boat without trying to catch bluefish.

We stow the provisions in the places we've now come to agree they should be in: Pepperidge Farm cookies in a cake tin on the bookshelf; Thomas' English muffins in the drawer at the fore end of the port bunk; cans of Pabst Blue Ribbon at the foot of the hanging locker. Everything has to be stowed carefully, because the weather has gone to pot. Today is gray and humid, with a sou'westerly wind already blowing 20 and forecast to blow 25; a "small craft advisory," as the federal weather-radio announcers call it, is in effect. "You can tell we're on the return voyage," says Margot. "The wind is on the nose." A tropical storm is also mentioned as being somewhere off the Bahamas and strengthening, though it's nothing to worry about right now. (Surely it is too early in the year for hurricanes in New England.) With a reef in the main and the number-three genoa, our smallest foresail, we fetch out around the breakwater and down Wellfleet Harbor on the starboard tack. We wriggle, quick-tacking, through the channel past Jeremy Point and stand south to the green buoy on Stony Bar to clear Billingsgate Island, before going about again and heading westward. Our foul-weather gear keeps much of the spray from penetrating, but as always we get damp inside our supposedly waterproof jackets and trousers from sweat, condensation, and—where we sit on damp cockpit seats—what feels like osmosis.

I try to steer sensitively, ducking the worst of the waxy

green waves by turning *Lochinvar* slightly away from them; but some can't be avoided and shower us heavily. No wave is the same as the one before. When after an hour of this the Billingsgate Shoal buoy appears ahead, I tack south for the Cape Cod shore, seeking quieter water in the lee of the land. Under the lee, we turn westward again for another hour until we reach the red-and-white buoy off Barnstable bar. This will do for progress today. As we tack, just laying the tricky entrance channel into Barnstable, Margot spots a large fish a boat length away, a big globular creature apparently standing on its head and waving its stumpy tail. It is happily absorbed in its own motion and oblivious to us. "No fin," Margot says; it is therefore not a shark. (Maybe a sunfish, we later decide, after consulting the fish book.)

This entrance into Barnstable isn't one I'd attempt in this weight of wind if it was blowing onshore. The water is shallow over the bar. With a wind from the north and the seas heaping up, the likelihood of broaching would be considerable. We would have an excellent chance of leaving the narrow channel and striking the sands on either side. You would need God with you, as Hilaire Belloc had when he crossed the similar bar at Rye, in Sussex, in his cutter *Nona*. Four times he touched, but never struck. Even today the buoys marking the Barnstable channel are hard to see. The chart tells us that the channel is "subject to continual changes," and not only does it seem to swing to the east between buoys 4 and 8 but buoy 6 is missing, as some of the marks in one's course through life tend to be. We hurriedly examine the water ahead. We also remember that the twin water tanks on the distant skyline behind Barnstable make a handy range, and we attempt to line them up with the sandy point on the western side of the entrance to the harbor. *Lochinvar* heels in a rain squall and both point and water tanks disappear from view, but I try to keep her on the compass heading I've just taken. Fortunately even in this weather the deeper water is apparent as darker; the lighter areas on each side are clearly the no-go shallows. And the water smooths out as we round Beach Point with its collection of modest, old-fashioned summer cottages. These are presided over by a small abandoned lighthouse, but it is no longer close enough to the present point to serve as a useful mark.

Barnstable Harbor, more than any other place I know on this coast, has the feeling of old England; but it is the feeling not, as the Devon name might suggest, of the West Country but of East Anglia. Once we get around the point we're confronted by a wide expanse of fairly shallow water, enclosed by dunes and salt marshes. The tides rush in and out, changing the landscape by exposing or covering the mud, sands, and marsh, and changing the light. I associate the place with certain Essex creeks, where you need to anchor with precision, picking what might be an exposed spot but one that has the depth required to prevent a grounding at low tide. You have to plant the hook so that when the tide surges and the wind blows against it, you don't (as I've confessed we did once in Nantucket) swing into other craft—though here the moored local craft are few. The East Anglian feeling may also spring from a fine loneliness, for no town or village is visible from our anchorage and we are the only cruising boat at anchor here.

Most of the local craft are powerboats with swordfishing pulpits and tuna-spotting towers. Many tie up at the slips, finger piers, and wharves off Maraspin Creek, a narrow gully with a dredged basin that runs south from the harbor toward the town of Barnstable, half a mile inland. These sportfishing boats charge past our anchorage on their way home, creating wakes that threaten to dislodge our safe-in-port cups of tea. On several occasions we've rowed up Maraspin Creek, turning east under a low concrete road bridge (disturbing the pigeons which roost beneath it) and following the extension of the creek that winds into the marshes. One calm night we came in from *Clio* to the restaurant which stands near the powerboat slips, glad for food we didn't have to prepare in the cramped cabin, grateful for friendly service, and not too bothered by the live electric organ music. On another night, three years ago, we sat in the cockpit after a shipboard dinner on *Lochinvar* and watched an eclipse of the moon. It was a total eclipse, which began at 9:30. The moon was full, a huge candlelit pumpkin hanging over Yarmouth marshes to the east, and the earth's shadow slowly took a bigger and bigger bite out of it until it was gone and its face was in darkness. Then, magically, it began to remake itself.

Tonight we are grateful when the damp and grumpy wind drops away a little at sunset, though it is by no means a calm night, and I have to tweak out the separate halyards with shock cord and line to stop them pinging annoyingly against the mast. Later, a change of noise or motion wakes me at the turn of the tide. As the mass of water in the harbor runs out, the wind no longer bucks the tide and *Lochinvar* stretches back at ease on her phosphorescent anchor rode.

The wind is still southwest in the morning, but not yet as brisk as yesterday. We get under way at 8:30 and run out of Barnstable. There's a mist, and it will be hot. Under full main and the number-two genoa we make for the east end of the canal, cutting across the shallow concave curve of the beach which runs west to Sandwich. *Lochinvar* romps along, sheets eased a little, a touch free of close-hauled. The power station's huge chimney, which should be our landmark, remains resolutely obscured in the haze until we are close in. As we approach the shore, now beginning to bend north, the breeze freshens and heads us. Strong gusts, sometimes torrid, sometimes cool, tear away from the land toward us. We have to make several tacks to gain the canal entrance and are carrying more sail than we should for speed or comfort; we tell ourselves (unwisely) that we're so close to the canal it isn't worth putting in a reef or donning foul-weather gear. Several other boats that have approached from the north are beating in with us, and as we cross forward or astern of each other, carefully giving right of way to the boat on the starboard tack, the skippers take a hand from straining tiller or vibrating wheel to give a comradely wave.

In the mouth of the canal, damp but thankful, we start the engine, roll up the jib, and drop the main, so as to preserve its stitching from the shaking it would otherwise get, motoring into the wind. As we pass the marina of tears and the power station, we're joined by half a dozen porpoises. They are presumably fishing, not just gamboling, here in the warm water released from the power plant. They swim in formation with a constant semicircular motion, rolling over and under in the churning current with their backs arched. They seem to be having fun rather than working for a living.

At the west end of the canal we're met with a typical Buzzards Bay greeting. The air is a murky orange-gray; tall wind-against-tide combers corrugate the channel. After roller-coastering over these for twenty minutes with less grace than the porpoises had shown near the power station, we sidle southeast under main alone toward Wings Neck. I've been considering Marion, a harbor on the northwest shore of Buzzards Bay, as our destination for this afternoon, but somewhere closer now seems desirable. So we round the south end of Bassetts Island once again and run up the narrow waterway to Red Brook Harbor. This time, however, we do without a Parker's Boatyard mooring and anchor in seven feet of water in the sheltered bight east of Bassetts. Woods on the northern, private part of the island grow to the edge of the beach. Ten other birds of passage like us are anchored here, in the lee of the island, a safe roost for the night.

After a late lunch, I take oil, grease, plastic tape, wire brush, knife, marlin spike, and pliers, and subject *Lochinvar* to a detailed fore-and-aft, deck-to-bilges inspection. A boat is always slowly going wrong. Some items deteriorate visibly, some want to have you think that all is well and then suddenly sock it to you. The anchor shackles, the turnbuckles or rigging screws, the cotter pins holding blocks and bolts, all must be checked. I drop and squeeze oil into the winches, blocks, roller-furling gear, and the fitting which connects the tiller to the rudder post. I crawl headfirst into the hatch which gives awkward access to the starboard side of the engine and give a half turn to the greasing screw on the water pump. I unfasten the lid of the engine cooling-water strainer and lift out the wire-mesh cylinder which is meant to collect eelgrass before it clogs the system and the engine overheats— as it nevertheless does once a season. The throttle and choke mechanisms are oiled. Grease is rammed into the toilet seacocks and lubricating fluid is pumped into the valves. I fill the kerosene anchor light and the cabin lamp; this is a procedure which invariably extends smelly kerosene to one's hands and whatever surface the lamps are standing on, so it might as well be done now, when my hands are mucky. I also trim the ragged blackened tops of the wicks. Then I force some calking compound into a seam of the icebox, grumbling aloud about its continued propensity to leak.

"You must be having a good time," says Margot. She holds the belief—common, in my National Service days, among British army officers—that as long as the men are grousing, their morale is high.

Jobs done, I row Margot down to the publicly owned southern part of Bassetts. The lower leg of the island has a gently sloping beach on its eastern side, facing Red Brook Harbor, and a more shelving beach facing westward on the small bay between Wings Neck and Scraggy Neck. On the thin spine of the island grow scrubby little trees, beach roses, and poison ivy. On the inner beach, communities of winkle snails cluster around the borders of pools, which the tide has left. On the outer beach is a richer assortment of shells. The slipper shells take our fancy, and we find it hard to stop picking up the pale yellow, thin, and translucent ones. Here somebody has built a monster out of sand, its serpent scales formed by pressing a child's beach bucket into the fat lizardlike back, its eyes made of shells. I wonder if its creator has seen the Elihu Vedder Monomoy serpent in Boston; or do we all have a similar monster in the back of our mind? The next tide will cover it.

Rowing back to *Lochinvar*, we hail some of our anchored neighbors and wonder about staying here tomorrow. It's a good place. I don't mind losing our so recently regained momentum. Our company includes a handsome

32-foot wooden cutter and a big, seagoing blue ketch. One high-sided fiberglass sloop is managed by a spry, elderly, white-bearded man, and we set against the ungainly looks of his craft his single-handedness. The boat is called *Dulcinea,* the dinghy *Sancho.* His own first name must be Don. But we are all romantics or we wouldn't be here. As harbors go, the character of this has the right variety of houses, boatyards, and boats on the moorings. There are some fancy residences around Hospital Cove and on Scraggy Neck, but there are also modest summer houses with screened side and front porches. Looking at their upright, boxy façades, I can imagine the small, square rooms inside them. I can almost furnish them with old rounded-top refrigerators, matchboard wainscoting in the kitchens, linoleum curling up in the corners. The harbor is satisfyingly spacious, yet snug. After dark, lights come on in many of the houses we have been admiring, and also, dimly through the trees at the north end of Bassetts, from a house we hadn't noticed there during the day.

26

SUNDAY: We get up at 8:00, which is late on *Lochinvar*. The morning is overcast and already hot. The weather radio chunters while the coffee water boils. Thoughts of staying put today are rapidly displaced by plans to move on. The forecast for tomorrow, Monday, which we had thought of using to sail in a southwesterly direction down Buzzards Bay, is for southwest winds, 25 to 30. The forecast for today is southwest 20 to 25. No Sabbath rest, therefore, for *Lochinvar*. The radio mentions offhandedly that the tropical storm, Bob, now upgraded to the status of a full hurricane, may be heading for the Carolina coast. I had a close encounter with a hurricane while on the Outer Banks a few years ago and, while sympathetic to that area, would just as soon it went there rather than here. In any event, the forecast doesn't dwell on Bob, and neither do I. Today's wind is what matters and it is predicted to be slightly less bothersome than tomorrow's.

Out in Buzzards Bay the wind is quite strong enough for us. The Bay is surely the birthplace of the smoky sou'wester—the afternoon breeze of high summer. With the sun behind it, the spray-filled air is a yellow-gray haze. If the current is setting down the Bay, the waves are short, steep, and wet. In Buzzards Bay I'm often tempted to sail in the early mornings and stay in harbor in the afternoons, when it breezes up. Then while *Lochinvar* fusses around on her anchor rode, I can take a long walk or sit and read, say, Llewellyn Howland's *South by South-West of Cape Cod,* an account of growing up amid boating folk in the village of South Dartmouth, which most of the natives call Padanaram, west of New Bedford. I've heard people on this coast talk about giving up sailing; when questioned they often say that it isn't because they can no longer afford it or are fed up maintaining their boat, but simply because of some grim experience in Buzzards Bay—a split sail or a dinghy which broke loose and was lost. "Maybe we're just not up to handling it anymore," they murmur, intimidated by the blustery bay.

We thrash across it from Scraggy Neck to Bird Island, off the mouth of Sippican Harbor, before tacking southward. Bird Island, small and uninhabited, has a dumpy little lighthouse, restored, like many of these old structures, by local volunteers. Its uninspired name makes me think about the Bay's "buzzardets," as the early colonists called them, and which some authorities believe were ospreys on the grounds that buzzards didn't frequent these waters. However, two years ago Margot saw a buzzard wheeling overhead as we approached Padanaram from the Bay and said it was an ill omen, probably intended for us personally. Padanaram is our goal today, our friends the Hollisters having been told to expect us Monday or perhaps Sunday; and so I keep

Lochinvar going across the wide mouth of Sippican Harbor, at whose top end is the small town of Marion. Marion is a sedate place with many decorous old houses and an excellent general store with higgledy-piggledy shelves and a floor which slopes like the deck of a boat going to windward. It also has several good boatyards, the boys' school of Tabor Academy, and the Beverly Yacht Club, which was founded by yachting refugees from north of Boston who decided they liked Buzzards better. The harbor is thick with moorings and expensive yachts. Last year we anchored off Allens Point, near the entrance to Blankinship Cove, a bit too far from town for an easy row. The big waterfront houses on the point were all competing with one another to have the tallest flagpole and the largest Stars and Stripes. One huge pole and flag were actually floodlit at night, perhaps flaunting something other than patriotism.

We are soon a mile offshore again on this blowy morning. From here the Bay presents a northern-looking coastline: a band of dark blue-green trees above a line of rocky gray-brown beach. The indentations of the shore are smoothed out by distance, and you can pass scarcely aware of bays and harbors, or at least without feeling a strong impulse to enter them. So we sail by Mattapoisett, Nasketucket Bay, New Bedford, and Clarks Cove. Padanaram was the part of Mesopotamia, mentioned in Genesis, to which Isaac sent Jacob to get himself a wife. Our approach to its New England namesake is by way of Apponagansett Bay. The general anonymity of the shore is broken at the foot of this bay by a lofty steel-and-concrete structure which looks like a giant birdbath or martini glass. In fact, it is an early radar device put up in the 1940s by M.I.T., threatened not long ago with demolition but, by local demand, preserved as an excellent landmark. We keep the chart close at hand, since numerous rocks, ledges, and shoals are scattered in Apponagansett Bay. On occasion as we've sailed in here we've encountered Buell Hollister, sailing out to meet us in his ketch-rigged leeboard sharpie, the *Lark,* or in the *Lark*'s equally unmistakable successor, the *Olivebank.* The *Olivebank,* named after one of the last square-rigged sailing ships, is a chunky 30-foot British motor sailer. She used to belong to Buell's uncle, our Stonington neighbor Peter Tripp, who converted her rig from an ordinary Bermudan sloop to a junk-rigged schooner. But today *Olivebank*'s tan bat-wing sails aren't to be seen.

Just inside the Padanaram breakwater we round up into the wind and furl our sails. We motor up the channel, which takes us through the moorings of several hundred yachts and past the impressive docks and building of the New Bedford Yacht Club, situated several miles from the odoriferous and boisterous commercial fishing activity of the New Bedford waterfront. The yacht club's next-door neighbor is the Concordia boatyard, haunt of the Howland family and home of many beautiful wooden boats, including the narrow, low-freeboard Concordia 39-foot and 41-foot yawls, each of which has a Concordia star on each side of its pert bow. Not far beyond the Concordia yard a stone-faced causeway carrying a road crosses the harbor. The gap through which the channel passes is spanned by a low swing bridge. The procedure for gaining entrance to the upper harbor and Apponagansett River has changed over the years: different signals, different times of opening. When I telephoned Buell from North Truro to find out the current situation, he told me that the bridge opens these days every half hour. We are not alone; several other boats are circling slowly, awaiting the three o'clock opening. Before long, bells ring, barriers drop, cars halt, and the Sunday-afternoon fishermen move off the bridge onto the causeway. The bridge spins silently and slowly on its central axis. Two rather scanty gaps appear. We wave to the portly bridge tender and motor through the right-hand gap. We head up the channel for several hundred yards before steering toward the eastern side of the upper harbor, where the chart shows only two feet of water. Here *Olivebank,* drawing four feet, is moored, masts raked forward, her junk sails stowed like Venetian blinds. (She does sink into the mud a little at low water, Buell admits.) *Lochinvar,* let it be remembered, draws three and a half with the board up. Since the tide is still high, we rig fenders and mooring lines and raft up comfortably alongside *Olivebank.*

Our recollections of Padanaram are largely rose-tinted, centered as they are on visits to the Hollisters at their house on Gladys Street, which runs down to the upper harbor. But one less cheerful memory jumps to mind as I look over the shallows between *Lochinvar* and the shore and take in the surroundings. Little Island, also called Monkey Island by the locals, lies to the north; various motorboats are moored nearby, as are two authentic houseboats, which are really small wooden houses built on barge-like hulls. Many summer cottages and more substantial year-round houses line the shore and shelter among the trees on the slopes behind. Several landing places are also visible from *Olivebank's* mooring. Disembarking at the informal one at the end of Gladys Street involves scrambling over slimy rocks. The one at the foot of Hill Street is more organized, with wooden stairs down to a short sandy beach where a number of dinghies are hauled up.

A few summers ago, going ashore for dinner with Buell and Margaret, we decided to leave our dinghy at Hill Street. It seemed less trouble than Gladys Street, though it involved a longer walk. Returning to the landing at ten o'clock, we found the dinghy not quite where we'd left it, and without its oars. We explored the nearby beach and looked in other dinghies. But no sign of our oars. Hell hath no fury like that of a boatman whose oars have been stolen. It is the lowest of low tricks. I swore into the calm, starlit night. The oars were painted gray and were properly long, and their fine leather chafe guards had been fastened on with copper nails. I'd had them for years, and they had gone to sea with boats of mine with whose modest adventures they'd been intimately associated. I cursed the malefactor. May the oars snap when he is rowing in a fast ebbtide! May his dinghy wash up on rocks and shatter!

We walked back up the hill of Hill Street, along the main road, and down Gladys Street again to Buell and Margaret's. They were washing the dinner dishes. Buell lent us a pair of oars Peter Tripp had made, homely but precious heirlooms. I promised to return them on the morrow when I'd bought some new ones, assuming oars were available in Padanaram. Then we trudged back to Hill Street again and rowed out to *Lochinvar*. I slept badly. Several times I woke in a fury and thought up tortures for oar thieves. After breakfast, still full of useless spleen, we went ashore to purchase new oars. After a windless night, the morning was calm and clear. As I rowed toward the bridge, Margot in the stern facing forward said, "An oar! There's an oar in the water!" I rowed to where she was pointing. When I turned around I saw a gray oar, one of ours, floating half-submerged in the placid water. I was pulling it aboard when

Margot added, "And there's the other! Over there!"

We thanked the gods. We were lucky it had been such a calm night. Although the tide had gone out and come in, our oars had not wandered far. Whether they had been thrown in out of malice or stupidity, by drunken fishermen or young vandals, no longer mattered. It was pure chance we had decided to row down under the bridge to Davis and Tripp's chandlery. If we had landed at Gladys Street we wouldn't have seen them.

"*Lochinvar!*"

A 17-foot skiff is approaching under sail, with Buell at the tiller. We apologize for being a day early in arriving. Buell, holding on to our gunwale, says, "It's just as well. When do you think we should start getting ready?"

"Ready for what?"

"For Bob—the hurricane. It's expected to hit here around noon tomorrow."

27

GLADYS STREET is short, sloping, and lined with old trees and about a dozen houses that date from between the wars. Most of its residents have lived there for a long time—one old lady since 1906. Number 5, Buell and Margaret's summer home, has been extensively rebuilt since they bought it a few years ago; one of the improvements is an upstairs balcony or deck with a splendid wide-angle view to the opposite bank of the Apponagansett River, more than half a mile away. This is Padanaram's upper harbor. Panning from left to right, you can see from the western end of the causeway, over the moorings (including *Olivebank*'s), to Monkey Island. Buell works for the Massachusetts Division of Marine Fisheries as an information and research officer, and Margaret is a counselor for a service advising infertile women; most of the year they live in Boston. Also on hand today at 5 Gladys Street are Margaret's sister, Jane Russell, a financial planner, and her husband, Fred Gorman, a language teacher and archaeologist. Although they had planned to return home to Boston tonight, they have decided to stay. But another guest room is allotted to Margot and me.

After the evening weather forecast on television, Buell and I drive to buy flashlight and radio batteries, masking tape, candles, and pizza for six. Hurricanes can of course change direction at the last minute, but there's little doubt that right now Bob is coming this way. It is expected to reach land early Monday afternoon. It is reported to have winds of up to 120 miles an hour. This is a somewhat different forecast from the one we got from the weather radio this morning, as we lay at anchor behind Bassetts Island: Monday, SW, 25–30. Had we known Bob was heading for New England, we might have stayed put in the shelter of Red Brook Harbor. However, in threatening circumstances, there's a lot to be said for being among friends. The New England phones are busy tonight as warnings and reassurances are exchanged and plans for tomorrow explained. I call Betty Richards in Stonington to tell her where we are. Her daughter Amy works for a Mystic boatyard and in marine matters is wise beyond her years. I can hear her shouting to Betty, "Tell Tony to take off everything above decks that he can."

Buell and I are up in the dark at 5:30. We have a busy few hours. I bear in mind Amy's advice, for windage is crucial. On *Olivebank,* first of all, Buell and I lower behind the bulwarks the heavy junk-rigged sails with their many battens and hefty spars; we lash them down. *Olivebank* has unalterable windage in her two chunky masts, a full-headroom wheelhouse, and a raised poop containing her stern cabin, but she also lies to a 1,500-pound mooring and stout tackle. On *Lochinvar,* I take down both main and jib and bundle them into the fo'c'sle. The main boom is slid into the cabin. The ventilator air scoops, life ring, boat hook, fishing rod, and mop, all have to go below. I tie the halyards out away from the mast with double, no, triple lashings.

Buell and I power *Lochinvar* away from *Olivebank*'s side and prospect the surrounding waters of the curiously calm upper harbor. Finding the right spot to anchor her in the shallows isn't easy, among the many moored motorboats and the two houseboats. But eventually I choose a place where the depth is three and a half feet at low water and where *Lochinvar* will have room to lie back on her anchor lines when the wind comes in, as it's first expected to, from the southeast. We'll have to worry later on about what may happen if the wind goes around to the northwest. We put out three anchors in an arc of a rough 45 degrees: my 20-pound Danforth, my 30-pound Fisherman, and a 35-pound CQR plow anchor from *Olivebank*'s arsenal, each on some chain and much nylon warp, giving about a hundred feet of scope on each anchor. Because the main anchor cleat is now crowded with line, I take the tails of each rode around the mast and then around the cockpit sheet winches before making them fast. As we have done with *Olivebank*'s mooring pennant, we protectively wrap and bind the anchor lines where they come through the fairleads at the bow. For this we use some heavy rubber hose, meant for the job, on two, and for the third a stout piece of gray suede elk skin which Buell's uphill neighbor Al, a sailmaker, has given us. The tiller is lashed amidships. Before leaving, we look intently at our work and at the way *Lochinvar* is lying. Buell says, "Well, you're in as good a spot as there is here—in the lee of the land for a sou'easter, and in good holding ground."

Still, 120 miles an hour of wind is not your usual test. I
pat *Lochinvar*'s weathered teak cockpit coaming as we
climb into the dinghy and hope aloud my small ship will be
safe. Buell, I know, is too much of a sailor himself to con-
demn this as mere sentimentality.

At 8:30, as we row ashore, it's still calm, but gray and
heavy with it. Buell remarks that no one has been saying in
the last few days, "Sure feels like hurricane weather," the
way people often do toward the sultry end of summer. We
should try to remember, this is how it does feel, pre-hurricane:
it isn't much different from the atmosphere before other
stormy days in August. Margot, Margaret, Jane, and Fred
have been taping window glass, but they help us remove
our small boats from the outhauls off the rocks at the end
of Gladys Street. We roll the skiff up into the Hollister
driveway and carry *Olivebank*'s and *Lochinvar*'s dinghies
into the backyard, where they are tied to a tree. Then, after
a big 9:30 breakfast, we catch up with the weather on TV.
Bob is now not far south of eastern Long Island and heading fast on a northeasterly course that will bring its eye over
East Hampton and Block Island to Narragansett Bay. As
Buell points out, that puts us in the dangerous sector, east
of the eye. Tropical storms in the northern hemisphere spin
counterclockwise, so in the sector east of the hurricane's
core its revolving wind speed has to be added to its forward
speed to get the total blast. For example, to the 80 knots of
rotating wind you add 30 knots of forward speed and get a
cumulative 110 knots, or roughly 125 miles per hour. (In
the same way, west of the eye, the hurricane's force is less,
since the forward speed must be deducted from the rotating
wind speed.)

The 9:30 forecast is for 115 knots maximum. Tide levels

of ten to fifteen feet above normal are to be expected. We work out what this might mean for us. High tide is at 4:40 this afternoon and the worst thing will be if Bob strikes hardest then, blowing its maximum from the southeast and sending in a storm surge at the top of the tide. But it looks as if it will get here before then, shortly after midday. Let's hope so.

Margaret says that 1 and 3 Gladys Street have been evacuated. Number 2, the ramshackle waterfront house on the north side, is still occupied, she thinks; like Number 1, it sits about three feet above the level of a normal high tide. It belongs to an elderly man called Brad, whose large family of cats is fed on corncobs in summer. Once a year Brad is to be seen taking a dip, fully clothed, in the upper harbor. (He apparently likes to combine social decency with his annual clothes wash.) But there's no sign at his house that either he or the cats are taking hurricane precautions.

While Jane and Fred hold the fort, Buell, Margaret, Margot, and I walk to the village center at 11:00. There's a thin rain, high gray clouds, but no real menace in the air, though the wind is getting up. On the road, cars with boats on trailers are fleeing inland, headlights on. In some gardens guy ropes have been attached to young trees. At the junction near the bridge Padanaram's shopkeepers are nailing plywood over their plate-glass windows. The bridge tender tells us he opened the bridge at 9:00 to let in a couple of boats and let out a fishing boat whose skipper had decided to make a dash for New Bedford, hoping to get in before the port's hurricane barrier is closed. Perhaps prompted by an uncomfortable premonition, I say, "Wouldn't it make sense to leave the bridge open?"

"Can't do that," he says. "Emergency vehicles have to be able to get across the causeway."

We gaze out at the boats, facing fretfully into the wind—certainly southeast now. The outer harbor seems full, though Buell says that he thinks some of the three hundred boats have left their moorings to go through the bridge to the upper harbor. On the slipway inside the bridge about forty ducks have congregated; they look ready to fly, swim, or walk. As we walk back past the Hill Street landing we notice a motorboat turned over, already capsized, with a slick of gasoline all around it. Must be an insurance job, we agree. The rain is coming down more heavily and the gusts of wind are stronger; a few willow branches crack and fall. We hasten back to Gladys Street.

There, Buell and Fred and I take up the watch on the upper deck, facing west. We have front-row seats which, to begin with, are sheltered from the wind and rain. At 11:50 Jane comes up from the television to announce that the governor of Rhode Island has closed the roads in his state to all except police and emergency vehicles. The clouds are looser and lower. Whitecaps are racing diagonally away from us across the upper harbor. I recall Margot a little while back complaining, "We sail to the same places every year and nothing much ever happens." I look around to remind her of this, but she is loading the electric drier with some washed clothes—Buell and I have each gone through several pairs of shirts and shorts this morning. Buell has brought ashore *Olivebank*'s powerful binoculars, and through these we see at the far side of the harbor a man on the foredeck of a big blue sloop letting out more anchor line. The cockpit cover on one powerboat is already flapping loose and tearing. *Olivebank* and *Lochinvar*, a mere two hundred yards away, are easily seen without the binoculars. *Lochinvar* looks as if she is riding to two of her three anchors at once. I can almost feel the increasing gusts of wind hit my boat as she heels slightly and then bobs aside. I take a bearing on her, lining up the corner of the deck, *Lochinvar*'s mast, and a point on the farther shore, so as to tell if she starts to drag. The two bulky houseboats are worryingly near her.

Between noon and 1:00: Buell fetches bottles of beer up to the deck. Margaret and Jane are making sandwiches. The rain thickens, thins, thickens again. A cormorant continues to fish off the end of Gladys Street. The light changes from minute to minute, from bright gray to murky gray. As yet, there's none of the yellow-orange one associates with hurricanes, but Fred assures us it will come. Jane says the TV is now giving out emergency telephone numbers and the location of shelters at New Bedford area fire stations and schools. The bridges over Narragansett Bay are all closed and Interstate 95 between Boston and New York is shutting. People are being evacuated from shore communities along Buzzards Bay, but campers in the Bourne Park by the Cape Cod Canal are said to be sticking their heels in. Buell says, "The family we bought this house from told us that in the 1938 hurricane the water came just up to the front door." Green leaves begin to fly past the deck. A wet cat, maybe one of Brad's, chases a leaf along the low harborside wall, over which water is beginning to lap. On several sailing craft roller jibs are unfurling and flogging to pieces. Jane relays a TV report: Block Island is now recording winds of 70 miles per hour. "It's almost that here," says Buell.

At one o'clock, the surface of the upper harbor is hidden from time to time under spray being driven in horizontal streams; the wind sounds like a high-pitched engine with the throttle stuck open. Boats are beginning to drag or break loose: a powerboat on the far side of the harbor is moving backward, northwest; a green 30-foot sloop goes sideways up the middle of the harbor, disappearing behind Monkey Island. However, *Olivebank* seems to be taking it sedately; her raked-forward masts make her look purposeful, as she tucks in her chin like a boxer keeping up his guard. *Lochinvar*—smaller, lighter, and on greater scope—seems to be beating to windward under bare poles, first on one tack, then on the other, of course not gaining ground, but not losing it yet either. I keep reassuring myself of this by checking from another vantage point, moving from upstairs deck to downstairs window and back up again. Another worry is what may drag or simply blow against *Lochinvar*—one of the houseboats, for instance. One is lying downwind of her now, but may be in a more dangerous position if the wind shifts. In fact, it is already veering from southeast to south, and *Lochinvar* is less in the lee of the land on this side of the harbor. Her bow dives into the swollen waves. She heels violently, exposing much of her hull underwater. Can I stand the anxiety of watching this for several hours? And if it is this rough in here, what's it like in the harbor below the bridge?

Not long after one o'clock the TV reports that electricity has failed in Fall River. Then the green light of the screen at 5 Gladys Street fades. The drier stops. Outside, a six-foot section of back-garden fence blows down. The engine of the wind now sounds like a jet, screaming steadily. At 1:45 Buell—whose absence I hadn't noticed—struggles in through the front door, clad in streaming foul-weather gear, his video camera wrapped in a plastic bag. He has driven to the village. He says, shouting a little from being wind-deafened, "It's like a war down there. Trees falling everywhere. At least six yachts against the bridge, going to pieces, and many more along the causeway, I think—it was hard to see."

He gets out more beer from the dark refrigerator. "Better drink it while it's still cold," he says. (The beer is almost solidly frozen, it seems to me.) The radio is battery-powered, but stations are abruptly blotted out as their transmitters lose power. On those still broadcasting, commercials and pop music continue amid the advice and warnings. "Stay inside," says one announcer, as if he had noticed Buell coming back. "I will," says Buell. On the outside of the windows raindrops are being forced upward. Another section of fence blows down.

At 2:00 the wind has gone around so that the upstairs deck is no longer tenable. As I shut its sliding door behind me I can hear amid the fierce keening of the wind the awful sound of a sail shaking and tearing apart. A good deal of the harbor is coming up Gladys Street and the lower half of the fire hydrant at the foot of the street is underwater. Brad's house foundations are awash. From the utility poles all sorts of wires and cables are dangling. Inside Number 5, the air is as steamy as a bathroom and Margaret opens a few inches of window on the leeside. From the front windows we watch all sorts of things blow up the harbor. The waves are being decapitated by the wind, their crests snatched up bodily and subsumed into a harbor-wide layer of water that is flying northward. Fred says, "I think boats are beginning to wash over the causeway." We pass around the binoculars and get glimpses of masts at strange angles, keels pointing at the sky. A section of dock approaches *Lochinvar* and just misses her. Dinghies, crates, bait barrels, rafts, and pilings tumble past. "That hut had the New Bedford Yacht Club burgee painted on it," says Jane. A big table, four legs in the air, sails by *Lochinvar*. Boats I have been using as reference points have vanished, including a handsome old catboat. One of the houseboats—fortunately the one beyond *Lochinvar*—takes off upharbor. Through the thick dim air I make out a big sloop, at least forty feet long, going like a runaway horse toward the woods. If *Lochinvar* goes, it should be now, while there is mud and marsh to leeward. If she goes later on, with the wind still veering, she may not escape the rocks or a rocky seawall. But this kind of weak-kneed thought has to be pushed aside. She must hang on.

Just before 3:00, the water has reached the hedge next door. Several lifejackets and boat fenders have washed and blown into the front garden of Number 5. The cormorant is still flapping into the wind but not making any forward progress; perhaps he has decided that he's better off in the air than perched on a wave-swept rock or the spreaders of a mast about to collapse, as some have. The far side of the harbor appears for a moment. There's a glimmer of wild blue sky, even of sun, and a hint that the scream of the wind is a fraction less. Is this the eye?

Bob is now blowing from the west, across the harbor and up Gladys Street. *Lochinvar*'s stern is pointed toward us, but for some reason she doesn't seem too close to a couple of small motorboats moored there. I'd feared she might bump them as the wind swung. At 3:30, the wind continuing to veer into the northwest, the water level on the hydrant has actually gone down. There is still an hour before the forecast time for high water. But the wind continues to blow furiously and may in fact be blowing out the supposedly incoming tide. One advantage of this is that the boats we now see littering the far shore, heeled over, keels exposed, won't be floated off and then blow down our way.

At 3:50, six ducks paddle in convoy past the end of Gladys Street, close-hauled and heading for Monkey Island. On the radio, a NOAA weather report: "Hurricane Bob will make land on the Rhode Island and Massachusetts coasts this afternoon." It already has. There are more pertinent warnings of flash floods and tornadoes. On an advice program a woman asks if insurance will pay for the removal of a tree from her swimming pool. Two fishing vessels, *Lady of Grace* and *Sonia & Nancy*, are reported damaged in New Bedford harbor. The owner of 3 Gladys Street calls from Boston and wants to know how things are. Margaret tells him the water stopped just short of his ground floor. He says he just heard on TV that Padanaram has been hit the worst of all.

Bob, moving away north and weakening, still has howling winds and driving rain to hurl back at us. With the wind from this angle, the house mews like a cat. But I'm running out of zip. Nervous exhaustion, says Margot. While I take a nap, she keeps an eye on Gladys Street. More flotsam appears: half a dory, a life ring, boat sponges, shattered tree branches, many green apples, and a bottle of pills. A big tree up the street has fallen, bringing down power lines. Brad's garage door is open and cats can be seen squabbling inside. A dogwood tree in Al's back garden next door has split down the middle; half rests against his kitchen roof. Fred and Buell have also crashed out, but— testimony to greater female endurance—Margaret and Jane walk to the bridge.

When I regain consciousness, the wind is gusting no more than 60. Fat lumpy black clouds are racing low overhead. The sun, yellow and gray and hurricane-colored at last, gleams from the west. The sound of Jane tearing tape from the windows is what wakes me. She says at least forty boats are on the bridge and causeway, maybe more. It's six o'clock, so I make drinks. We toast the doughty *Olivebank,* brave *Lochinvar,* good old Gladys Street. By 7:30 the wind is 15 to 20 from the northwest, the sky is an ingenuous pinky-yellow, and it's a lovely evening. In the back yard, among tree branches, dinghies, and sections of fence, we cook hamburgers on the charcoal grill. The radio rounds up the coastal devastation: beaches, houses, ships, yachts, trees, powerlines. The National Guard is patrolling the bridge at Padanaram to prevent looting. Somewhere sandwiched in all this is the real news of the day, at least for the rest of the world: A coup in the Soviet Union—Gorbachev has been deposed.

The day after. Gray, thickening to heavy rain. Not at all the bright drying weather you'd hope for after a hurricane. But there is no wind. The calm is strange. Fred and Jane drive home to Boston. Buell, Margaret, Margot, and I walk to the village, stepping over and around fallen branches, fallen trees. There is no power; according to the radio, more than a quarter of Rhode Island and Massachusetts is without electricity and may remain so for several days. After a storm like this, overhead power lines seem a poor economy. On the bridge, where the armed, khaki-uniformed Guardsmen are stationed, the havoc is at hand. Wrecked boats lie everywhere. Half the moorings that had boats on them are bare; the causeway is lined on both sides with wrecked craft and more are littered along the roadway. "At least 96, by the last count," says a policeman on the bridge. (Later the count rises to 130.) As far as boats are concerned, Padanaram has

certainly suffered worst of all. The wind here peaked at 110
miles per hour.

Yet we were in the right spot. *Lochinvar* is unscathed.
Even in the galley cupboard, the olive oil and the marmalade are still in their separate containers. An open jar of
homemade raspberry jam stands among other jars, wonderfully unspilled. One book fell onto the cabin floor. The
main problem is retrieving the three anchors, which are
truly dug in. The rode of one has also wrapped itself several
times around an empty mooring buoy; this may be what
stopped *Lochinvar* from swinging into the nearest motorboat when the wind veered west. Buell and I, using the sheet
winches, at last get the anchors up; the Danforth has dug in
deepest. We untangle the mess of anchor line on the foredeck, pry away and mop off the thick black Padanaram
mud. Then, when *Lochinvar* has been rafted alongside
Olivebank again, we row back in to collect our partners for
lunch on board. Because the electric stove at 5 Gladys Street
is out of action, we eat canned soup warmed on
Olivebank's propane stove.

In the afternoon we take a voyage of inspection in Buell's
skiff. The upper harbor, though least affected, shows many
signs of Bob's passage. One 22-foot boat is upside down,
keel in air. Several yachts are high on Monkey Island and
many are in the marshes toward the head of the
Apponagansett River. A number of craft still on their moorings have been damaged by collisions; they display scarred
topsides, broken rails, bent stanchions. A Tartan 27, a sis-
tership of *Lochinvar,* has a broken mast. The bridge clearly
isn't going to open until the power returns; we row under it
and down the outer harbor, which is rimmed with wrecked
or stranded boats. Many have landed on rocks and are in

pieces or badly holed. Some are still recognizable as boats, but others are mere fragments of fiberglass, torn and splintered shards of white glass cloth. Some which arrived on sandy stretches are nestling tightly against one another as if for protection. Some have dragged their moorings with them; big mushroom anchors sit pathetically next to the beached vessels they were meant to hold in place. Some moorings are revealed as bathtubs full of concrete. On some boats, perhaps without chafing gear, mooring pennants have snapped. On some, the mooring lines have apparently jumped out of fairleads and sawn down through the skin of the hull. Boats with short, plank bowsprits—often installed for convenience in housing anchors—have been made to pay as these projections have failed, tugged down by mooring pennants as the boats were lifted by waves, and consequently their headstays and stem fittings failed. Most of the beached craft have sails or the remains of sails still rigged on booms and luff-groove furling systems. All that windage. I thank Amy once again for her advice, Buell for his plow anchor, and the Apponagansett for its sticky mud.

For the next few days we are indeed stuck in Padanaram. No power, no bridge opening. The weather goes on being gray, damp, and hot. Buell and Margaret leave on Tuesday for work in Boston. We cook either on *Lochinvar* or in the Franklin stove at 5 Gladys Street at the cost of sooty saucepans. We wash in cold water and read by candlelight. I repair the back garden fence. Margot cleans out the silent refrigerator and makes life-and-death decisions about thawed food. We walk, row around Monkey Island, and speculate with the neighbors about when the power company will reach South Dartmouth and Gladys Street. Chain saws racket away in streets and gardens. Many trees are stripped or are changed in color, the leaves bleached or browned by the salt wind; fall has come early for them. Even Brad, the recluse, has got clean-up fever and makes perfunctory attacks on his undergrowth, sending cats scurrying, though his yard, with storm-flattened grass, looks tidier than it did before Bob. Al, next door, who will be busy into next year repairing sails, offers to drive us to the New Bedford supermarkets. But we make out well enough with the ship's stores and canned food and bread bought in the village.

There, the shopkeepers begin to know us. "You still here?" they say cheerfully. We mark the phases of recovery. The numbers of boats on the causeway dwindle as cranes lift them and huge trailers haul them away. Thursday morning, on my way to get the morning paper, I notice the second hand of the electric clock in a realtor's window. It is moving! The power is back on, at least in the village center. But at the bridge, where we have been checking in daily, the assistant harbormaster tells me that it may be another day or so before the machinery is overhauled and approval is given for reopening. We talk on the phone to Betty in Stonington, to Paul in North Truro, and to Al and Janet in Vineyard Haven, comparing notes on our hurricane experiences.

On Friday afternoon Buell and Margaret return. Buell, seeing I'm beginning to feel trapped by the bridge, suggests we fit sheer legs and a lifting tackle on *Olivebank* and pluck out *Lochinvar*'s mast. Once under the bridge, we can stop at the Concordia yard and have them restep the mast. Envisaging hard work, problems, and expense, I decide to hang on to our mast another day or so. I'm sure the bridge will open soon. With this optimism, we go shopping in New Bedford at the largest supermarket I've ever been in. Women stand in the aisles chatting in Portuguese as though on village street corners three thousand miles away. We buy ice, and are thus all ready to go. On Friday evening a power-company crew finally reaches Gladys Street, hauls away a downed tree, and restores some of the lines, though no power reaches the houses. A violent thunderstorm strikes during the night.

Saturday has to be our day of thanksgiving, come what may. We breakfast at the village luncheonette: pancakes, eggs, sausages, and a plethora of newspapers. Hot showers are available at 3 Gladys Street, where the water is heated by gas. The sun comes out properly for the first time in six days. In mid-afternoon, sitting on the upper deck, we see the bridge turning. I row immediately downharbor to find out what the opening schedule will be tomorrow. The mechanics assure me the bridge will be left open for several days for boats to pass through, since the road on the western part of the causeway is still blocked by wrecked craft. At 5:00 p.m. lights come on at 5 Gladys Street and the refrigerator starts to hum. We celebrate with dinner in Padanaram's fanciest eatery. By the second bottle we are reliving Bob. No doubt about it, getting through a hurricane takes more than good holding ground—you need good friends.

28

AT 7:30 NEXT MORNING, the bridge *is* still open. As we motor out, I resist the urge to go at top speed in case it suddenly closes again. Beyond it, our sense of liberation is tempered with gratitude and also with guilt. How good Padanaram was to us is made clear by a glance at the wrecks still littering the causeway and shores of the harbor. But there is no point in stopping on the way to the breakwater. It will be a while before fuel, ice, and water are available from the New Bedford Yacht Club's dock. Our block of ice came from the New Bedford waterfront, our gas tank has been topped up with jerry cans filled at a local gas station, and our water supply has been replenished by courtesy of the garden faucet at 5 Gladys Street.

The morning is calm, pink-gray. We hoist the main and unfurl the jib in a light easterly that greets us just outside the breakwater. The crafty sea has refashioned itself once again. Here last Monday was screaming wind, raging waves. Hard to picture when you are surrounded by little wavelets tripping down Buzzards Bay in a breeze which heels *Lochinvar* no more than 5 degrees from the vertical. The artists of former times who painted matching pictures of *Calm* and *Storm*, showing the same patch of coast in each extremity of weather, were clearly filling the need for reminders that heaven and hell can exist at different moments in the same place. Our course is southward across the bay toward Quicks Hole, the gap between the islands of Nashawena and Pasque. As the sun rises, the wind slowly builds, though to nothing more than a full-sail breeze. It's a close reach, with a current running west which has to be allowed for. We don't want to be set down below Quicks and have to claw back up. These are historic waters for us. It was off Pasque that *Clio*'s centerboard pennant failed. Not far from here our dinghy decided to go it alone. And it was while approaching Nashawena a couple of years ago, as we made for Cuttyhunk in a brisk sou'wester, that a large white sloop came beating down the bay in our general direction. We were hard on the wind, on the starboard tack. The large sloop was also hard on the wind, but on the port tack. These differences of tack aren't always significant but I registered them because it seemed to me, after peering under our boom for a while at the big sloop, that we might be on converging courses. *Lochinvar* was rollicking across the bay at 5 knots. The white yacht—about 65 feet long, I reckoned—was plowing along at about 7 or 8 knots. It was flying the British Red Ensign.

As we drew closer to one another, at what seemed an ever-increasing speed, I couldn't help casting nervous glances under our mainsail and around our jib at the big sloop. Surely the crew on a yacht that size knew what they were doing? Surely they realized they didn't have the right of way? It's a basic rule of sail: the boat on the port tack gives way to the boat on starboard. Perhaps they expected to pass clear ahead of us. Or for some reason they were assuming that a smaller vessel like ours would tack out of their way. I changed places with Margot so as to be down on the leeside, with a clearer view of the onrushing white monster. "I can't believe this," I said. I could see the matching sweatshirts of the white yacht's crew; they, too, were on the leeside of their cockpit but were looking at us blankly. Their helmsman stood proudly at the wheel, staring ahead. The yacht's powerful bow wave surged aft.

As we converged, calculations raced through my head. If I kept on, if the other yacht held on, she would impale us on our port side. We would undoubtedly lose the mast and sink. I shouted at the top of my voice, "Starboard!" The yacht's crew continued to stare at us, showing no sign of any reaction. She was enormously powerful, big, heavy, and fast. We had about five seconds left.

"Coming about!" I yelled, mostly for Margot's benefit. There was no time to release the jib sheet. But *Lochinvar* pivoted, her bow swung. As we fell over onto the port tack, our jib aback, the big white sloop roared by. She was so close I could see the colored braid in her jib sheets. We were being tossed about by her bow wave. "What about starboard tack?" I called. A young man leaned over her rail and said plaintively, "We were going to pass astern of you." Then they had thundered past.

I was white and shaking, then red and furious. I said to Margot, "There was no way they could have gone behind us—not unless they'd changed course much earlier. If we'd kept on, they'd have hit us. We'd have been swimming by now, or drowning."

"And they're flying the Red Duster, too," said Margot.

On the wide, retroussé counter of the big yacht, heading on toward Penikese, was its name, *Jaguar*.

Very little of my past life passed before me in those fateful seconds. But as we sorted out our sheets and settled for the port tack for the time being, following in *Jaguar*'s wake, I thought of how Peter Tripp would have sketched this encounter: *Lochinvar*'s jib pinned against the port spreader, her ensign wrapped ignominiously around its staff, her skipper steaming from the ears while he shook a useless fist . . . I could see a short item in *The Boston Globe*, that excellent but not invariably Anglophile newspaper, with the headline TWO BRITISH BOATS COLLIDE IN BUZZARDS BAY—ONE SINKS.

There have been other times when we have nearly been sunk. I recall a rainy morning in Rhode Island Sound when a tug with a barge in tow was—we ultimately realized—not going to acknowledge the rule that power gives way to sail in the open sea. Then there was a sparkling clear afternoon in Block Island Sound, about a mile off the entrance to Great Salt Pond, when one of those big steel floating motels with patriotic names that call themselves coastal cruise ships all but ran us down. We were in *Clio*, reaching along under full sail, and by a last-second maneuver like that with *Jaguar* avoided the collision that would have sunk us. There seemed to be no one on the ship's bridge or at her helm. Were all the officers of the watch downing g-and-t's with the blue rinse set on the promenade deck aft while an autopilot steered her on a set course? Again, there had been a strange lack of response from the offending vessel. The indifference from the people looking out at us, floundering a few yards from the tall, flat flank of the cruise ship, was eerie. I shouted, "You stupid idiots!" And then, as the stern passed and the credits rolled—"*America*. Wilmington, Delaware"—I shouted again, "Drunken idiots!" There was no response. Nobody at all on that ship was wondering why that small blue sailboat was going around in circles with its skipper jumping up and down. This is the way the end may come, blind, stupid, impersonal.

On that occasion with *Jaguar*, Margot—interrupting my fevered recollections—said, "They've gybed around and are coming back." She was pointing southwest. Sure enough, there came the big yacht, running back toward us. Off our starboard quarter she hardened up, came about, and sailed along about two boat lengths to leeward of us, with her jib slackened. There was a different man at the helm. Possibly they'd put the previous one below to study the rules of the road. The same young man as before stood up and called to us: "We're—very—sorry."

I was so surprised by this apology that no words came to me. However, I waved in as noble a fashion as I could manage, acknowledging their gesture. Then they winched in their jib sheet and *Jaguar* quickly pulled away from us again. When we anchored in Cuttyhunk Harbor half an hour later, we saw *Jaguar* on a mooring there. But we anchored at a tactful distance. I thought the sight of *Lochinvar* might be a humiliation for her crew. Less generously, the proximity of *Jaguar* might have kept me blazing mad at them all night.

This morning there are no impediments to our passage to and through Quicks Hole. Ahead, the Vineyard spreads its flanks invitingly. Our course into Menemsha Bight is a touch east of south, and a few small draggers and lobster boats remain at a distance. We reach the entrance breakwaters of Menemsha an hour after high water. This can be a place to concentrate the mind on occasions when a strong wind is blowing against the current, creating tide rips and overfalls. But our only cares tóday as we motor in are the fishing skiffs in the entrance and the already fast-moving ebb current. We avoid the main thrust of this by clinging to the side of the channel, though it isn't made easy by the outstretched lines of anglers on the breakwaters. *Lochinvar* shoulders her way over the tide and past the entrance to Menemsha Basin. This little dredged cove off the east side of the channel provides wharfage for the local fishing fleet and a few facilities for transients, if they can find room. Fuel and ice, fish and lobsters, are to be bought here. Another smaller cove which cuts into the dunes on the opposite side has moorings for a few small boats. But at this stage I'm concentrating less on the scenery and more on my approach to the shoal across the channel leading up into Menemsha Pond.

From previous excursions here, I know that there's about two-and-a-half feet of water over this bar at low water. Normally there should be about four feet of water at half tide, and it's still nearly two hours until then. But my confidence isn't bolstered by a young man windsurfing down channel who asks, "How much do you draw?" as he approaches, and shakes his head doubtfully when I tell him three and a half. An hour into a falling tide is not the right time to run aground. As we pass the Coast Guard Station I keep my eye on the depth sounder and the channel buoys. I adjust the throttle so that *Lochinvar* is just edging forward over the tide; if we don't hit the shoal too hard, we may be able to back off. On the other hand, the longer we take, the more the tide will fall and the shallower it will be. The bottom shows clearly, a few clam shells lying there, the odd bit of weed floating quickly past over the sand. The depth sounder's red bubbles of light glow against the numbers on the dial. Approximately a foot and a half must be added to the depth indicated by the machine, to take account of the transducer's position well underwater, but nevertheless I'm nervous as the numbers sink: 5—5—4—4—3. The biggest bubble hovers at the 3 for a moment, almost dips to the 2, and then starts climbing again. We're over and in.

The channel of Menemsha Creek: mud flats and marshes and low islands to our left, the east; a sandy beach backed by little dunes to the right, the west. The contrary tide is an advantage, slowing us so that we have a chance to observe the beach. A few abandoned lobster boats lie hauled up on the sand, with KEEP OFF signs to suggest that someone, someday, is planning to restore them. But the signs are fading. Oystercatchers and terns swoop low, ignoring us. I like this stretch of channel even though each time we come in here the beacons and buoys marking it seem fewer and farther between. But we safely reach the far end, at Long Point, where the channel debouches into Menemsha Pond a body of water about a mile square. Straight on from the creek a pair of pilings forms a gateway into the southern, deeper half of the pond. In some years we've anchored off its eastern shore, where Jan, now of Vineyard Haven, used to rent a cabin; today we turn west and anchor in about five feet not far off the western hillside. This will provide a lee if the wind as predicted blows from the southwest. Here, as at the Head of the Harbor in Nantucket, other cruising craft are rare. The bar at the north end of Menemsha Creek serves to deter all but shoal-draft boats. Today there's just one, a good-looking black sharpie ketch. We anchor about a quarter of a

mile from it, a distance that recognizes the privacy, the solitude, each of us has come here for but still confirms this as
an anchorage that our two boats have successfully got to—
which makes for an unspoken companionship.

Sun all afternoon. Margot says the boat smells and that
either I don't notice this or (typically) find it romantic. Can
it be true? Bunk cushions and sleeping bags go on deck to
rid themselves of the damp residue of Bob. Locker doors
and hatches are left open. Then we set off in the dinghy,
leaving our ark to air itself out. Once or twice we've rowed
into the southernmost reaches of Nashaquitsa and Stonewall
Ponds which wind from Menemsha Pond to the south shore
of the island. At this point only a thin, 200-yard-wide isthmus of marsh and sandy beach, together with a low road
bridge, holds Martha's Vineyard in one piece. Snowy egrets
frequent these ponds, but to see them one must brave the
small boys who drop pebbles from the bridge into the
dinghies passing below. We've also rowed in the other direction, up to the basin for supplies, relying on the last of the
ebb to help us there and the beginning of the flood to bring
us back. (Supplies do not include wine, beer, or spirits; like
Vineyard Haven and Cuttyhunk, Menemsha is dry.) Rowing
to the northeast corner of the pond, we landed once to visit
Jan, whose cabin was half a mile up an overgrown lane;
before we returned in the darkness, I wound plastic wrap
around Margot's bare ankles to keep off poison ivy.

Generally we row to the northwest corner of the pond
and walk north to the beach which faces out on Menemsha
Bight and Vineyard Sound. There we swim and walk either
along the beach or the track through the dunes of
Cranberry Lands to the entrance channel and the creek. We

watch the boats coming in, and people fishing, and feel briefly different, seeing this activity from a landsman's rather than a sailor's point of view. In the first years of this century Joshua Slocum kept the *Spray* somewhere in these parts, when he was having a go at being a hardscrabble farmer in Chilmark, at this end of the Vineyard. That was after he became the world's first single-handed circumnavigator. Standing by the little cove, on the west side of the creek across from the Coast Guard station, you could almost see the *Spray* moored here. A clumsy-looking former fishing smack, which he had rescued from final collapse in a field near Fairhaven, opposite New Bedford, she went on being sailed locally by the pioneering captain in summer and voyaging south in winter, though some who saw her tied up here thought her increasingly ill kempt. On one trip he brought an immense lump of coral from the Bahamas to the American Museum of Natural History in New York and some rare West Indian orchids for President Theodore Roosevelt. But in November 1909, when he was sixty-five, he sailed alone from Vineyard Haven in a rising gale, bound for South America, and the *Spray* and her captain were never seen again.

Today we row close along the shoreline of the pond, nosing into tiny coves and miniature harbors among the high grass, shrubbery, and reeds. A few small sailing boats are disporting themselves in mid-pond. Several clammers are tonging from battered workboats in the northern shallows. On the low-hilled shores of the pond, houses stand primly separated from one another by rural rather than suburban distances and are well set back from the water; they sport neither ostentatious flagpoles nor flamboyant flags.

In the evening as usual I write up the day's log in a school composition book. I consult *Eldridge* for the morrow and note times of tides and changes of current in a smaller red notebook. From here our radio only just picks up WFCC, a station in Chatham which broadcasts classical music; we must be on its transmitter's western limits. Before we acquired our present multi-waveband radio and special weather-only radio, we put up with a cheap set the size of a cigarette pack. Finding a weather forecast on this involved listening to a lot of other things: baseball games, hot lines for people with emotional difficulties, horoscopes, financial advice about tax shelters. All kinds of ghastly music came between us and so-called Accy weather reports. These summarized, not always accurately, the federal forecasts. Now the BBC World Service news and WFCC's music gain our gratitude. Tonight, as I do my end-of-day chores, filling the lamps, taking in the ensign, checking the anchor line, and Margot cooks pork chops, zucchini, and rice, we hear of the crumbling of the coup in the Soviet Union and then listen to a Haydn symphony.

After dark, we explore the Milky Way through binoculars. The Northern Cross is high in the sky to the east, and with the help of a star chart I try to identify Deneb, Delta, Gamma, Beta, and Altair. Menemsha lies beneath various flight paths, and high overhead pass the pulsating lights of planes bound for London, Boston, and New York. The lights of stars and planes are reflected on the surface of the pond almost without a tremor. The shores of the pond are now a bumpy black rim, the edge of our small universe, and the flame of our anchor lamp scarcely flickers in the breathless night air.

29

TOWARD THE END of August the light begins to change. This sunny morning, when we motor out of the Menemsha entrance channel, it is already a September light, clearer and crisper, with the summer haze all gone. From Vineyard Sound the muted brown, red, and yellow cliffs of Gay Head stand tall at the western tip of the Vineyard. As *Lochinvar* gives the reef called Devils Bridge a wide berth, under sail in a light southwesterly and steering west-northwest, the visibility is as good as it can be. The small uninhabited island of Noman's Land is in clear view to the south. Northward we can see beyond Cuttyhunk and the rest of the Elizabeth Islands to the main Massachusetts shore.

In the days of coasting trade under sail, Devils Bridge and its fellow reef, Sow and Pigs, off the west end of Cuttyhunk, claimed many a victim. Perhaps the most notable disaster was the loss of the packet *City of Columbus,* which struck Devils Bridge in January 1884 with the loss of 103 passengers and crew and a number of Gay Head Indians who tried to save them. Numerous vessels have been swept off course by the unexpected currents in this area, first recorded by George W. Eldridge, the Chatham chartmaker who founded the *Eldridge Tide and Pilot Book* in 1854. Eldridge wanted to help the masters of sailing vessels avoid being swept onto the reefs, rocks, and shores of the Elizabeth Islands between Sow and Pigs and Naushon, the section known as the Graveyard, toward which both ebb and flood currents tend to set the unwary. The annual *Eldridge* guide continues to emphasize these dangers and to reprint George W.'s sketch map showing the main pattern of the currents. I wonder if a copy of the book was in the navigation room of the liner *Queen Elizabeth 2* in August 1992 (a year following Bob and most of the events in this account). The big ship was steaming west down Vineyard Sound when she hit an underwater ledge south of Sow and Pigs and was badly holed. The ledge is shown on the Vineyard Sound chart at a depth of between 39 and 55 feet, but unfortunately at its highest the ledge proved to be thirty-four and a half feet below the surface. However, since the QE2 draws 32 feet she ought to have cleared it. Why she did not became the subject of much speculation. One marine expert pointed out that a large vessel moving at speed—a vessel 963 feet long doing 26 knots in this case—squats more deeply in the water. This should surely have been taken into account by captain and pilot. Blame has not yet been apportioned as I write, but Buell and I agreed when we discussed the matter that, apart from the sloppy surveyors or cartographers, the people who should be in the firing line are Cunard's cruise planners—who dreamed up the notion of sending the huge ship through

Vineyard Sound to give the customers a thrill.

In George W. Eldridge's time a lightship marked the approaches to Vineyard Sound and Buzzards Bay. Today our seamark is the light tower which replaced the lightship and which, outward bound, we didn't see because of the thunderstorm. A so-called Texas tower, it's a spindly-legged structure rather like an oil rig but even more like a giant robot designed for walking around Mars. With *Lochinvar* hard on the wind (now an ideal 10-knot southwesterly), we leave the Buzzards tower a quarter of a mile to port and count our blessings. The wind has often before come dead on the nose as we headed west from here, as if anxious to keep us in Massachusetts waters. Sometimes it is blustery and the current foul, and we thrash back and forth, making a very slow and wet westing. Today, with our goal the nearest part of Rhode Island, the gods of the winds have given us a clear homeward slant.

Inshore are the approaches to Westport, the last harbor in Massachusetts. Not the easiest place to enter, with a mean current to buck on the ebb, though I have it on my mental list of harbors I want to visit again. We sailed into Westport many years ago in *Caliban*. Managing to wriggle around various shoals and presuming on our two-and-a-half-foot draft with the board lifted, we ascended a long way up the west branch of the Westport River. This is the kind of place where you go with either local knowledge or good luck. Only skiffs, dinghies, and small catboats appear there, and a sylvan calm reigns from bank to bank. We were therefore surprised during the night to hear a sudden loud vibrating sound. Waking, I thought at first it was a powerful motorboat approaching. But the noise was coming from around and below the hull, and it was even louder inside the boat than when heard on deck. We decided that it was fish, thousands of fish, making the din.

We home in today on Sakonnet Point, or rather on Schuyler Ledge, the underwater obstacle off the point. As we get closer, it becomes a challenge to sneak past the rocks of the point without tacking. We have been close-hauled on the port tack all the way from Menemsha, and it seems a pity to spoil this with one short hundred-yard tack on starboard. The thought of having to winch in the sheets is also off-putting. But by sailing in a series of long arcs, bearing off a little and then with added momentum slowly squeezing close to the wind before bearing off again, we get near to Schuyler's. We slide by just inside the red bell buoy—not to seaward of it, where we should be—but still at a safe distance from the big brown rocks of Sakonnet. The restored iron pepper-pot lighthouse, white as a sail, stands on its own huge clump of boulders, with surf splashing around. Nearby, what look like several prehistoric standing stones are, I think, the chimneys of a ruined house. The lighthouse marks our passage from sea to relative shelter. From here, the mouth of the Sakonnet River opens out before us, two miles wide, stretching across to Sachuest Point. This point is the southeastern tip of the island, shaped like a crayfish with one claw, which was once called Rhode Island—from which the entire state took its name—and is now called Aquidneck Island. The broad river, in fact a long bay or fjord, runs directly inland.

We've sailed in here on less benevolent days, in fading light and deteriorating weather, busy reefing and looking out for fish traps and marks. We've saved contemplation and thanksgiving until we worked our way into Sakonnet harbor. This cove, less than a mile upriver from Sakonnet

Point, is open to the north but has a breakwater on the west protecting it against seas blowing in from Rhode Island Sound. Entering the river not from the west but from the south, as we do today, is the best way of avoiding the pesky hard-to-see lines of nets strung out here by the fishermen of Sakonnet in hope (it would seem) of catching not just fish but yachts.

I don't have many fond memories of Sakonnet harbor, even though it has furnished us refuge on occasion. Friendly, knowledgeable locals, the sort who readily direct you to an unused mooring for the night, are in short supply. There are precious few spots to anchor in; one we chose proved to have an adjacent underwater rock against which *Clio*'s rudder bumped when the wind shifted from northwest to southwest. Everywhere in the harbor you're liable to be rocked violently awake at 5:00 a.m. as the fishing boats charge out. And what, several years ago, appeared to be a characterful waterfront with restaurant and handy facilities for mariners turned out to be less felicitous. The restaurant was closed, possibly forever. A strong smell of fish overhung the dockside. When, at 8.00 a.m., I asked a man washing fish with a hose spewing salt water if I could buy some gasoline, he said I needed to ask Frank. Frank, short, stocky, smoking a cigar, and pushing fish boxes around, said there wouldn't be any gas till "maybe 11:00." As if to preempt further requests, he went on: "There ain't no fresh water or ice, either." He took a reflective pull on his cigar and exuded a cloud of smoke. Then he uttered what was clearly his last word on the subject: "Sakonnet is the asshole of the universe."

A year after that encounter with Frank, we blundered into Sakonnet again. We were bound from Block Island to

Cuttyhunk and the weather was threatening. Our arrival was well timed. The Rhode Island rainfall record was about to be broken. We picked up a weedy mooring pennant just as the monsoon began. Torrential rain fell from 5:00 p.m. to 9:00 a.m. Water bounced off the bridge deck into the cabin via the companionway, where I'd been forced to leave out the top slide-in board for ventilation. The dinghy filled until its gunwales were awash. As I mopped the damp interior, Margot cooked spaghetti for supper. When the pasta was al dente, she put the plug in the sink and thriftily poured the boiling water into it, adding Joy washing-up liquid ready for doing the dishes later—our working principle on boats being that we always try to use things twice. I decided the spaghetti needed to be strained a second time. I was tipping it over the sink when the pan lid slipped and the spaghetti plunked into the soapy water. I tried rinsing a strand and eating it, but it tasted only of Joy. The decision was taken (crossly) to start again. Boil the water. Cook the spaghetti. Keep the sauce warm. And don't be such a clumsy idiot, Tony. The rain kept coming down, and next morning, with lightning stabbing the water around us, Margot leaned over *Clio*'s side to bail out some of the water in the dinghy and then climbed into the dinghy to bail out the rest, presumably preferring the job to staying in the cabin with me while I made coffee.

Sakonnet, I'm told, now has a small marina with hot-and-cold-running everything, and Frank may have changed his tune. But it may not surprise the reader to learn that today, after passing the lighthouse, we do not bear right into Sakonnet harbor but steer for the next bell buoy and thence northward for the other side of the river mouth. Beyond Sachuest Point we turn left, avoiding the rocks of

Flint Point Ledge, taking our direction from a prominent church tower on a hill to the west, and coming to anchor in Third Beach Cove, also known as Sachuest. This is a more open anchorage than Sakonnet, but is well protected from the west and south, from where whatever wind there is tonight may come. The cove has numerous moorings, many empty of boats, but we rely on our own hook. We plant it at the north end of the mooring area, close inshore, in the lee of a little rocky cliff.

Third Beach is so called because it follows two other beaches on nearby Sachuest Bay and Easton Bay. This Monday afternoon, as we walk the crescent of sand, it isn't overstocked with humanity. A few novice windsurfers are struggling to retain their balance in the fading breeze; loud recorded music blares from a snack bar; the beach club for U.S. naval personnel is closed. We find some small mussels on rocks near the Point and remove them for a sauce for tonight's pasta (spaghetti still being an essential part of the Sakonnet experience). At nightfall, which comes clear, still, and suddenly cool, the lights of Sakonnet harbor can be seen across the river. Although they have the poignancy that distant lights across water always seem to possess, we'd rather be right where we are.

30

AUGUST, abbreviated by Bob and the Padanaram bridge, is hastening to an end. I'd like to sail next morning up the tranquil Sakonnet, but we're running out of days. Cruising makes you fit your ambitions to wind, weather, and available time. It makes you adaptable, putting aside hopes and intentions with good humor and making advantages out of what circumstances dictate. Last year we had time to spare and ran up the unspoiled Sakonnet. On its blue-green banks, meadows and vineyards await a Virgil to sing their bucolic charms. We tucked in for the night neither at Sakonnet harbor nor at Sachuest but behind Fogland Point, a stumpy spit which curves out from the east bank of the river a few miles upstream. The cove on the north side of the spit shoals into clam flats, but we didn't enter it beyond the moorings of a few local boats. After a quiet night at anchor, we woke to a cockerel crowing at a nearby farm. Creamy-brown Jersey cows grazed a thick-hedged field in the midst of which was a square patch surrounded by a dry-stone wall. It was a lit-tle graveyard, with four gray gravestones. In mid-morning, when it was already hot, we swam from the public beach which runs along the south side of the spit. Rowing back to *Lochinvar,* we passed cormorants standing on unoccupied mooring buoys, looking like German imperial eagles as they dried their outstretched wings. One of these days I mean to find out about cormorants. For one thing, why don't we ever see baby cormorants? Are they nurtured in Southern climes before being brought North fully fledged? Perhaps they look bigger than their parents, the way young gulls do. Or possibly we just don't notice them because they aren't cutely fluffy like the offspring of the ducks and geese who paddle toward us on panhandling missions.

At noon we ran upriver before a genial southerly, under main alone. After several unhurried miles the Sakonnet nar-rowed abruptly. A stone bridge once spanned this pinch point, but through the gap in its now ruined structure boats can pass into what is called a cove but is really a strait between the top end of Aquidneck Island and the small town of Tiverton. We arrived purposely at the stone bridge just after low water. The flood current was with us but wasn't swirling us out of control. Tiverton, on our star-board hand, stood on a wooded hillside, white clapboard houses and churches above a waterfront of boatyards and fish docks. We had to concentrate, however, on our immedi-ate future, our passage through two more bridges, one road, one rail. We'd never been this way before. The chart showed the road bridge as having heaps of vertical clear-ance, but the railroad bridge, north of the road bridge but not quite parallel to it, was of the "swing" variety, with only twelve feet underneath when it was closed. The question was: Would it be open? The current was now running strongly and any changes of mind and course would need to be well premeditated. As we got closer, it seemed to me that the railroad bridge was abandoned. It was indeed open, and appeared to have rusted in that position. The cabin with gingerbread trim from which the bridge tender had controlled the opening and closing of the span was derelict and possibly haunted. Faced with a channel on each side of the central bastion on which the span pivoted, we sailed through the western one. This proved to be the proper choice, for after we had passed through, we saw a sign on the bridge, facing north, which said, USE WEST CHANNEL, CABLE CROSSING. No sign faced south.

Like a cork popping out of the bottle which was the Sakonnet, *Lochinvar* shot into Mount Hope Bay. The "Mount" is a mere 200-foot-high bump on the otherwise level shore to the north, but in the afternoon heat haze, the Bay seemed a big blurry expanse stretching far northeastward into Massachusetts. The former mill city of Fall River lay around the corner on our starboard hand, but we decided to save for another occasion the place where in 1892 Lizzie Borden allegedly "took an axe and gave her mother forty whacks," and was later acquitted of murder. We turned to port under the lofty suspension bridge which connects the north end of Aquidneck Island to Bristol Neck. The afternoon breeze was piping up. We unrolled the jib and, hard on the wind, just weathered the tip of Bristol Neck before bearing off into Bristol Harbor. This is a deep cul-de-sac, chockful of boats, open to the south to Narragansett Bay, and obviously a place where it is preferable to moor rather than anchor. We gave the harbor a rapid once-over. Bristol is a famous yachting place, haunt of the Herreshoffs, who designed and built their brilliant craft here, and the town still builds boats and manufactures boat wares. However, with the wind funneling strongly into it, Bristol didn't strike a note of welcome for casual callers. A cruising guide to Narragansett Bay we had on board referred to two state guest moorings but suggested the Bristol harbormaster had taken them over for his own purposes. We reached back and forth in the area where they were said to be and saw no sign of them. Deciding to put the Herreshoff museum and the colonial streets of Bristol on our "one of these days" list, we beat out of the harbor.

I say "we," though Margot chose this moment to take a nap below. I had the solitary pleasure of trying to catch a 30-foot Nonsuch catboat, which had made a similar inspection tour and was now similarly heading out. My tacks to the southeast were restricted by the shoals of Middle Ground, by Castle Island and Hog Island. My tacks to the southwest were abbreviated by Popasquash Neck, which forms the west side of Bristol Harbor. Moreover, *Lochinvar*'s acceleration after each coming about was diminished by the helmsman having to sweat in the jib single-handed. These were my excuses for the fact that the big catboat, of course without a jib, got around Popasquash Point before *Lochinvar*. It headed north toward Barrington and Providence. *Lochinvar*, turning the other cheek, reached across the ship channel in the direction of Prudence Island, an eight-mile-long pear-shaped chunk of benign neglect and thoughtful conservation set in the middle of Narragansett Bay.

In Potter Cove, at the northwest end of Prudence Island, Margot came on deck, rubbed her eyes, and took the helm while I dropped the hook. We anchored in the southwest corner of the cove, sheltered from the promised nighttime southwesterly, but somewhat exposed to wake and swell from the bay. The cove is an isolated spot, free of all amenities except peace and quiet, ringed with marsh, low woods, and a beach, and with only one house in sight. Yet it is absolutely littered with moorings, apparently planted by Narragansett Bay yachtsmen who come here at weekends and don't like getting their hands dirty with anchor and chain. On this occasion four out of some fifty moorings were in use. But we were loath to borrow one in case the rightful owner turned up. Our night was in any event calm, if foggy.

In the morning, as the fog burned off, we rowed the dinghy to the nearby dock and first walked northward into what a sign told us was a National Estuarine Sanctuary and Rhode Island state park. We walked on a rough car-wide track with trousers tucked into socks against the ubiquitous ticks. The trees were unusually old and tall. A farm looked inhabited but unworked. An apple tree offered its fruit— "tart," said Margot; "sour," said I. Among the wildflowers we saw flax, Indian pea, daisies, black-eyed Susans, clover. We passed the empty remains of a big stone house, with two intact wings, one shuttered up, one with glass windows, both wings vacant. According to Lynda and Patrick Childress, my authorities for Narragansett Bay, this house was built early this century by a wealthy yachtsman named James Garland, who during a sail from Providence to Newport took shelter in Potter Cove from a bay blow. Like many who have chanced on pretty places, Garland decided this was the spot for him. While living on his yacht in the cove, he had his mansion constructed of stones found on the site. But before it was finished, Garland died. What of is not mentioned by the Childresses, but we thought it could have been malaria. Our walk north was halted by mosquitoes.

We had neglected to bring insect repellent ashore with us and the winged beasties zoomed down in squadrons, each Concorde-type nose or proboscis bent down for immediate biting and bloodsucking. We beat a fast retreat.

North of the cove, we'd begun to feel a bit Crusoe-like, and thought it was time to look for natives on the island. We walked south, past Potter Cove, heading toward a settlement promised by the Childress guidebook in three-quarters of a mile. This proved to be a misprint for three to four miles. The grassy track became a gravel road, long and winding and hot. Two cars went by and the drivers waved at us. Finally we reached a paved road. On some gates in a wire fence a sign said DUMP. Civilization was presumably at hand. Sure enough, the road was soon lined with simple summer cottages of the sort that get named Hideaway and Happy Landings. We came to Homestead Wharf, where the ferry from Bristol loads and unloads passengers and cars. At the wharf car park, a sign declared: WAITING LIMITED TO SIX WEEKS. Many of the vehicles looked as if they had been there much longer than that and might even have died there. Many were without Rhode Island registration plates but had instead hand-painted numbers, up to three figures—an island perk.

Next to the ferry wharf stood Marcy's Grocery, a simple structure which also housed the post office. The windows were small, the interior dim, but no lights were on. We peered at the sparse stock of provisions. Margot found some small cartons of juice and I found a lurid and gooey Danish pastry. A very large woman surveying the bakery section and wearing a kind of boondock muumuu said to me, "I see someone bought that chocolate cake." It had apparently been tempting her for some time. I wondered how long my Danish had been on the shelf, but didn't put it back. Marcy, surnamed Dunbar, was an elderly lady with gray hair tied up in plaits over her ears. She totaled our little bill on a Model A cash register and told us, when we asked about the ferry service, that the first boat to Bristol went at 6:30 a.m. and carried "quite a few" Prudence Islanders who worked on the mainland.

Margot and I sat on the wharf, read *The Providence Journal,* and consumed our goodies. The bay was flat and airless; a sailing boat, mainsail tight amidships, motored south. As we lingered, in no hurry to face the hike back, a car with Florida plates pulled up and a woman said, "You waiting for the ferry?" No, we said, we were from a boat anchored in Potter Cove and had walked here. "You want a ride back that way?" she asked. Why, yes, we said, that would be wonderful.

We climbed into a Mercury Grand Marquis, an imposing automobile that spoke grandly of a world before Honda and Toyota. It had seats covered with a vivid blue plush velvet. Our chauffeur, a grandmotherly sort, introduced herself as Mrs. Laura Phillips. She wore very dark, thick-lensed sunglasses with blinker screens at each side, and when she found that we were new to Prudence Island she proposed making a tour before she took us to Potter Cove. Mrs. Phillips drove very slowly, stopping on the way at her son's house to deliver some mail. She told us that about fifty people lived year-round on Prudence Island and maybe fifteen hundred in summer. Some came here summer after summer, the way their parents had, the way their children would; it was a family thing. The mail delivered, she turned south down a road that ran along the west shore of the island. She halted in one place so that we could walk a hundred yards up a path through straggly woods to a rock nine feet tall. From this eminence, known as Pulpit Rock, Roger Williams preached to the local Indians, Mrs. Phillips said. (Williams was the early settler who purchased the island from the Narragansetts in 1637 and was perhaps softening them up for a low offer. He named the island Prudence, and either named or set the pattern for naming the other nearby Bay islands called Hope, Patience, and Despair.)

From here Mrs. Phillips took us south past small coves and rocky beaches to an area of scattered summer houses she called the New York section. Here a ferry used to land from Wickford, across the Bay to the west, bringing vacationers from the great metropolis. The wide paved road that ran nearly straight across the island from here was Broadway. "You can't see them," said Mrs. Phillips, "but back in the woods are old farms, old stone walls, cranberry bogs, swamps, a whole mess of white-tailed deer, a vineyard, and even some sand dunes which we call the Desert. Don't ask me what they're doing there in the woods." Halfway along Broadway she paused outside the two-room schoolhouse. "The teacher comes from Bristol every day," she said. "Sometimes she has to stay the night if the weather is bad." For junior high and beyond, Prudence children commute to the mainland.

The southern third of the island, a former U.S. Navy base, is now a state park, and as the Grand Marquis sashayed slowly along the neat concrete roads, Mrs. Phillips pointed out sheds used by naturalists, picnic tables, and the so-called T-wharf, where visitors can land from their boats to hike along the island trails. The navy had left behind not only the roads and the wharf but many storage buildings and ammunition bunkers. The latter were steep-sided, grass-covered barrows, with deep alleyways running into their interiors. Mrs. Phillips drew our attention to new metal railings which ran over the mounds, protecting the edges of the fifteen-foot drops into the alleys. "Just installed by the state," she said, "to stop stupid people falling in. Taxpayers' money. A real waste."

We trundled up the east side of the island and Mrs. Phillips talked happily about her family: children on honor rolls, a son in the Coast Guard. On retirement, she and her husband had sold their house in Massachusetts—"the market being what it was, we lost a bundle"—and had gone to live in a mobile home in Florida in winter, spending their summers here in a rented cottage, close to their children. At a section called Sandy Point, near a lighthouse, she pulled over to chat with a woman who had just come out of a cottage. Mrs. Phillips said, "These are my new friends, the Baileys." The woman gave her a basket of freshly picked vegetables and Mrs. Phillips, dropping us at the dock at Potter Cove, made us take some tomatoes and a handsome yellow squash.

In the afternoon there was a dulcet breeze from the southeast. We beat down the hazy East Passage of the Bay close to the steep-to Prudence Island shore, just weathering Homestead Wharf, Sandy Point, and the south tip of the island. An immense tanker, presumably bound for Providence, materialized out of nowhere and took our wind for several minutes. Much of the time *Lochinvar* sailed herself to windward. Newport, our destination, is a place we come to less often than we did. This may be in part because of Newport's identification with the Big Time in yachting. Newport can remind one a bit too forcibly of the connection between yachts and money. To be comfortable with this, one should arrive in the right manner and mood, prepared to participate in or look in on sailing at an upper level. I've had exciting visits to Newport, once to take part in the Bermuda Race, which starts from there, as a crew member on the Alden yawl *Mistral,* and on several occasions as a journalist writing about America's Cup contests, going to press conferences and parties and on trips out to sea to watch the dueling yachts. In the days when we lived in Stonington, we also drove to Newport from time to time to show family and friends the great nineteenth-century holiday houses of the very rich. On Ocean Drive and Bellevue Avenue, the Belmonts, Vanderbilts, and Astors erected their French châteaux and Renaissance palazzi, as if to show who had the greatest amount of money and power and thus the best right to impose their secondhand taste on the landscape. Like beauty queens in Marie Antoinette and Lucrezia Borgia costume, the mansions jostle for attention.

In the sixties and early seventies we also sailed to Newport occasionally in *Caliban.* In those days there was room to anchor in Brenton Cove. From there we would row ashore, find an old wharf to tie the dinghy to, and saunter along the shabby downtown streets. In its early days Newport had done well out of slave trading, molasses, and rum. Its legacy of colonial and revolutionary architecture was a good deal more humble and affecting than that left by the robber barons of the Gilded Age. There were also shops where modest boating folk like us could buy a red-painted Chinese hurricane lamp for $3.99 or a folding canvas bucket (ex-U.S. Army) for even less. There were bars for sailors and cheap jewelers for gifts for sailors' girlfriends. Back in Brenton Cove we felt no pressure to perform as yachtspeople. Canada geese came scrounging. At night the gloomy big houses on shore seemed deserted, and the moored yachts silhouetted against the waterfront lights were at a comfortable distance.

By the early eighties, Newport was being fixed up to suit its position as a Yachting Capital. Brenton Cove filled up with moorings. Boating boutiques had replaced the surplus shops. Blocks of condos rose along the once-tatty waterfront, forcing out boatyards. Tour boats carried visitors around the harbor, loudspeaker commentaries pointing out the lawn where Jack Kennedy married Jacqueline Bouvier and the house General Eisenhower used as a summer White House. We were encouraged to phone ahead to reserve a slip or mooring and expected to go ashore by launch; money changed hands.

Ashore, the done thing was a tour of the wharves where the Twelve Meter yachts contending for the hideous cup were being primped and polished by young men in matching rugby shirts while the helmsmen and afterguard smeared on their noses a war paint of white sunblock. On one such wharf I encountered an elderly American wearing a peaked cap with a New York Yacht Club badge. Detecting an English accent, he said, "I wish you'd win the thing and take it away and perhaps there'd be a little peace again in the nice old town of Newport." Well, we Brits never managed it, though our brash cousins, the Aussies, certainly did. But Newport, despite having lost the cup to the Antipodes and San Diego, has gone on being a hectic high-tech yachting town, a mecca for boat shows and regattas, and the "little peace" has never been recovered.

Our last visit to Newport before this up-the-Sakonnet and down-Narragansett Bay voyage was with Buell Hollister. We left *Lochinvar* in Padanaram over a weekend and joined *Olivebank* for a jaunt to watch a match race between two of the surviving J-class yachts, the enormous craft which were the America's Cup contenders between the wars. We motor-sailed westward into a blustery sou'wester. *Olivebank* has her engine exhaust on her starboard quarter, and with her tan junk sails full, heeled over on the port tack, the exhaust is submerged and there is no indication that her big diesel is ticking over. *Olivebank* trundles to windward, surprising out-and-out sailing craft with her speed. "Those Chinese really knew something!" we like to think of them saying to one another on the overtaken yachts. In Newport, we hunted unsuccessfully for a spot to drop the hook in the so-called anchorage area north of the Ida Lewis Yacht Club. (Ida Lewis was the woman who in the second half of the nineteenth century used to look after the little lighthouse, on a rocky outcrop, that is now part of the clubhouse; she is said to have saved the lives of eighteen shipwrecked mariners.) Buell finally anchored in 27 feet of water not far from one of the wharves of Fort Adams, the glum granite fortification at the harbor entrance. We reckoned that *Olivebank*'s heavy anchor chain would allow us to lie to a relatively short scope in that depth. And we had an undisturbed night. But as we breakfasted a harbor launch came alongside to let us know that a ferry from Block Island was soon arriving. It was accustomed to turning right where *Olivebank* was anchored, in order to back in alongside a wharf. We took the hint and moved to a nearby vacant mooring, which fortunately no one else wanted for the next few hours.

In mid-morning *Olivebank* joined the procession of boats which followed the J-yachts past the fort, Hammersmith Farm, Castle Hill, and Brenton Reef. *Shamrock V* was the last of Sir Thomas Lipton's challengers; *Endeavour,* the first of Tommy Sopwith's pair. *Shamrock* green, *Endeavour* blue: great single-masted yachts designed for one absurd but splendid purpose; both boats British, restored by American money; the successful American defenders *Enterprise, Rainbow,* and *Ranger* all broken up. It was more than half a century since *Shamrock* and *Endeavour* had raced in American waters, and a thousand boats had turned out to watch this friendly sparring match between the aged giants. The Coast Guard was also out in strength, attempting to keep the spectating fleet at a respectful distance from the J's. The skipper of each spectator boat had to try not to collide with any of the other boats, which were of all shapes and sizes. At one end of the spectrum was Donald Trump's mega–motor yacht, the *Trump Princess,* formerly owned by the Saudi arms dealer Adhan Khashoggi. As *Olivebank* passed it, a helicopter was landing on its upper deck or top story. Buell commented, "I don't think Donald ever gets his feet wet." At the other end was a 16-foot-long boat like a child's idea of a submarine, with a single sail on top and a Swedish flag. According to the yachting press, it had just crossed the Atlantic. A bearded man stood aft, propelling the boat with a wooden sweep. Beneath a Plexiglas dome amidships appeared a blond female head. (Margot, sympathetically: "Do you think he ever lets her out?") We came near and saw that the Viking barely had room for a foothold on his tiny deck, where he could stand to scull his craft. I called over to him, "Where's your helicopter pad?" He replied, with Scandinavian solemnity, "My boat is too small."

It was a listless morning, the breeze needed for the race taking a long time to arrive. The Coast Guard rushed around, sirens wailing, blue lights flashing, admonishing various craft to keep clear of the J's, which were lying pensively still in the water. "*Olivebank*, sir!" bellowed a loud-speakered stentorian voice, "I request you do not pass in front of the bows of *Shamrock V!*" As it happened, we were passing a long way in front of said bows (which were dormant at that moment); Buell was muttering that he was unable to change course because half a dozen boats around us were doing the same. Eventually the breeze filled in gently from the south. The ten minute gun was fired. We believed that *Olivebank* was now at the correct spectating distance, but *Shamrock*, maneuvering for the start, came charging toward us under full sail, the Coast Guard in manic attendance. At the last moment, when we were fully stretched between admiration of the magnificent sight and a fierce desire to leap overboard out of its way, the huge yacht gybed and headed for the line with *Endeavour*. In fifteen minutes the pair were almost hull down, halfway to Block Island. Recalling Ring Lardner's remark that watching America's Cup racing was as exciting as watching grass grow, we decided we'd already experienced the thrills on offer and set off for Buzzards Bay.

Sailing *Lochinvar* down the East Passage of Narragansett Bay from Prudence Island last year, we passed the base at Melville where the U.S. Navy now concentrates its forces in this area. There is still a lot of gray paint about. The suspension span of Newport Bridge, carrying traffic across the East Passage, was so high above us it seemed to cast no shadow. We downed the main and furled the jib off Goat Island—once a goat pasture, then a navy torpedo station, now condos and marinas. As we circled Brenton Cove, wondering which mooring we should take, with no helpful or avaricious launches in sight, we came on another small sloop whose crew were obviously troubled by the same question. We conferred. "I guess you just pick one up and wait for them to come and demand the rent or else throw you off," said our confrere. I said to Margot, "Keep your eye open for a really weedy pennant."

That was the kind we found. I went forward to offer a form of recompense by removing the slime, proto-jellyfish, and green creepy-crawlies. Later that evening, we were hailed by the other craft, which had taken a nearby mooring, motoring by, looking chastened. "You were lucky," the helmsman called. "The owner of our mooring just came back."

The signs of disuse on our mooring didn't give us immediate confidence to go ashore. We dined on board and listened to social noises rising from the Ida Lewis Yacht Club. But next morning, more sure of our berth, we took the launch in, made contact with a New York friend who summers in Newport with his family, and lunched at the Sporting Rock Beach Club on Bailey's Beach. Although Margot and I had put on our best daytime shore gear, we felt a trifle underdressed. The club men wore yellow linen jackets and bright green trousers. The ladies were exceedingly pale under broad-brimmed hats. We swam with our host in the club pool, a few yards from the beach and the sea, but we were the only people in the pool and I wondered whether we were doing the right thing. Like a character in a Dostoevsky novel I had a violent urge to make a public confession: "I am on a mooring in Brenton Cove for which I haven't paid a cent." But fortunately I managed to keep a grip on myself. No one would have had the remotest idea what I was going on about.

31

IT COMES GRAY and breezy in Sachuest. I know on rising just what sort of day it's going to be. A strong sou'wester—a deep reef in the main—damp foul-weather gear—everything below needing to be stowed properly, which means coffee filters in a dry spot and Granddad Molony's long ebony parallel rules used to jam in place odds and ends on the navigation shelf. The halyards, despite restraint, are strumming against the mast as we breakfast. Our course will be a touch west of southwest. As I brush my teeth, I feel the same suspense in the stomach one has before standing up in a public meeting to make a complicated point. The seacocks are rechecked. I make sure the oars are tied down in the dinghy. I try to give an honest answer to the question: Should I lower the number-two genoa and hoist the number-three? This would mean unfurling the number-two, wrestling it to the deck, and stuffing it below. With luck the sou'wester may ease a little and then we'll need the drive of the bigger sail. Am I shirking a struggle?

With the main hoisted and reefed, we get the anchor up and slouch off in the direction of Sakonnet lighthouse. Then, anchor made fast in its chocks, anchor line fed below, and the jib unfurled, we thrash out of the river mouth on the port tack, just clearing Cormorant Reef and its associated rocks. In the puffs, the lee rail dips under; I let the mainsheet traveler down to the lee quarter. This tack can't go on indefinitely. We would land on the rocky cliffs below the great Newport houses on Bellevue Avenue. But even before the hard fact of the land there are other impediments on this course. I have a sudden all-encompassing sense of déjà vu. We have done all this before. I know, even, that Margot and I are about to embark on a conversation we have already had. She says, "You are remembering the fish traps, aren't you?" I say, "I don't see them yet—maybe they've finally removed the bloody things."

These fish traps are an absolute nuisance and indeed a peril of these waters. Apart from those we passed when entering the Sakonnet, long lines of them are strung out from the Aquidneck shore, farther out to sea than you'd expect. They are huge nets hanging from thick cables and floated by barrels which the Sakonnet fishermen, who own them, camouflage with dark blue, green, or gray paint, as if intentionally making them hard to spot. Nearly every time we sail past here—almost always into a sou'wester, having to tack inshore and out—I fail to see the traps and decide that sanity has at last prevailed: the fishermen of Sakonnet have been compelled (by regulation or the threat of grievous violence) to adopt other methods of harvesting their local seas. And nearly every time Margot shouts, "There the buggers are! Dead ahead. You're heading right into one!"

Sometimes we've tried to go inshore of these fiendish obstructions; this was a mistake. Once I tried to zigzag through them. Margot thinks my native bloody-mindedness makes me seek them out and attempt to do battle with them, like the Don against the windmills. Certainly I've found myself wishing for a razor-sharp centerboard, which would cut through the nets and cables. Occasionally we've felt boxed in by the confounded things, have tacked and gybed and almost panicked before deciding that the only way out of the maze was by the way we came in, if we can find it. How do the fish feel? One morning like this we made our usual blunder and were chased away by the mother ship of the nets. Yellow-oilskinned Sakonnet fishermen made menacing gestures at us, and we muttered salty curses back at them as we tacked out to sea. This morning there are no witnesses to our incursion. Margot calls: "A line of barrels ahead!" I have learned not to think that I am greater than the fish traps. I shout back, "Ready about!" She casts off the starboard jib sheet from its cleat and holds the line steady on the winch until I shout "Lee ho!"

We have a wet plug to windward past Brenton Reef and across the entrance of Narragansett Bay. The tide is setting us up the Bay, where we don't want to go. We claw across to the west shore of the Bay, to Narragansett Pier, a little resort town which has had no pier for many years. Then we make a lengthy series of short tacks in the lee of the land along the shore of Point Judith Neck. This is another of those stretches that generally seems longer than you could wish. We eat lunch. Margot has astutely made pita bread and tuna-fish-salad sandwiches, which are further enclosed in cellophane bags; thus not too much of the contents drop into the cockpit. Then we face Point Judith itself and once more feel the weight of wind and sea unmitigated by the land.

Point Judith is another of our milestones: at least we've got as far as this! It also figures in our mental chart as a Point of Storms or, just to fool us, as a Point of Strange Calms. Here the currents oppose one another; the waves become shorter, higher, and more confused. Here the second reef often gets pulled down, or we suddenly find ourselves slatting in a great swell rolling in from the Atlantic while a malign eddy sweeps us toward the rocks. As the lighthouse creeps awfully close, we look at the tormented lobster-pot buoys for guidance. Surf breaks high and loud on the breakwaters of the Harbor of Refuge. Ferries and fishing boats charge in and out of Point Judith Pond, adding to the maelstrom-like conditions.

Today the waves off the Point are small but steep. I call them billows, as in Shakespeare's "inconstant billows dancing" (*Henry V*). Margot, heroically cranking in the jib sheet as we tack offshore, pauses to say, "It sounds as if it means big pillows." But these are nothing feathery or soft; they jolt and judder us as we bang into them. In the early afternoon, the sun breaks through to encourage us. The sandy green shape of Block Island appears to the southwest. Our test after another hour or so of windward work is to find the buoy off Block Island's north reef, and to arrive at it in such a way that we are uptide of it. The current is about to change and push eastward. In similar circumstances we've got here before without being far enough to the west and the tide has pushed us back around the tip of the reef, seemingly on the way back to Martha's Vineyard or (who knows?) the Azores. This afternoon I get it about right. We overstand the north reef bell on the port tack, and then, after coming about, the starboard tack brings us southward nicely west of the buoy and on the windward, tideward side of the reef. On the sandy north point of the island, the little lighthouse marks our arrival; the lantern and balcony sit directly on the roof above a gable end. From here it is a mere two miles to the breakwater at the entrance to Great Salt Pond.

Block Island is a pork chop–shaped piece of moorland dotted with ponds large and small. It is about seven miles from north to south and a bit over four from west to east at its broadest point. Adriaen Block, one of the many intrepid Dutch mariners who ranged the world in the early seventeenth century, is given the credit for landing here in 1614, since he left it first his Christian name—Adrian's Island— and then his surname, which has survived despite later attempts to rechristen it New Shoreham, among other things. The native Manisses could muster three hundred warriors in 1662 but slowly faded, pestered out of existence by petty restrictions; they weren't allowed to walk out at night and an act of 1719 prohibited them from keeping dogs. (Nonetheless, by 1860 there were too many dogs on Block Island; they had gone off their staple diet of leftover fish and were making do with the island's geese and sheep.) The island historian, the Reverend Livermore, a man of hopeful wit, points out that Block Island was a stumbling *block* on this coast for many ships. It got in the way of sailing vessels, and at least one steamship, and thus provided a livelihood for "wreckers." The poet John Greenleaf Whittier was among many who assumed the worst of the islanders on this score. His 1860s poem "The Palatine" gave the impression that the immigrant ship was lured into stranding and then pillaged after it struck on Sandy Point in 1738:

Into the teeth of death she sped:
(May God forgive the hands that fed
The false lights over the rocky Head!) . . .

Down swooped the wreckers, like birds of prey
Tearing the heart of the ship away,
And the dead had never a word to say.

And then, with ghastly shimmer and shine
Over the rocks and the seething brine,
They burned the wreck of the Palatine.

And of course the *Palatine* took its revenge by producing an eerie light thereafter, seen now and then off Sandy Point, a ghostly reminder of the wicked islanders' crime.

In fact, says the Reverend Livermore, the "wreckers" were Christian men who banded together to save ships and their cargoes from ultimate destruction. It seems that many of the passengers of the *Palatine* had been sick and malnourished because the crew would sell them food only for exorbitant sums. Although some of the weaker died after the wreck, and were dutifully buried on the island in a spot still called the Palatine Graves, others were looked after until they had recovered. In the case of the schooner *Laura E. Messer,* which also stranded on Sandy Point, the God-fearing wreckers eventually relaunched her with her cargo intact and the crew's possessions unmolested. As for the Palatine Light, modern opinion ascribes it to the decay of undersea marsh, producing methane, which ignites in certain atmospheric conditions. However, some Block Islanders are rightly reluctant to believe this, wanting to keep the light among the "haunts" the island is proud of—others include a headless figure and a dancing mortar.

In the nineteenth century, this isle of farmers, fishermen, and wreckers began to attract holidaymakers. The venturesome first party was seven men from Newport who came "a-fishing." Steamboats brought tourists, a government-funded harbor was built on the east shore, and the first "public house for boarders and excursionists" opened in 1842. Soon other big clapboard structures with surrounding porches were being erected: the Spring House in 1852 and the Ocean View Hotel in 1873 were two of the most notable. By 1875 Block Island had so caught on as a summer place that the locals were already somewhat jaded with visitors. President Ulysses M. Grant landed for a short tour of the island in August that year. Reverend Livermore has to admit that although "all the available flags were flying, never, probably, was there less excitement on the arrival of so distinguished a visitor." Fishermen mending their nets didn't bother to look up as the great man went by. Few children turned out to greet him. The President "dined, shook hands with those introduced to him, affectionately beckoned to a bright little girl to come to him, visited the new lighthouse, and took leave for Cape May about three p.m."

Although the channel into Great Salt Pond lies east-southeast, sailing vessels entering in the prevailing sou'westerly often find themselves hard on the wind. So it is today: the wind is being funneled out against us from the demi-Paradise within. It's touch and go whether we will have to tack across the channel, an anxious-making maneuver in view of the many boats motoring out and in. But it is also part of our Block Island routine to sail in here, and sail we will, sheets right in, pinching in the puffs, standing by the center-board pennant so that we can haul up the board if we are forced out of the dredged channel, and gaining the reluctant attention of the beach fishermen casting into the channel. Possibly they are hoping something will go wrong; the wrecking instinct dies hard. However, we weather the port-hand buoy abreast the Coast Guard station, and once inside the pond we free the sheets. Then we roll up the jib so that we have more time to get the anchor ready and find a suit-able spot to anchor.

Great Salt Pond nearly spans the island. Once it was a true pond, completely enclosed, but the barriers to the sea east and west were narrow; salt water leached through or washed over in storms and gave the pond a briny taste. The first settlers saw at once its possibilities as a harbor on an island which didn't have one naturally. They dug a channel through the west beach, but it soon silted up. It wasn't until 1897—some decades after the first small artificial harbor now called Old Harbor had been built out from the east shore—that government funds made it possible to hire the heavy engineering equipment for dredging a channel into the pond and building a breakwater which would stabilize the opening. New Harbor came into existence but went on being called Great Salt Pond.

We first sailed in here in the *Billy Ruffian* in the 1960s. We saw at once that the pond was indeed "Great"—at least a mile broad and a mile tall; a little bigger than Menemsha, though less regular in shape. In those days the spaciousness of the pond wasn't sullied by the presence of many yachts. Perhaps a score would be at anchor in the southeastern corner, near Champlin's Dock or Payne's Dock, where the New London ferry then landed. Above the shores of the pond infrequent houses were scattered in stone-walled and relatively treeless meadows. Indeed, our first impressions of the island were of unkempt fields, often with little family cemeteries in them like that on the Sakonnet, of houses in need of paint, and of certain beaches under cliffs where the natives dumped their old cars when they wouldn't run anymore. Those still roadworthy often plied for hire as taxis or, in private hands, stopped to offer a lift to anyone walking. Old ladies wore long flowered cotton dresses and ankle socks. On the roadsides black-eyed Susan, blue chicory, and blackberries grew in wild profusion.

But by the early 1980s Block Island had become the major summer attraction for boating people on this part of the coast. You could sit at anchor in Great Salt Pond and watch a seemingly unbroken procession of yachts arrive. One Fourth of July weekend more than twelve hundred boats were here. Conditions have often been so crowded that boats anchored too close together or on too short a scope; they bumped and dragged. We've had favorite anchoring spots in the pond, but lately have been grateful for any room at all in water of reasonable depth. Some of the pond's deeper areas call for uncomfortably long lengths of rode or chain; some of the shallows have their own difficulties. We once anchored with *Caliban* well into the little bay west of Champlin's, and when we came to leave couldn't retrieve our anchor. The Danforth had apparently hooked under a pipe carrying a cable along the bottom to the Coast Guard station and wouldn't budge. This was before Margot's subaqua apprenticeship. We had to cut the line. (We pictured Block Island skin divers swimming along the pipe at least once a summer collecting anchors, which gave us additional pain.) To get away from the crowds, we've sometimes turned hard right after the entrance channel and gone into Cormorant Cove. Once you've avoided a rock in the shoal-constricted mouth of the cove, you're in a safe little anchorage, though one with a long walk to the commercial center of the island at Old Harbor. One of our fancied spots in the main body of the pond is in relatively shallow water near the east shore, with another nearby rock that may keep the fainthearted at a distance (at least those who notice the rock on their charts). On the little sandy cliff overlooking this spot stands a Victorian cottage. The house seems to be almost entirely green-shingled roof; the small downstairs is surrounded by a white-railed porch. We've rarely seen anyone on this porch, though one evening it became clear that a small girl called Lorina was in residence. An irate adult male voice could be heard shouting, "Lorina! You do what you're told!"

Today, the pond isn't too densely packed. Late August has its cruising advantages, since families with children are now pondering the imminence of school and college. This year Bob has no doubt had a deterrent effect; a week on, the impact of the hurricane is visible along the shores of the pond, with the small trees and shrubs browned or bare, and much salvage activity still going on—two big barges with cranes are at work lifting off stranded yachts; a number of boats are lacking bowsprits and masts or looking in various ways bashed and battered. Unfortunately "our" anchorage off the green-roofed house is fully spoken for by boats on recently planted moorings, and we're forced to sail a few hundred yards farther north. But this has the advantage of putting us close to the isthmus, or neck, that connects the north and south parts of the island and across which, a very short walk, is Scotch Beach, part of a longer strand called Crescent Beach, which I call (privately) the best beach in the world.

However, the beach is for tomorrow. This evening the sou'wester goes on venting its bluster; nasty little gusts come buffeting across the pond. We're content to sit in *Lochinvar*'s cockpit for a combined anchor watch and happy hour. We watch late-arriving boats sail in and gaze warily at those that look as if they might be anchoring too close. One couple—older man, younger woman—take their big sloop into very shallow water not far from us and make eleven attempts to get their anchor to hold. It is an object lesson, which I attend to as humbly as I can: he goes astern too fast and doesn't let out enough scope before snubbing up on the anchor line. But the twelfth time is lucky. We watch the sun setting, long lavender-pink beams lighting the east shore of the pond. On a nearby elderly motor cruiser, an elderly man we have seen here before steps onto his foredeck, bagpipes under his arm, and pipes a Caledonian lament.

32

IF THE LAST POST in Great Salt Pond is the sound of bagpipes, reveille is the raucous shout *"Andiamo!"* Two young men from Aldo's Bakery in a small outboard skiff are hawking their wares around the fleet. And if *"Andiamo!"* doesn't bring the customers on deck, a further call of "Wake up, everybody!" follows. The trouble from our point of view is that, despite the picturesque solicitations, Aldo's blueberry muffins, Danish, doughnuts, and fresh bread are too sweet, too mushy, and too expensive. But the number of willing buyers always seems to exceed that of the disappointed or disinclined, for *"Andiamo!"* goes on being the wake-up call in Great Salt Pond.

The morning is calm and sunny. Among the many things we want to do on Block Island are walk to town, meet Peter Wood, and go swimming on the best beach in the world. Before doing any of these, I row into the Block Island Boat Basin, one of the three marine facilities in the Pond, to fill the water jugs and buy two bags of ice cubes. (The block ice tends to be either sold out or reserved for slip customers, but the cubes will see us through our last couple of days. Another advantage of the end of August is that the ice you pay so much for doesn't melt so fast.) At the Basin shop I pick up a free copy of *The Block Island Times,* the weekly paper which Peter Wood edits and publishes. Then I phone Peter and arrange to meet him later in the day.

In mid-morning Margot and I (carrying a small backpack for purchases) walk to town. The island roads are fairly narrow and mostly without sidewalks, and we stroll along the sandy margins, keeping a cautious eye on people on mopeds as they weave and wobble along at high speeds. Mopeds are also a blight on the Vineyard and Nantucket, but they are particularly so on this smaller island. Any visitor can disembark from a ferry, cruise ship, or yacht and rent one of these noisy and perilous machines. Several local entrepreneurs got into the moped rental business in a big way in the mid-1970s and many islanders were aggrieved. Campaigns have been conducted to limit the mopeds and even ban them. Bumper stickers on island vehicles declared NO PEDS—which wasn't a denunciation of pedestrians. Legal cases were fought to get rid of mopeds, and when the campaigners lost in the Rhode Island courts, there was a movement to secede from Rhode Island. The number of rental outlets is now limited to six, and the number of mopeds to three hundred, but there continue to be too many accidents and a lot of injuries as vacational high spirits and hard asphalt meet at speed. Peter Wood's paper recommends renting bicycles instead and conveys the island rescue squad's straightforward advice to those who insist on mopeds: Know the difference between the throttle and the

brake. Wear a helmet. Stay off dirt roads. And give a dona-
tion to the rescue squad, which provides its help for free.
(The air ambulance to the hospital in Westerly, Rhode
Island, costs real money.)

We walk uphill on Ocean Avenue, which overlooks
Trims Pond as well as the Atlantic, and then downhill past
the Block Island Power Company. Diesel generators spew
dark gray-brown smoke into the air from rusty stacks. The
noise is like that of a hundred mopeds. An immense wind
generator, like that in Cuttyhunk, used to stand on the hill
behind, intended to reduce the island's fossil-fuel consump-
tion, but for some reason a connection to the system proved
impracticable. Dark hints from some locals that the power
company's difficulties in this respect had something to do
with the fact that it was also at the time in the diesel and
heating fuel business were strenuously denied.

Another five minutes brings us to the post office. On the
grass in front cupcakes and brownies are being sold in aid
of the Fire Department. Then it's uphill again past another
landmark, the building that used to house Rose's, a real
hardware store before it became a restaurant called
Tiffany's; presently it is a boutique. Where the road bends,
at the end of the long porch of the Surf Hotel, we look out
over Old Harbor.

Here, Block Island as always seems shakily balanced
between its desire to be the Bermuda of the North and the
inclinations of a few merchants (and moped moguls) to
turn it into the Coney Island of New England. But at its
heart, Old Harbor is just plain funky. Past the Surf, with its
gingerbread woodwork and wicker-seated rocking chairs,
and the National, an even larger clapboard hotel, we pause
in a scruffy little park overlooking a scruffy parking lot

beside the small harbor. This is where ferries land from New London, Point Judith, Providence, and Newport. A few yachts and fishing boats are moored close to one another and the stone north breakwater. Old hands as visitors, we are glad to see the Star Department Store is still in business, same as last year; it sells postcards, T–shirts, and table mats, with or without Block Island motifs. The frail privet hedge survives in front of the terrace of the Harborside Inn. The white-painted female statue called Rebecca presides as always over a fountain and dog-watering basin at the mini-roundabout at the end of Water Street. We sample the cold drinks and eponymous products at the Ice-Cream Place. Alas, the Empire Movie Theater—one-story clapboard—has closed, it looks as if forever. We walk up onto the knoll overlooking the harbor and the sea where the stone foundations of the Ocean View Hotel lurk under the coarse grass. The Ocean View was built in 1873 by a local man, Nicholas Ball, who had done well in the California Gold Rush. For a long time the hotel claimed to have the longest (287 feet) bar in the world, with bartenders wearing roller skates. The roller skates weren't evident in 1965, when Margot and I (staying down the road at the dry Surf) had a drink there. There was only one bartender, and the six people at the bar sat close or even huddled together for human company.

With a *Boston Globe* and essential supplies in the backpack, we wend our way to New Harbor and out to *Lochinvar*. After lunch, we row to the isthmus of Indian Neck. We anchor the dinghy, tread barefooted the grainy old planks some thoughtful person has laid across a soggy stretch of marsh, and step quickly across the hot asphalt of Corn Neck Road. A few steps more bring us to our favorite beach. Surf of just the right playful height rolls in from the southeast. Beyond the little Scotch Beach parking area there aren't many people on the sand. We stride north, sometimes on dry sand, sometimes with feet in the inrushing water. Beyond a section called Mansion Beach the sand narrows and there are even fewer swimmers and sunbathers. Near Clay Head, at an area the locals call Pots and Kettles, the cliff is unstable: chunks of congealed stone, sand, and clay lie like large lumps of crunchy cereal among the rocks at the water's edge. We make this our turnaround point and walk back to an untenanted spot on the sand where the off-lying waters aren't too dangerously rock-strewn for swimming. Margot dons her mask, snorkel, and fins, and swims far out. I swim for a shorter time closer to the beach and then sit on the sand. I keep her snorkel tube in view as long as I can, but at last a sun-induced sleepiness overcomes worry. We've been coming to this beach for thirty years to walk, swim, and doze. It is one of those places that marks the passing of time—here we are again, another summer— but also makes time pause.

Remembering to leave the anchor light rigged and burning, we row ashore again from *Lochinvar* in the late afternoon. We wait for Peter Wood on the raised outside deck of The Oar, the Boat Basin bar. From here the variety of craft in the pond is manifest. Old gaff schooners, new plastic racers; sedate motor cruisers and Cigarette-type powerboats. Some people go to sea in floating kennels and some in floating mansions. Some camp out on the water, others have captains and stewards. Some take baths; others stand under cockpit shower bags. The biggest private vessel in the pond today is *Platinum,* a huge motor yacht which has a funnel, twin helicopters, and a Red Duster flying at her stern, where Gibraltar is given as her port of registry. At the Boat Basin, most of the boats are sportfishermen, squat transoms backed in to the floats, plugged into shore current for their microwaves and TVs.

As we sit here, a man wearing a peaked Popeye-the-sailor's cap rows a battered dinghy ashore. I recognize him as the owner of a boat anchored near us, sleeping bag draped over its boom, cardboard cartons on the cabin top, jerry cans tied to the shrouds; it is clear that he is a "live-aboard." Several dinghy-lengths behind him as he rows in swims a Jack Russell terrier, getting its exercise. Ignoring the dinghy float, the skipper ties up at the main dock below a NO DINGHIES sign. While he is filling a Clorox bleach bottle with drinking water, his dog emerges from the water onto the pebbly beach below The Oar, but sees a big ginger cat snoozing on one of the rocks and retreats into the briny. It dog-paddles farther along before landing again. Then it shakes itself dry and trots out on the dock after its master, pausing only to defecate in mid-dock, where the pedestrian traffic is at its most intense. At last it spots the skipper heading toward The Oar and scurries after him. The dog is tethered outside the bar by an old piece of line while Skip has a drink inside.

Dogs remain a feature of this evening. Peter's two curly black Portuguese water dogs, Niño and Annabel, are in his Jeep. Peter has been spear-fishing. Niño and Annabel, damp and sandy, climb onto the seats to sit with us, even on us. We think they recognize dog lovers; Peter—wearing baggy white shorts and a bandanna around his brow—says they do this with everybody.

After a career as a New York journalist, Peter moved out

to Block Island in the 1970s with his wife, Shirley, and the two of them took over *The Block Island Times*. Although Shirley died tragically several years ago in a plane crash en route to the mainland, Peter continues to run the paper and keep Shirley's name on the masthead. At his house on Old Mill Road, as far backcountry as you can get on the island, we stroll drinks in hand across the lawn to a neighboring field. There Peter introduces us to Guido, an Italian sheepdog. Guido looks like a cross between a small polar bear and one of the dozen sheep he is guarding. He barks in a powerful baritone to let us know he's on the job. Peter says Guido at times thinks he is a sheep. Recently he took all his charges out of the field and led them on a long ramble across the island. His owners feed him on pasta, says Peter, because they feel he might get homesick and start swimming toward Italy.

While we chat in the living room, the sun sets. Members of Peter's staff appear from the basement office, where the next issue of the paper is being put to bed. (To make up for the lack of daylight, a friendly artist has painted blue sky and white clouds on the basement walls and ceiling.) *The Block Island Times* may not be as venerable as the Provincetown *Advocate* or have the broadsheet elegance of the *Vineyard Gazette,* but it does an impressive weekly year-round job of covering the local scene; a fortnightly free supplement appears only in summer. Like many small papers, *The Block Island Times* has to balance the need for advertising with the dictates of its editors' consciences. On Block Island, the confrontation between developers and conservers is sometimes fierce. Peter has seen both sides, since Shirley also ran one of the island's four real-estate firms, and he and she donated some land to help establish a permanent green way across the island for walkers. Many of the paper's stories deal with the sale of old farms for sub-divisions and the outcry which ensues. On Corn Neck Road, a large complex of suburban summer homes was recently erected, against the protests of citizens' groups like HUSTLE (Help Us Save the Land and Environment). Roughly ten new summer homes are built each year. Some, like one going up on the southern ridge overlooking Great Salt Pond, are grotesquely out of scale.

"We haven't done quite as well as the Vineyard and Nantucket in protecting land from development," says Peter, "but about 20 percent of the island is now covered by conservation easements, which I think is pretty good. A great deal of federal, state, and private money has been channeled to help save our ponds, meadows, and beaches. And though a lot of the merchants complain that progress is being stifled, the island has experienced tremendous eco-nomic growth over the last twenty years. We have our own bank, two law offices, four big hotels that once were on the point of being boarded up, mushrooming B&B's, more and more visitors, and a waterworks that's no longer full of dead birds."

The problems of the larger world are here, writ small, but sounding just as serious. How to dispose of more and more garbage. How to prevent pollution in Great Salt Pond. Whether to appoint an out-of-towner as police chief. And for the editor-publisher of *The Block Island Times,* who unlike the editor of *The New York Times* is likely to meet those he writes about next day in the post office or grocery, the question: how to get across to some of his reader-adver-tisers that they should be content making an adequate living in an idyllic place? Peter counts himself lucky in that, unlike his New York counterpart, he can commute to work by walking down into his own cellar.

In the cellar of Peter's barn across the yard, I remind him, his workbench and tools once helped me. After dining chez Wood, we had sailed away the following day in *Clio* and got as far as the bumpy waters off the north reef. Here a mast spreader snapped. We hurriedly came about to save the mast itself and limped back to Payne's Dock in Great Salt Pond. Borrowing the dock's homemade ladder, I unshipped the rotten pieces of ash, took a taxi up to Old Mill Road, and fabricated a new spreader from a piece of oak in Peter's scrap pile. Back to Payne's; up the mast again; fix the spreader; thanks and a tip to the good-natured dockman; and then off to anchor before resuming our voyage next morning.

Tonight Peter has an end-of-season party for his staff to attend. He drops us at the Payne's Dock end of Ocean Avenue, outside Deadeye Dick's Restaurant. Our farewells are always the same: "See you next summer!" It's an end-of-August ritual for Margot and me to dine at Deadeye Dick's. Given a choice between the outside porch (cooler but buggy) and inside (noisy, warmer, no fans), we eat inside. The food and wine are dandy, our waitress— Annette—amiable, the napkins not paper. In a week or so this place will be shuttered for the winter and Annette will be in college. We walk back to the Boat Basin and row out to *Lochinvar*, looking for our anchor light burning for real among the electric masthead lights of the floating city in the pond. It helps us to spot it. Margot lights the cabin lamp. I stand for a while in the cockpit. On the south wind the racket of the island power plant can just be heard, as can the disco music from Champlin's Dock. The yachts that tie up there must know what they're letting themselves in for. On a few nearby craft, halyards ping lightly. An inflatable dinghy goes by, its outboard pop-popping, the couple in it unaware of me. She says to him, "I told you to leave a light on." He to her: "I'm sure the boat's in this direction." She: "Next time I'll stay at Ballards." I recall Thoreau: "Many an irksome noise, go some way off, is heard as music." For tomorrow, the weather radio promises south to southwest, 10 to 15. Nothing could be better.

33

"GOING TO AMERICA" is how Block Islanders describe the mainland journey. Our course is 310 degrees, the reciprocal of the 130 degrees we would steer when coming out here from Watch Hill. The forecast was no lie. Balmy light airs from the south become a perfect full-sail breeze from the southwest. The early haze burns off. As *Lochinvar* reaches along at nearly 5 knots in a calm sea, we look back now and then at Block Island getting smaller and mistier, already turning into memory. Well, there's next year. Perhaps it's bad luck to think such thoughts; something might break and we'd have to wend our way back to Payne's Dock and Peter's workbench. On the other hand, worrying about something sometimes seems like a way of forfending it: the mast can't fall down when you've just visualized such a calamity. Meanwhile, I trim the sheets for an extra tenth of a knot, and when Margot comes on deck with sunscreen goo and hat, I tell her happily, "We're beat-

ing that Catalina 30 which came out of the pond with us."
(I don't say anything about how the dozy crew of the
Catalina are letting their genoa luff and flap, thus reducing
their speed.) Half a mile away the ferry from New London
crosses our course, making for the north reef buoy on its
way to Old Harbor. A fairly new vessel, it is more shiplike
than its predecessor, which resembled a roasting pan. And
possibly because I've got *Lochinvar* in the groove and all is
right as it can be in our small section of the world, Margot,
after a five-minute stretch-out, says, "Isn't it time we tried
Paul's fishing rod?"

Apart from a short stay below decks during Bob, the rod
has been strapped to a cabin-top handrail ever since it came
aboard. Margot attaches a lure which looks like half a herring: pink and silver, with a grapnel of three rusty hooks.
She works out how to let the line out and how to crank it
in. Then she sits down with the rod over the starboard
quarter and watches the lure skip and dance and burrow in
our wake, about forty feet astern, well clear of the dinghy. I
lose interest in it after a while. The Catalina crew have
noticed their unproductive jib, have sheeted it in, and are
sailing through to windward of us. Margot will have to
move so that I can get at our starboard jib sheet winch to
make a tiny adjustment for greater speed.

Before I can ask her to do this, she exclaims, "My God!
What's that?" "That" is a strong hit. In her excitement she lets
out more line. Then, having figured out which lever or knob
to push to reel it in, she winds the crank. Slowly the line
comes in. One moment there's nothing visible and the next a
great heaving and splashing. I slacken the mainsheet and then
the jib sheet to reduce our speed. Margot reels in the fish. It
comes up, shiny silver blue: a bluefish, still threshing as she

lifts it into the unbuoyant air. How is it that it doesn't leap off the hook? I seize it in the burlap bag Paul said was part of the necessary equipment. Margot gets the hook out from a mouth of bared sharp teeth. The wretched thing is panting and lashing about inside the bag as we lower it into the stern locker.

"How big was it?" asks Margot, as thrilled as I've ever seen her.

"At least seven pounds," I say. "Maybe eight."

Of course, one is never enough. Truly bitten, Margot lets the lure run again. As she settles down on the cockpit seat, I look past her shoulder at the water gliding past the lee rail. An enormous something catches my eye. Now it's my turn to yell.

A flattened snout. A vast menacing mouth. The beast is yellow and greeny-black and seems to go down vertically for at least ten feet. I shout again, "For God's sake, Margot, haul in that line!" The idea of hooking this giant is appalling. He rolls over in the water for a look at us and dips under. Astern, his triangular black fin appears for a moment. The shark was perhaps drawn by the struggle of our bluefish. We decide we've done our fishing for today.

On other occasions in Block Island Sound we've sighted sunfish and swordfish. Once I spotted what looked like a gaudy baseball cap floating on its side. I steered for it and was about to reach over and pick it up when Margot, on the foredeck, screamed, "Don't!" It was a Portuguese man-of-war. "Contact," said our guide to sea life, which we consulted later, "may be serious, though human fatalities have not been verified." I recall it now as a white-and-purple ruff, with a crimped border like a pie, raised in a beautiful high arch. It was actually sailing to windward. So far we've seen no sea serpents.

•

The haze thickens again as we approach the mainland shore. The flood current, now sweeping us westward, has to be allowed for. I need to keep in mind the broken chain of reefs and rocks lying just underwater between Watch Hill and Fishers Island. But we know we're on the right course for Watch Hill Passage when we see the large yellow-painted hotel rising from the modest heights of Watch Hill. Then we catch sight of the big green gong buoy to port and the big red bell to starboard that marks Gangway Rock, with Watch Hill lighthouse on the spit curving out from the base of the hill. The gong and the bell toll competitively, as if for rival congregations. We trim sheets for the close-hauled fetch through the passage.

The wind is on the light side here, maybe preparing for a midday calm, but there's enough to whisk us along Napatree Beach. Once around Napatree Point, Stonington outer breakwater is visible. We're two miles from our moor-ing. Already I'm feeling both glad and sad to be back. Margot, I know from experience, dislikes these homecom-ings more comprehensively than I do. By this stage in our cruise, her home is *Lochinvar* and she doesn't want to go permanently ashore. So I say, as I have done in previous years, "How about Sandy Point for a late lunch, and then a swim?" It is a way of postponing a landing. She always replies, "Good idea."

Sometimes we put off our return by dropping into East Harbor, Fishers Island, for lunch, a swim, and even a last night on board. But more often Sandy Point is our penulti-mate stopping place. Although still called a point, from being attached to Napatree until the 1938 hurricane, it's now an island sandbar which protects Little Narragansett

Bay and provides a base for many restless terns and many more tough, possessive gulls that make a good living from the Bay's natural resources, scraps from Stonington fishing boats, and pickings from the Stonington dump. On weekends Sandy Point is a place for boating parties to swim and picnic. Today, in early afternoon, we're likely to have it to ourselves. We anchor in view of the bottom, five feet down, fifty yards off the low middle of the island. Lunch first and then a job I'm not looking forward to—filleting Margot's fish.

I place the chopping board on a newspaper laid over the teak hatch of the lazaret. Our galley's all-purpose carving knife is a wooden-handle Norwegian fish knife, but its stainless-steel blade is not brilliantly sharp. Margot photographs the bluefish; a copy will go to Paul. Trying to remember how Paul and the Jamaican lady in Nantucket dealt with their fish, I make a considerable mess. Now I know why I've resisted fishing for so long; this is what you have to do every time you catch one. But in ten minutes the surly gulls have been propitiated with head and carcass, the gore has been washed overboard, and two rather hacked fillets of bluefish are wrapped up in our icebox, trophies of today's voyage.

After rigging the boarding ladder, we swim ashore and walk around Sandy Point. Bob has carved out an abrupt little cliff on the northeast side of the island, which once shelved gently. Masses of weed and eelgrass are matted around empty clamshells and the wreckage of horseshoe crabs, those prickly mementoes of early creation. In the years we lived in Stonington, we used to come out here to celebrate with a single birthday picnic the late August birthdays, two days apart, of two of our daughters. Sand inevitably ground its way into the sandwiches and wind blew out the candles on the cake. "Why did we do it?" Margot and I ask one another, though that of course is a question about parenthood itself and there is no original answer. But those picnics were, by and large, fun, and perhaps that goes for parenthood, too.

Under mainsail alone we ghost around Stonington Point and into the harbor. The village on its stony promontory seems half asleep, apart from a few children paddling off the beach at the Point and a lobsterman hauling his pots near the inner breakwater. The lad driving the Dodson Boatyard launch gives us a cheery wave as we slide through the crowded moorings, but fortunately we aren't seen by anyone who might announce our return. In spirit we aren't quite back. We pick up our mooring off the club dock. There's still plenty of daylight and time to go ashore, but it's better to have one more night on board. After all, there's no need to go anywhere, and we have fresh bluefish for dinner. It's a night of perfect calm, during which I wake once or twice to hear the hooting of the trains, reminding me that *Lochinvar* is in her home harbor.

SEPTEMBER

34

FOR SEVERAL DAYS, although we've moved ashore, I still wake up thinking that I'm in my fo'c'sle bunk. The cruise drifts in and out of mind. I look at trees to gauge the strength of the wind. I imagine that the tides are still moving us up and down, this way and that. In Stonington, unwelcome intimations of the land's reality nudge us: an overdue gas bill, sent on from Greenwich, makes small-print threats of disconnection; the date for our return flights a few weeks hence has not by divine intervention been changed. Work and domestic duties await. As far as this rapidly waning season is concerned, it's now or never to make use of *Lochinvar*. Visiting friends and family are taken aboard. Returns of hospitality take the form of lunches afloat, afternoon sails, and evening drinks in the cockpit. We sail, for example, to Napatree via the inside passage north of Sandy Point and across the shallows of Little Narragansett Bay, then land and walk along the sandspit to the old poison-ivy-guarded fort. In the other direction, we walk to Watch Hill, to the little line of shops by the harbor, to buy ice cream and browse in the Book and Tackle Shop and stand by the silent carousel, for which summer has already ended. We pay our respects to Ninigret, sachem or chief of the Niantic tribe, whose bronze statue overlooks the harbor: he kneels, a feather in each of his twin braids, and a codfish in either hand.

Some afternoons I sail alone up Fishers Island Sound. I take pleasure in the glittering water and deep-shadowed September light, the buoys standing up tall and the black cormorants flapping fast. A sweater is needed for the long tack up the Sound when the mainsail shades the cockpit. The sound of a lobster boat makes me realize that the throbbing of powerboat engines in all directions, which makes a sort of tinnitus all summer, is no longer to be heard.

On one such afternoon, starting early, I sail to Noank and up the Mystic River to visit my friend Stephen Jones. Jones is not only a writer and professor of marine literature but the proprietor of a small boatyard which caters to the needs of a charter boat, an ex-Maine sardine carrier called the *Sylvina W. Beal*. I anchor off a little West Mystic cove behind Willow Point, a few hundred yards south of the railroad bridge, where the *Beal*—a bowspritless knockabout schooner—has just moored, and row ashore. The Jones headquarters are in a small frame building with an upstairs balcony to sit on, beer in hand, watching the boats pass in the river and trains clattering across the bridge. Jones and I are doing precisely this and discussing recent events (Bob), boats (the *Beal* and *Lochinvar*), and books (the collected works of Joseph Mitchell), when a message arrives from the

Beal: "Geoffrey has hurt his back. Can you help bring the passengers ashore?"

Geoffrey, Stephen's son, is owner and skipper of the *Beal,* which has been on a three-day trip to Greenport. Stephen and I board a launch used for ferry work, but the engine balks. We proceed to Stephen's pride and joy, an ancient fishing boat called *Lawrence,* which has a small stand-up wheelhouse and a raised foredeck, from which I cast off the bowline. We chug out into the river and alongside the *Beal.* I make fast the bowline again and hand down the suitcases and grips of the half-dozen passengers. Geoffrey slowly rises from a prone position on the *Beal*'s deck and hobbles to the rail, over which Stephen helps him. He climbs down to the *Lawrence*'s deck, face tight with pain. (I know how it feels. My own disks and lumbar muscles ache in sympathy.) Despite the temporary loss of their captain, the passengers appear to have had a good voyage. At the dock, I lift some of the bags ashore, but have to make it clear to one young woman, who seems to think I've been impressed into full-time service before the mast in the Jones fleet, that this is as far as I'm taking them.

In the office, the passengers gone, Geoffrey watches me demonstrate, flat on a bench with my knees up, a set of back exercises a physiotherapist taught me the last time my back seriously "went out," and which I've been performing morn and night ever since, to some avail. But Geoffrey is too riven by his own back pain to pay much attention. He is driven away to an osteopath. Stephen says he has noted the exercises and will remind Geoffrey of them. I tell Stephen as I get up to leave that if lifting all those bags proves to have done in my back, I'll expect workman's compensation. Stephen points out that when my back originally collapsed, on a winter morning some twenty-five years ago, after I lifted a sailing dinghy with a man who turned out not to be doing his share of lifting, he—Jones—had come to my Stonington bedside with a bottle of Barbados rum, just landed in Noank from the world-circumnavigating ketch *Sandafjord*. Which leads us back to then, and then to questions about Patrick Cullen and Tim McGinnis, two of *Sandafjord*'s crew, and what they're doing now . . .

It is twilight and a purple-silver calm as I take *Lochinvar* downriver. I stick to the buoyed channel past Noank, remembering that the last time I steered *Lochinvar* on a shortcut across the shallows I spent a day unblocking the engine cooling system. Despite the water-straining device, it was thoroughly clogged with eelgrass. The navigation lights, little used as they are, make a welcome glow on the side decks, green to starboard, red to port. I pass the railroad bridge which spans the entrance into Beebe Cove, where for several winters after her Orient sojourns *Clio* was laid up in Bruce Avery's small boatyard. Noank church tower is lit up, white clapboards once painted by Cullen and McGinnis as they raised funds for the next stage of their voyage. I take the inshore passage between Ram Island and Mason's Island. It is soon night, but there's a half-moon and starlight. The Atomic Four rumbles industriously beneath the cockpit and the exhaust water splashes astern. White Rock is something to watch for, smack on the rhumb line course to Stonington west breakwater. The clock on the Congregational church tower (a brother to Noank's) is chiming 8:00 as *Lochinvar* goes up the silent harbor, past the yachts dozing at their moorings like dogs that have given up all hope of being taken for a walk. It's suddenly chilly and I pull on a jacket over my sweater. I have an urge to wrap myself in sounds, smells, and sensations—of marsh grass, mud, sand, and surf; water moving beneath the boat; the sail quivering; sun bright on the deck; the rattle of unleashed anchor chain; the pungent whiff from the doused cabin lamp. All thoughts to keep me going through winter ashore.

Lochinvar will hibernate in the club parking lot, tucked in beside the tall hedge along the railroad tracks, a few hundred feet from her mooring. Dodson's will prop her up there on five jackstands. Betty's daughter, Amy, will put more of her boatyard expertise to work by helping me with saw and hammer in constructing a frame and covering *Lochinvar* with tarps, tying them securely against the weight of snow, rain, and wind to come. And as we take off from Logan over the drumlin islands in Boston harbor and listen to the jumbo's captain tell us that tonight we have a strong jet stream with us on our six-hour flight to London, part of my mind lingers behind in Stonington with an empty mooring in the harbor; and part—as the jet engines ease back from the frantic roar of steep ascent—is coasting forward to next summer. Next time we must nose our way into Lake Tashmoo on the Vineyard and venture across the shoals to Madaket.